To Discuss
w/ Jeremy
+ Jenn

Value of
Visuals

Building
a
Boutique

Digital Marketing
strategy & tactics

Jeremy Kagan

Managing Director

Eugene Lang Entrepreneurship Center

Columbia Business School

Professor

Marketing Department

Columbia Business School

www.wessexlearning.com

Wessex Press, Inc.
www.wessexlearning.com

Noel Capon, R.C. Kopf Professor of International Marketing, Columbia Business School, founded Wessex Press, Inc. in 2007. Wessex is a small publisher with global reach focusing predominantly on marketing, management, and other higher-education textbooks. Wessex's goal is to provide top-quality learning materials at affordable prices. Publishing under the Wessex Press and AxcessCapon brands, Wessex Press, Inc. offers titles in multiple print and digital formats. Wessex also offers video books.

Library of Congress Cataloging-in-Publication Data

Kagan, Jeremy

    Digital Marketing: Strategy & Tactics / Jeremy Kagan

        p. cm.

    ISBN   978-0-9994861-8-4 (hardcover)
            978-0-9994861-9-1 (softcover)

    1. Digital Marketing. I. Title: Digital marketing: strategy & tactics. II. Jeremy Kagan

Design/Production: Anna Botelho
Editor: Lyn Maize
Index: Judi Gibbs—Write Guru®

Dedication

This book is dedicated to all of those who educated me in this industry of digital media — my friends, clients, and colleagues; and to all of my students over the years who have kept me on my toes and on the cutting edge of the latest and greatest. I'd like to offer special thanks to my family, who never doubted and put up with the late nights, the early mornings, and the general craziness.

Brief Table of Contents

Table of Contents

Acknowledgments

In the preparation of this book, I have benefitted greatly from the comments and expertise of marketing colleagues and digital entrepreneurs around the world. I'd like to offer particular thanks to all of my industry colleagues and partners, especially the ones who took the time to come into my classes to speak over the years, from regulars like Brian Hecht, Patrick Ambron of BrandYourself, and Joe Guzik of Red Bull Records, to other friends who may have spoken just once but made an impact. It's also important to note the exciting guests like Brian Halligan of Hubspot, Brian O'Kelley of Appnexus, Ben Lerer of Group Nine Media, David Jones of You and Mr. Jones, and so many others, who educated the students in what happens in the real world of digital marketing (and made me look good in the process). They may consider it a small contribution of an evening or an afternoon, but it was invaluable to me and the students.

Also deserving of my heartfelt thanks are all of the chapter partners, and those who provided images and examples for the book. In particular, Moz.com and BrandYourself in *search*; the IAB in *display*; MailChimp and Movable Ink (thanks Vivek!) in *email*, Hub Spot and Statista for *social media* and *inbound marketing*, and the many resources Google and Facebook have made available for use across the board, from research and education to tools and tips.

Thanks are also due to my colleagues associated with Columbia University Undergraduate, EMBA, and Executive programs. Noel Capon, R.C. Kopf Professor of International Marketing at Columbia Business School, author, and department head who gave me my start at Columbia Business School; David Rogers, colleague and author of "The Network is Your Customer" and his newest title "The Digital Transformation Playbook" at Columbia Business School, who runs the BRITE conference, and who graciously includes me in his Digital Strategy Executive Education programs; and Sree Sreenivasan, former Chief Digital Officer of New York City, Chief Digital Officer at the Metropolitan Museum of Art, long time Professor at Columbia University and former Dean of the Journalism School, who has been a friend and colleague since we taught Master classes together. And, to all my students over the years who have given me great feedback (intentional and accidental), taught me about so many new things, and continue to make me so proud as they venture out into the industry at large.

It's critical to note that this book couldn't have happened without the support I have drawn from my family. When you have three small children, it's a team effort. Carving out quiet time for Dad to write means Mom has triple duty with the kids. Kathy, this book wouldn't be here without you; Alexis, Rose, and Jacob, for all the times I hustled you out of my office to get some work done, I would have rather been playing with you too! And special thanks to my Mom, who always believed in me, supported me, and bragged when she could, even though she can't always describe what I do for a living.

Last, but certainly not least, are the people at Wessex Press, Inc. who believed in this project and provided amazing professional assistance over the last two years in bringing my ideas and vision to life. Paul Capon, President and CEO; Lyn Maize, my editor, who tolerated and nagged me about deadlines and missing them in mostly equal parts — you made sure that my voice came through, the big picture stayed in focus, and that I worked on the most important things. The constantly updated requests for new checklists were straight out of absent-minded professor central casting. And of course Anna Botelho, design and production whose unenviable job of making the visuals in my head real and come out so well. Though I didn't always know what I wanted, you gave me a lot of options to change my mind. I resisted the temptation to jokingly describe a vision of a 'scratch and sniff' cover because you might have just pulled it off.

Foreword

The irony of writing a book on digital marketing is not lost on me. Indeed, as I developed the material that first became the course, then became this book, the one constant has always been change. Updating lectures the night before, continuously adding innovations from my consulting and research as well as "In the News" references to keep my lectures fresh and relevant, change is definitely the norm, not the exception.

This, in turn, has forced me to think of digital marketing from a principles perspective, and why it is so important to the modern professional's tool kit. This book approaches digital marketing in two ways: from the point of view of the strategic thinker — who might guide the vision in their organization requiring an understanding all of the options available as well as how to evaluate them; and the tactical perspective, for the roll-up-your-sleeves practitioner, who wants to dig in to the details and may even launch campaigns themselves.

Each chapter is designed to present frameworks for thinking broadly and structurally about the channel being discussed, but with many examples and exercises to bring the practical deployment of digital marketing into a real world focus. I've also made an effort to provide context, so the reader can understand how these channels interact, combining for a cohesive, measurable strategy for using digital channels in their broader marketing programs.

Additionally, it's my hope that the book can be used not just as the backbone text for a foundational digital marketing class, but ultimately *remixed* — to support classes on related topics. A half term class on paid digital ad channels? Use the first 6 chapters. A class on Inbound Marketing? The introduction, and chapters on SEO, Email, Social, and Mobile might be the material you need. A class on digital business models or entrepreneurship could also use the introduction, plus chapters on social, shopping, mobile, and business models, as well as emerging channels, to discuss topics relevant to a startup.

Importantly, each chapter is supported in another key way. Most chapters have an Industry Partner or even two — showcasing relevant, active and successful companies in the fields explored throughout the text. They provide applicable support for the core text — but even more notably — ongoing content for learning, including updates on what's new and noteworthy. We've added extensive case studies and examples, and tools, resources and certifications available online to supplement and support the lessons from the text, ensuring that it's always applicable and never outdated.

I am also committed to updating the text frequently for students, faculty and practitioners. Indeed, as I use it myself at Columbia, I am updating the text and supporting materials every semester for classes as well! These updates will be available to the online support community in the form of a password protected website, and ultimately make it into the next edition.

In the spirit of community and sharing of user-generated content, I encourage and look forward to feedback and suggestions from anyone using the text for their own work!

Supplemental Materials for Students and Faculty

For faculty, we provide a comprehensive selection of visuals in the form of PowerPoints, lecture guides with class exercises and teaching notes, and test questions for each chapter. For students, faculty, and practitioners we provide access to the proprietary website referenced earlier, where they can access both primary and secondary source documents and research to enhance their knowledge, new examples and visuals as they are published and other updates tied to the *Tools and Resources* available at the end of chapters in the book.

About the Author

Jeremy Kagan is the Managing Director of the Eugene Lang Entrepreneurship Center at Columbia Business School, where he oversees the entrepreneurial curriculum and programming, the multimillion dollar Lang Investment Fund, and the Columbia Startup Lab. For over a decade he has also been a Professor at Columbia Business School, Department of Marketing, in the MBA, EMBA, and Executive Education programs, teaching in the areas of Digital Marketing, Strategy and Innovation, and Entrepreneurship.

He previously founded *PricingEngine.com*, a SaaS marketing technology company helping small businesses manage search marketing (SEM) and digital advertising, with peer benchmarking, a simple, unified platform for deploying and managing campaigns, and many other features to save them time, money, and acquire more sales and leads.

In his consulting capacity, Jeremy works as a mentor with numerous accelerators, such as the ER Accelerator, Innovation Norway, the German Accelerator, Dreamit, XRC Labs, as well as advising individual startup companies.

Kagan has held executive positions at Sony Music Entertainment in the Global Digital Business unit handling Global Mobile Accounts; as Vice President/Director, Strategy and Customer Insights in advertising at Publicis Modem, where he was head of Strategy and Innovation; and as a strategy consultant at IBM and Dean & Company. He holds an MBA from Columbia Business School and both a BS from the Wharton School and BA at the College of the University of Pennsylvania.

Kagan now lives with his wife and children in Greenwich Village in New York City — just down the block from where he used to promote Indie rock concerts and parties. Life's funny that way.

David Rogers, a faculty member at Columbia Business School, is a globally-recognized leader on digital business strategy. He is author of four books, most recently *The Digital Transformation Playbook* (in 6 languages). Rogers delivers keynotes at conferences world-wide on the impact of digital technologies on business. David advises global companies such as Google, Merck, GE, Toyota, Cartier, Visa, China Eastern Airlines, and Pizza Hut on digital strategy and has led workshops for executives in hundreds of companies from 66 countries.

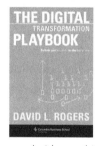

www.davidrogers.biz

"For marketing to succeed in the digital era, we need to stop thinking of customers as targets (to market at) and start seeing customers as networks (to connect <u>with</u>)."

— David Rogers, faculty – Columbia Business School, and best-selling author, *The Digital Transformation Playbook*

CHAPTER 1

Digital Marketing and the 4 P's

Digital Marketing has become mainstream. No longer is "digital" the parsley on the marketing plate at a fancy dinner, an afterthought, or a cool extra to add some sizzle to a marketing plan. Digital is now the main course of the marketing meal — the connective strategy that pulls all the elements of an integrated marketing program together, ensuring that all messaging and communications strategies are effective at reaching the customer. Yet in many organizations, the digital marketing mix is still handled arbitrarily, after the fact, or managed by a junior member of the team who has some personal familiarity or a willingness to learn how to work in the digital medium.

This book is designed to bring the educated layperson — the typical marketer or business professional familiar with the topic — to a point where digital methods become an essential element of their integrated marketing strategy from the onset. We will approach the topic strategically, but also dive into elements of tactical execution across all the major digital channels: search, display, email, social, and mobile.

Our approach will focus on the ultimate business goals and results of a marketing strategy — and how to frame these objectives and measure them for success — rather than just showcase every "shiny new object," app, or social network. Given the rapidly changing subject matter in the book, we'll provide extensive examples, tools and resources for use outside the confines of the text, and in a special section at the end of each chapter.

Digital Is Different

Ultimately, this sea change in marketing, driven by digital, requires a more quantitative and thoughtful approach to marketing strategies — reaching the right person, at the right time and place, with the right message. Less than a decade ago, senior marketers could dabble in a few experiments with digital, or in many cases ignore digital altogether in favor of more traditional and comfortable personal or mass media channels. Fast forward to today, and marketers who ignore digital do so at their own peril. New competitors in every business and industry have been born and are flourishing in the digital and mobile world. Even the very investments in traditional media channels that have been trusted for so long, now require an integrated digital component to truly leverage them. Even the well understood traditional media investments themselves — television ads for example — require a complementary digital component to leverage the online activity generated by them, like searches for more information or social network activity.

One needs to only look at the billion-dollar acquisition of *Dollar Shave Club* by Unilever[1] — a startup company that was essentially built on a viral video[2] (more on this company later in Chapter 6).

Dollar Shave Club CEO Michael Dubin from his YouTube video; over 25 million views!

From the early viral marketing experiments (Hotmail launched with a tagline offering a free email account), to ride sharing apps like Lyft and Uber that give you credit for recruiting friends, to the new mobile food delivery apps offering discounts and loyalty benefits in exchange for using them, digital marketing has become an essential component to launching and growing any new company. Today, even when utilizing a more traditional approach, no marketer would launch a branding campaign on television without a website to drive traffic to, a coordinated search and social strategy for leveraging the campaign, and plans for digital touchpoints to keep your prospects engaged throughout digital and mobile channels.

As Wayne Gretsky famously said, "A good player plays where the puck is. A great player plays where the puck is going to be."

If you've chosen to read this book, it's clear you already know that any marketer or business professional must understand these changes and be able to plan and integrate the power and potential of digital marketing channels.

Digital provides many destinations for marketers to consider.

Digital Continues to Grow

This new reality is shown in the sheer amounts of budget being deployed to the digital channel. As seen in Figure 1.1, digital marketing now represents the single biggest channel of any marketing budget — passing venerable categories such as newspapers, magazines, and radio. Only television — when broadcast and cable are combined — is larger. According to projections, digital made up 36.7% of total media ad spending in 2016 and will account for around half by 2021.[3] Sources from eMarketer, Forrester, to ZenithOptimedia anticipate digital becoming the undisputed champion — the largest channel by revenue — in just a few short years.

■ Figure 1.1 Media Ad Spending by Share

U.S. Total Media Ad Spending Share, by Media, 2012–2018 (% of total)							
	2012	2013	2014	2015	2016	2017	2018
TV	39.1%	38.8%	38.1%	37.3%	36.9%	36.2%	35.7%
Digital	22.3%	25.2%	28.2%	30.9%	33.2%	35.3%	37.3%
Mobile	2.6%	5.7%	9.8%	14.0%	18.7%	22.6%	26.4%
Print	20.7%	19.0%	17.7%	16.5%	15.5%	14.7%	14.0%
Newspapers*	11.5%	10.2%	9.3%	8.6%	8.0%	7.5%	7.1%
Magazines*	9.2%	8.8%	8.4%	7.9%	7.5%	7.2%	6.9%
Radio**	9.3%	8.9%	8.6%	8.2%	7.8%	7.5%	7.1%
Outdoor	4.0%	4.1%	4.0%	3.9%	3.8%	3.7%	3.6%
Directories*	4.5%	4.0%	3.5%	3.1%	2.8%	2.5%	2.3%

* print only

** excludes off-air radio & digital

Source: Kagan 2018, based on data from eMarketer.

Throughout this book, we will approach the discussion of digital marketing to be suitable for any marketer beginning their career, or one looking to increase his or her longevity; the direction is obvious.

In Figure 1.2, we can see that every digital channel is growing at double-digit rates. This is fueled by a torrid pace of innovation in both technology and execution that makes it possible for anyone to carve out an area of expertise.

The relative youth and dynamism of these channels offer huge upside potential and opportunity for marketers. For example, Snapchat launched advertising with a handful of partners in just the last couple years; Instagram went from zero ad revenue at the end of 2013 to over $3 billion today.[4] Dozens of apps break through to popularity each year. How many people aside from a few teams at their respective brands even claim to be familiar with something so new? And, the first movers keep getting bigger. According to Gartner Inc., by 2021, 20% of every activity an individual engages in will involve at least one of the top-seven global digital giants (Google, Apple, Facebook, Amazon, and globally Baidu, Alibaba, and Tencent by virtue

■ Figure 1.2 Digital Marketing Growth by Channel

U.S. Digital Marketing Forecast, 2014–2019

	2014	2015	2016	2017	2018	2019	CAGR
Email marketing	$2,067	$2,266	$2,466	$2,665	$2,865	$3,067	8%
Social media	$7,518	$9,736	$11,724	$13,511	$15,359	$17,342	18%
Display advertising	$19,801	$23,680	$27,916	$31,281	$34,477	$37,547	13%
Search advertising	$27,899	$31,622	$34,995	$38,470	$41,890	$45,386	10%
Total	$57,285	$67,305	$77,101	$85,928	$94,593	$103,370	12%
Percentage of all ad spend	24%	27%	30%	32%	33%	35%	

Source: Kagan 2018, based on data from Forrester Research and eMarketer 2017.

of their home market size and dominance).[5] Most of the enormous growth in digital advertising accrues to existing giants Google and Facebook, who continue innovating and acquiring upstart challengers to stay on the cutting edge. As new channels, technologies, and gatekeepers relevant to their business continue to emerge, there are always fresh opportunities for the savvy digital marketer to become the organizational expert.

Digital Marketing is Effective

There is no disputing the power and potential of achieving sales goals through digital channels. From the branding power of a viral video, the sales generated through shopping and search ads transacted through an e-commerce website, to the qualified leads generated from expert content marketing, digital offers the most cost-effective way to reach and target customers.

Digital also offers firms unique ways to build superior customer relationships through email, social media, and collaborative communities. Even the word of mouth from online reviews, blogs, games, or contests all drive huge business outcomes for marketers that master their methods. We will discuss both strategy and tactics for all these channels in subsequent chapters.

Digital effectiveness is driven in part by an enormous and democratized access to the unprecedented amount of data about the factors driving success. Department store magnate John Wannamaker purportedly said, "Half the money I spend on advertising is wasted; the trouble is I don't know which half." For the digital marketer, this is decidedly different. Proper *tagging* (snippets of code allowing the tracking of consumer activity, interest and data) of ad campaigns and their components, emails, social media monitoring, and the website data from Google Analytics provides better information for decision-makers on their digital advertising campaigns.

This means that the ads that work are shown more often, that budgets can be planned more effectively, and the return on advertising spend can be tracked and managed with greater accuracy. Digital also allows for optimization and improvement on an ongoing basis, rather than waiting to the end of a campaign to evaluate performance and make improvements.

Sadly, this has led to the eclipse of the "Mad Men" era of the "big idea" in creative advertising — but excitedly to a new "Revenge of the Nerds" era of quantitative marketing. The hot new driver is not the creative director but in many cases the data scientist. In the era of "big data" and analytics, understanding campaigns and performance rapidly equates to success.

Digital Marketing is Dynamic

All of this tracking, monitoring and optimization is in sharp contrast to mass media's much slower pace; leading to a variety of new ways for customers to buy and marketers to measure their activity. For example, the traditional concept of the "upfront" in television allowed major mass media buyers to receive discounts for buying in bulk in advance. The more you buy the more you get, but there's no practical way to test and refine. With digital, committing budgets in advance is at odds with basic principles of optimization that digital offers across all advertising channels.

A digital campaign may run *dynamic creative* (flexible ad content, message and imagery) across multiple destinations against highly segmented audiences, all at the same time. This allows for experimenting with and optimizing for all three simultaneously, learning what works best, and buying more media only when the combination of message, media, and audience proves its value. Contrast this to the old school rate cards, advance discounts based on estimated audience, limited inventory, and opaque and time-delayed understanding of the effectiveness of a traditional television commercial and you clearly understand the value to today's marketer.

Pricing is also significantly different in digital media. Most traditional media prices are based on some combination of real estate (how big or long the ad is), audience size (potential versus actual people who could see the ad), and some measure of the quality of the demographic reached. There are only so many commercial spots in a half hour show. *The CPM* — an acronym for Cost-Per-Thousand impressions — has been the standard that rules all. In traditional media the *potential* that someone sees the ad, based on consumer research, is enough, and it the scarcity of inventory that keeps prices high.

In the dynamic world of digital, pricing can sell on a CPM basis as well, but the audience size is not usually the limiting factor. Existing inventory can be sliced and diced by volume and audience segment, with no real limit on the number of advertisers. And almost all ad inventory is sold in some form of real time auction, which finds the market price based on demand.

Because of this, the majority of online ads are sold on some basis of performance such as cost per action, like a click. This allows the marketer to, in theory, only pay when someone demonstrates genuine interest in the advertising message. And with the advancements in analytics just discussed, it makes it much easier to understand the link between the price paid and the return gained. (Figure 1.3)

■ Figure 1.3 Digital Ad Revenues by Pricing Model

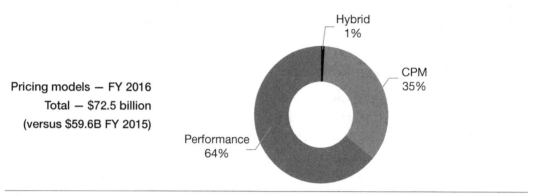

Pricing models — FY 2016
Total — $72.5 billion
(versus $59.6B FY 2015)

Hybrid
1%

CPM
35%

Performance
64%

Growth in *performance-based pricing* is also driven by the almost ubiquitous auction-based pricing models of digital. Search, display, social, and other channels use sophisticated reverse Dutch auction bidding that clears the market at prices advertisers can determine based on their returns. An additional layer of complexity is waged between tools and technologies designed to work within these auction environments to minimize price for the advertiser on one side, or maximize yield for the publisher on the other. (We'll cover programmatic and auction pricing models in detail in later chapters on display ads and social media). All a far cry from the rate card of yore.

The ability to buy and target much smaller and specific groups has also allowed for an explosion of niche marketing. While a retailer specializing in all kinds of hot sauces might never have a way to reach target customers effectively using mass media, digital provides the ability to target searches, context, and discussion in a way that aggregates up demand into profitable sales.

Finally, when surveyed, professional marketers make it clear that they are adopting digital channels in force because of these very factors. As seen in Figure 1.4, advertising budgets of the future are moving to where people are spending their time; and they are spending their time in digital and mobile media. If the collective plans of those managing the marketing budgets of the future are an indicator, the secular move of budget dollars from traditional media — directories, magazines, newspapers, and television — has only just begun.

■ Figure 1.4 Increase of Digital Tactics

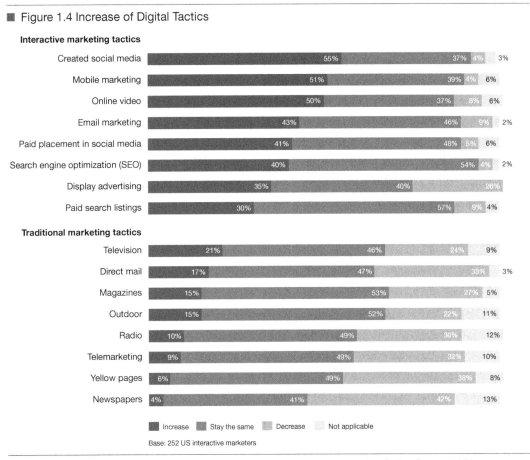

Interactive marketing tactics

Tactic	Increase	Stay the same	Decrease	Not applicable
Created social media	55%	37%	4%	3%
Mobile marketing	51%	39%	4%	6%
Online video	50%	37%	8%	6%
Email marketing	43%	46%	9%	2%
Paid placement in social media	41%	48%	5%	6%
Search engine optimization (SEO)	40%	54%	4%	2%
Display advertising	35%	40%	26%	
Paid search listings	30%	57%	9%	4%

Traditional marketing tactics

Tactic	Increase	Stay the same	Decrease	Not applicable
Television	21%	46%	24%	9%
Direct mail	17%	47%	33%	3%
Magazines	15%	53%	27%	5%
Outdoor	15%	52%	22%	11%
Radio	10%	49%	30%	12%
Telemarketing	9%	49%	32%	10%
Yellow pages	6%	49%	38%	8%
Newspapers	4%	41%	42%	13%

■ Increase   ■ Stay the same   ■ Decrease   ■ Not applicable

Base: 252 US interactive marketers

Source: Data from Forrester Research, Inc., U.S. Interactive Marketing Executive Online Survey, 2010.

It's important to understand that digital marketing is not a monolithic area of similar spend like television. Whereas television is primarily dominated by the 30-second spot, digital represents a wide array of distinct channels for deploying marketing messaging. Search marketing, display advertising, social media, email, and mobile all broadly capture the attention of marketers and their budgets, and each has its own challenges of creative, targeting, and measurement. In this book, we will review each in turn:

- *Search Marketing*, reviewing both Search Engine Optimization and search advertising,
- *Display Ads* across banners and video,
- *Social Advertising* including community and content strategies,
- *Email Marketing* from customer acquisition to retention and loyalty, and
- *Mobile* with all its Apps and channels.

Marketing's 4 P's Revisited

One might think that with the drastic differences noted for digital marketing, we're planning to "burn the ships" and march into a new land ... but our previous marketing experience actually provides an excellent foundation for change. Traditional marketing has relied on models of the four P's: Product, Price, Placement, and Promotion. Each of these broad areas has been dramatically impacted by the advent of digital and mobile channels and the changes and opportunities they provide. Digital marketing has forced marketers to rethink many of these fundamental assumptions from past eras, when marketing was all about mass audiences, repetition, and broad-based metrics. Now the marketing toolkit favors new approaches for targeting and segmentation, customization and personalization of messaging, and new and better ways of measuring effectiveness. The toolkit also offers ways to *optimize* messaging in real time to be more effective with current and prospective customers. Reviewing the four 'P's with this new perspective provides an excellent foundation, as well as a 'jumping off' point for building our digital marketing understanding.

"Product" as we know it has changed from a one size fits all volume play for the mass market, to a mass customized and personalized platform approach. The fundamentals of product features and design have changed too. Price is notable not just for its unrelenting transparency, but for the emergence of new models of auctions, group buying, subscription models, and direct to consumer. Placement has forced a reckoning of the advantages and disadvantages of brick and mortar versus online, as e-commerce takes more and more revenue away from traditional methods — drastically disrupting some categories like travel and retail for example. And finally, with the rise of the Internet and mobile media, so too have our methods for reaching potential customers moved to match and take advantage of the advertising potential of the channel. Not just *where* brands advertise, but *how* they do it continues to change.

Product

In the digital world what constitutes a product — and what we can do with it — has changed dramatically. It used to be that products were produced and sold to a mass market with a one size fits all approach. Product design and feature decisions were made by the company based on the best information they had from consumer feedback — or none at all. And equally important, a product once sold was the last point of contact the company had with the consumer unless they decided to buy more.

Online business models and services have transformed this approach. Even physical products in the digital world have changed dramatically with the advent of more interactive and adaptive market strategies. Companies are creating better products designed to be platforms for personalization and customization, and developing new products using the data and feedback from the customers themselves.

Consider Apple and its original mass market computer, the Apple II. The computer was the same for everyone — a beige box with limited customizability. The company's connection with the customer ended when the box was sold to a consumer they never knew through a retailer who had the customer connection. Today, the iPhone is the beginning of Apple's relationship with the consumer. The product itself is defined as much by its ability to download apps, access services and social media as its primary function of the 'computer' in the box. Want to win a bet? Ask everyone in a given classroom to pull out their smartphones. Even among those with the same brand of phone, it's an easy wager to bet that not a single one has the same applications downloaded, services accessed, or accessories used to personalize their device. Apple's ongoing relationship with customers through its App Store — a multibillion dollar business that didn't even exist ten years ago — closes the loop with the consumer, allowing them to have a continuity of engagement with them they never had before. Apple can collect ongoing service revenue, function as a software marketplace, a data clearinghouse for advertising and commerce, and of course suggest upgrades and new hardware based on a user's individual profile.

What a difference a few decades make!

The changing value proposition of what defines a "product" and the opportunity of brands to finally connect to their end consumer in a more ongoing relationship is altering the way even traditional brands approach the market. Nike is best known for selling athletic shoes and apparel. In the past, it might have been fine to think of themselves as an apparel manufacturer and approach their marketing by pushing clothing and sneakers to everyone at every consumer touchpoint. However, Nike has invested a great deal in high quality, broad based digital content that suggests it is adopting a new approach that's more targeted, responsive and consumer friendly. Nike sees itself not as a company that just sells you athletic shoes and gear, but *as your partner in reaching your health and fitness goals.*

Is this too broad a definition? Not at all. A company's message "selling" you something is only relevant when that consumer is *in the market for that item*; and their advertising messages are ignored or annoying when the consumer isn't searching with intent to purchase. But a company supporting your broader goals or needs — in this case, fitness and health — can message with you almost daily in a welcome way, if they approach it properly.

Look at the *Nike Training Club* program shown in Figure 1.5. It consists of a well-designed website, a large investment in high quality video content, and a mobile app allowing access on the go to experts in various areas of fitness. The program is aimed at women and allows them to register and design an exercise regimen, compete and train with friends, and track their progress. There's no cost, yet the investment in the site, app and quality content is significant. Are they crazy?

■ Figure 1.5 Nike Training Club

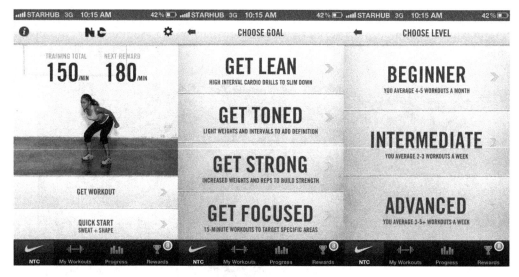

The workout partner to Nike+ Run Club, NTC has a huge variety of workouts, from yoga to gym moves. Nike sells shoes, not app subscriptions, so everything including the workout plans are free, *https://www.youtube.com/watch?v=2I9x59ibKEQ*.

Nike realized that by becoming a woman's partner in achieving her fitness goals — whether specific like running a marathon or more general like getting more active and into shape — it has permission to interact with her as a brand on an almost daily basis. If the message was a simple sales message, it would be ignored. But by providing a branded environment of support, encouragement, instruction and learning, Nike can be there every day. When the program participant does finally need athletic apparel, the goodwill and countless branding opportunities ensure that Nike is "in the running" for this purchase opportunity.

Nike has also created a unique window into its customers' behavior that it previously never had — and the data gathered can be used in many ways. Participants using the app or website provide information of incredible value: how often they exercise, with whom, and what sorts of things they do. This information can help Nike design better products, target sales messages to the right people, and generally refine its strategy.

And why a mobile app? The best website and content in the world is useless if the customer can't or won't use it. While consumers rarely exercise next to their desktop or laptop computer, it's almost impossible to pry the typical consumer away from their mobile phone. It's with them at the gym, in the park, on the beach — indeed anywhere they might want to exercise. So, the content investment almost necessitates the app to ensure usability and access.

Another example of a company that gave away software in order to drive sales of high margin and unique items is LEGO. LEGO's "Design by Me" (original name) program allowed a user to download free computer-aided design software to create their own LEGO models. You could, for example, create the very building you are reading this in. The software, based on your design, was able to store your design, calculate the bricks needed, order and ship the bricks enabling you to construct it as a custom product.

LEGO then gets interested parties to invest their time and energy in designing a unique product tailored exactly to their tastes. Likelihood of conversion to a sale? High. Chances of comparison shopping — zero — it's unique. This, combined with the high perception of value for something you have spent so much time designing, leads to a high-priced, high-margin, and high-satisfaction product.

Another new initiative in the toy industry is from Hasbro, called "HasLab," a crowdsourcing platform that hopes to put dream products into the hands of fans. Fans of Hasbro products can interact with the company and one another by providing input and financial support for a limited edition toy. If the goal is met, Hasbro will produce the toy and they'll receive it. According to an announcement April 2018, HasLab is kicking things off in a big way with a big Star Wars playset from *Return of the Jedi*, "Jabba's Sail Barge."

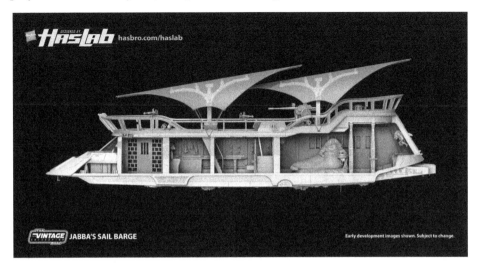

The benefits that LEGO and Hasbro also get — even if these toys and designs never become a sale — is one-on-one engagement with their customers and a sense of what they want. The data and insight are invaluable.

Leveraging the "Long Tail"

There are quite a few examples that reflect this fundamental change in how we can address markets and expand business models. It's no longer about a mass customization model; it's about the ability of the digital world to eliminate or remove the challenges of the physical that forced a mass market model in the first place.

The removal of the limitations of real estate and shelf space allow near limitless selection. This encompasses the ability to be open 24/7 with infinite "shelf space" to capture incremental sales; and the ability to aggregate demand from locales not within drivable distance to a store, but where we can ship to. These new models are thanks to the Internet (and our excellent payment and logistics infrastructure).

This new reality was noted best in 2004, by Chris Anderson, in an article "The Long Tail" in *Wired* magazine (and expanded into a subsequent book in 2006).[6] *The Long Tail* is referring to the distribution of popular products and services offered by retailers. For example, in the traditional media world, a music retailer or bookstore often carried just the most popular artists or titles. A movie theater shows just the blockbusters. This makes sense from an economic standpoint — only the popular titles sell enough to justify keeping them on the shelves and paying "rent" for the space to store them. Thus the "Fat Head" of the distribution channel becomes self-reinforcing and those with more eclectic tastes may simply miss out.

The *New York Times* bestseller that introduced the business world to a future that's already here, by Chris Anderson, former Editor in Chief of *Wired* magazine.

Internet-based retailers, however, have no shelf space for their online stores, just database entries. The least popular song, movie or book can be downloaded from a server at the same cost as the most popular. The cost of technology is very low and dropping. However, shipping

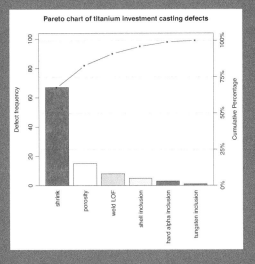

Pareto chart of titanium investment casting defects

The Pareto Principle (also known as the 80/20 rule, the law of the vital few, or the principle of factor sparsity) states that, for many events, roughly 80% of the effects come from 20% of the causes. Management consultant Joseph M. Juran suggested the principle and named it after Italian economist Vilfredo Pareto who showed that approximately 80% of the land in Italy was owned by 20% of the population.

It is a common principle in business management; e.g., "80% of sales come from 20% of clients." Richard Koch authored the book, *The 80/20 Principle*, which illustrated a number of practical applications of the Pareto principle in business management, leading many business professionals to cite the "80/20" rule as a tool to maximize business efficiency.[7] Most recently the Pareto principle has been linked to the long tail theory in its explanation that products that are in low demand or have low sales volume can collectively make up a sizable market share that rivals or exceeds the best sellers.

a physical good implies a warehouse facility with a much wider selection of product. Even if this is located in a very low cost area, or at a partner's site, it adds cost to each transaction. For this reason Amazon has helped support the growth of e-readers and on demand technologies to lower their cost base further.

Movie theaters have the same challenges. With a limited number of screens, each theater must show movies that appeal to a broad audience; people who can drive to the theater, pay for tickets, and fill the seats. Despite a large demand for independent films, or documentaries, or Bollywood films, there's simply not enough audience density except in a few major cities to allow for them to appear on the big screen. Similarly, even with hundreds of channels, television stations must build mass audiences to show advertising to justify the 'screen time' they give a show. Old shows, cult hits and shows that simply don't have time to find their legs all fall by the wayside.

Netflix shifted the paradigm first with DVDs to your mailbox but now with streaming video and multi-device access, binge-watching is becoming the norm. Viewers choose when and what to watch, and can select anything available on the companies' servers.

The long tail phenomenon is not just limited to media and digital products. The Internet has changed the game for physical products too. Google for search, Facebook and social media for word of mouth and crowd reviews, and e-commerce pioneers all contribute key enabling technology which allows people to find every needle in the haystack or niche product they can think of — with a retailer ready on the other side willing to service that need.

A great example can be seen in Figure 1.6. If you're an enthusiast of spicy food, you may find the selection of hot sauces at a local supermarket somewhat limited to Tabasco and Sriracha. Going online, a simple search turns up several "Hot Sauce Superstores" with thousands of selections to sizzle your palate. Savvy marketers attempt to redirect these search behaviors so their superstore can capture the majority of attention, and sales, from these dedicated niche buyers.

■ Figure 1.6 Optimized Search Results for "Hot Sauce"

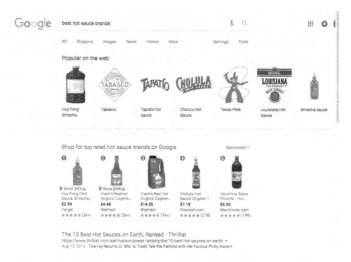

Screenshot of Google search results for digital hot sauce options.
Google and the Google logo are registered trademarks of Google Inc., used with permission.

We even see changes in the development of products as companies recognize the ability to provide options to increase sales. Dell Computer is famous for being one of the very first to sell customizable, personalized computers where you design the features, select memory options, screen size, and the like. Originally manufacturers selected all baseline features. When Dell created a website called IdeaStorm, the idea in part was to let customers suggest (blue sky) features or items that they would be interested in buying but did not exist. A forum was created by which customers could suggest what they wanted in a detailed posting. Other customers could then vote "up" or "down" if they liked it. The result? A few customers made specific suggestions; but many more voted. The best were adopted and offered for sale. And the first people to be notified? The "crowd" of thousands who had made or voted on the suggestion in the first place.

Every day new companies and products turn the process on its head. It used to be that developing a new product involved a great deal of money to design, test market, and launch — and it still could flop. The discovery tools of the Internet, virtual prototyping applications and the ability of the web to spread word of mouth have now been harnessed in the form of sites like Kickstarter. On Kickstarter, aspiring filmmakers, musicians, product designers, and the like can propose a product and presell it to the public — before launch and production — raising funds and generating demand at the same time. The process has gotten the notice of consumers looking for novel new products as well as venture capitalists looking to find the next big thing. Since their launch in 2009, 4 million people have backed a project, $35 billion has been pledged, and 137,865 projects have been successfully funded.

And with continued evolution in tools and innovations, the demand curve gets a little flatter and the tail a little longer every day!

Price

In the world of commerce before the Internet, there was little to no price transparency. Retailers and middlemen had much more information and experience with the market and transactions, and consumers had to work hard to get pricing information they needed to comparison shop. For many, the time-consuming effort to find the best price, already limited to the local retailers, was simply not worth the effort.

Particularly problematic were very important but infrequent transactions. Products and services like travel, real estate, auto sales, and even job hunting all had arcane and opaque pricing. Often, purchase required domain expertise, with the penalty for being wrong quite high. Take a terrible vacation with your family and you might not get away for another year. Thus, reliance on middlemen, the travel agent, the real estate agent, the car salesman, and the recruiter became the norm.

Sadly, these middlemen were not only more experienced and better informed than the consumer — they were also not always incented to keep the consumer's interests at heart. On the most basic level, these were commissioned sales people with a vested interest in making the deal — and often greater negotiating experience. Finally, sales contests and commissions skewed the very offerings they provided. Travel agents, for example, received healthy commissions from the major airlines. Without access to the available flights from smaller discount and regional airlines, often at lower prices, consumers were forced to pay the higher prices of the bigger airlines, with a commission to the travel agent.

Real estate agents were even more opaque. With exclusive listings and proprietary databases on market sales, knowledge of the neighborhood and other buyers, they had quite an advantage. For a customer, it was the single largest purchase in their life, and their first and last time with this complex process. For the agent it was one of many commissions. Research has even shown that real estate agents take longer to sell their own homes to get a higher price.

The Internet, however, brings a new transparency to pricing. It became possible to compare retailers and prices on similar products quickly and easily. Renting an apartment and viewing listings on Craigslist allows prospective renters to know the market level of rents before committing to the time and effort of visiting. Travel sites make it easy to find alternative airlines and routes, and even check on user reviews of destination hotels.

Travel sites display almost all airline choices between two points allowing easy comparison of prices and other factors. Commissions on airline tickets have essentially vanished; online agents make more money cross-selling hotel rooms and rental cars then tickets these days. And many travel sites make their money only from ads, eliminating any conflict of interest with the consumer. Sites like Kayak.com compete on "efficiency" by getting consumers to use them as a travel search engine for all their options. Sites like Hipmunk have innovated further by adding new data to the decision process. Hipmunk allows ranking of flight choices, for example, on a proprietary "agony" factor, which indexes price, comfort, and on-time performance among other factors. No wonder travel is one of the categories that has moved completely online.

Hipmunk offers travel planning inside your email and calendar. Their unique tools, display and AI bots make it easy to visually compare results and choose what's best for you.

Insurance is another industry that has become extremely price transparent. No one expects to see a local drug store also tell you what the same product costs across the street at their competitor.

Yet with both home and auto insurance, personalized pricing is what the market now requires. As the insurance industry moved online it realized how very simple it is for customers to leave one website to comparison shop. To keep hard won visitors, companies now provide the information they seek — price comparison or pricing calculators — on their own storefront.

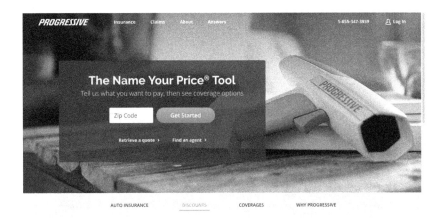

Part magic. Part smart shopping. Only from Progressive.

Just get an auto insurance quote, use the Name Your Price Tool and POOF! We'll show you a range of car insurance coverage options. Forget hunting discounts, calculating rates or tinkering with coverages. Instead, use the Name Your Price Tool and jump straight to the rate you want.

The Progressive Name Your Price Tool Campaign, 2017

Ironically, all of this price transparency actually appears to reward products with strong brands. When comparing prices on a Samsung television online, for example, it is the trust of the brand that makes a consumer choose to buy the same television from an unknown online retailer at a much cheaper price, rather than simply select a no-name brand from a larger but more expensive retailer.

The "digital" effect on pricing is not limited to the list price. Coupons and discounts, long tools of the trade, have been majorly impacted. In the past, more price conscious customers would be the ones motivated to clip coupons, which often involved circulars in the Sunday paper, then remember to bring them for redemption to the store. Only the truly price sensitive would take advantage and this allowed price discrimination of a sort for many branded products

Now coupon codes, alerts, and digital coupons have replaced this friction with a simpler, sometimes personalized process. Sites like RetailMeNot and Coupon Cabin make obtaining a discount as simple as a search on the product or retailer in a different browser tab. Want to save a lot of money? Every single time you see a form field for a discount or promotional code — check one of those sites. Free shipping and 20% offers abound for those who seek them. There are even browser plugins that will *automatically* search for and apply these codes at checkout.

For the brand trying to seek advantage by offering different pricing levels using discounting tactics, a much larger group of customers will now be taking advantage of them.

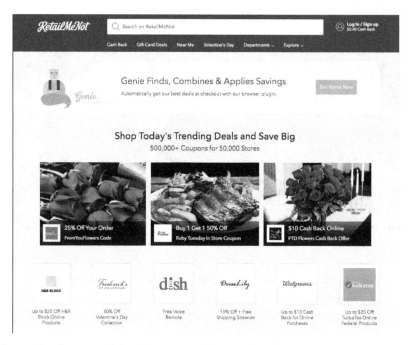

Leveraging the power of data-driven promotions, *RetailMeNot* provides a digital coupon marketplace where industry experts help companies optimize promotions to drive new business.

Mobile's ubiquity, of course, makes this trend even more dynamic. The challenge for retailers used to be getting the prospective buyer through the front door. Consumers now carry around an Internet enabled computer that can scan bar codes in real time, check prices, and direct them online or across the street for a better deal.

Placement

Placement always seemed like the "P" that they forced into the 4 P's framework — because we are really talking about sales and distribution channels. But, in the digital world, "placement" takes on a whole new meaning. Certainly, digital channels are new places to sell product — but they are far more than simply the digital equivalents of supply chain intermediaries or catalog sales. Digital channels combine great advantages in contrast to brick and mortar; with some completely new ways of doing business.

Brick and mortar retail still has a larger majority of sales due to the many advantages of a better in person "customer experience." But even in channels with a strong "touch factor," failure to recognize the influence of online or offline sales is a major mistake. A recent report by Forrester Research states that by 2017, 60% of all U.S. retail sales will involve the Internet in some way, either as a direct e-commerce transaction or as part of a shopper's research on a laptop or mobile device.[8]

The continual merging of e-commerce research and transactions.

E-commerce is growing at a healthy rate and m-commerce (e-commerce on mobile devices) is grabbing more share each passing quarter. Despite this, e-commerce has only just broken through to the double digits in overall retail/B2C/B2B sales. This might suggest that the marketer at a brick and mortar incumbent might breathe a little easier, with time to adjust to the new reality. Nothing could be further from the truth!

While the overall trend seems to suggest vigorous growth there is a long way to go. Even if a particular sector seems immune, the actual influence of online — search, customer experience, collaboration, price comparison — is far greater on the purchase process than might appear. Even if the transaction takes place at a brick and mortar location, the purchase process is more likely than not critically influenced by online along the way.

Cars, for example, are a natural for brick and mortar sales — who wouldn't test drive the car before the expensive purchase? However, the digital influence here is extremely pronounced. Online research determines which cars to consider, from review sites to manufacturer information; price ranges and features are explored before ever setting foot on a lot; and even financing options may be lined up well in advance, removing the favored tool of the salesman to close a deal.

Recent research (Figure 1.7) indicates that more than two thirds of consumers conduct some online product research before stepping foot in a brick and mortar location, amplifying the need for retailers to optimize their customer's digital experiences.[9]

"Companies should be channel agnostic, meaning it does not matter if they start with online or offline, what matters is that all channels are interlinked to give consumers the convenience they need. Online plays a major part in the customer journey or ROPO (research online,

■ Figure 1.7 Online Product Research Study

Source: Retail Dive 2017.

purchase offline). The most successful multi-channel companies established their online channels as early as the late nineties, went on to establish 'click and collect', eradicated silos across the entire organization, and established a channel agnostic incentive program so retail staff do not consider online as a separate business." — Paul Martin, UK Head of Retail, KPMG in the UK[10]

Digital commerce is well established but continues to face significant technical challenges as e-commerce and m-commerce become more sophisticated. The mobile friendly site, designed for viewability and providing the user interface for simple purchase, is critical to convert customers with smartphones. Perhaps even more challenging is the necessity of seamless tracking and identification of customer's preferences and purchases across multiple devices. The digital consumer demands that the item placed in a shopping cart or "wish list" on her office desktop computer be reflected on their home tablet or smartphone, and vice versa — or the sale may be lost. Weaving together user profiles is a technical challenge that must be met for customer sales and managing the relationship management in the long run.

New models of retail are also being enabled. In the past, the biggest customer of a manufacturer like Proctor & Gamble wasn't you — it was Walmart (and still is). Brands rely on retailers to move product and have only a tenuous relationship with and understanding of the customer. Vast marketing expenditures every year merely serve to re-capture and retain the demand for the products that are already in the customers' closet.

With online channels, brands can now go direct to the consumer. A toy manufacturer, paying large licensing fees for this year's movie tie-ins, faces two tough customers with low prices in Walmart and Toys"R"Us — but needs their volume to make its holiday numbers work. What if by going direct, they can sell at a far higher margin? This *cream-skimming* strategy is already being seen online, despite the channel conflict.

Other companies are experimenting with *subscription and replenishment models* with varying success. Offering discounts in return for commitments to monthly deliveries of sundries seems a fair tradeoff to capture and cement lifetime relationships for products like deodorant and toilet paper. (Remember Dollar Shave Club's $1B price tag?)

Social media has also begun to influence e-commerce in many ways. Levi's experimented with a store that only displayed items that had been liked by enough people in your circle of Facebook friends. If you are a teenager nervous about wearing the right outfit to a party on the weekend, selecting from a rack of blue jeans already screened by your peer group may be one of the most important features!

Social *buzz* is not just influencing online retail. Nordstrom has disclosed that their marketers actively monitor Pinterest and other sharing sites and select the more popular styles and products to dress their mannequins. Social buzz translates into real world displays and influences sales decisions even at the physical locations of their retail store.

Promotion

Last but certainly not the least of the "P's" is *promotion*. With a vast move of consumer attention to online media, budgets are slowly following. As we saw in an earlier chart, the trend suggests that literally over $100 billion of advertising dollars in the U.S. alone will inexorably follow the eyeballs of potential customers into the array of online media channels. These channels and the strategies and tactics needed to utilize them will be explored throughout the rest of this book. IAB research shows that mobile now accounts for 50.52% of this revenue (Figure 1.8).

■ Figure 1.8 Shift from Desktop to Mobile

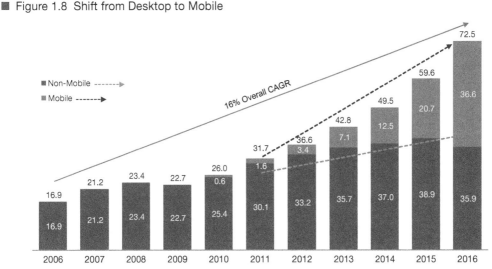

Ongoing Engagement and Customer Relationship Management (CRM)

Beyond the 4 P's and the changes to them are perhaps an even more critical change to marketing: ongoing customer relationships can be maintained and improved using digital tools better than ever before. In the past, customers might call a company when they had a problem; get the occasional catalog or promotion in the mail; or even have a 'loyalty card' providing a discount for repeat purchases. While some retailers and catalog merchants used sophisticated tools to try and optimize their performance, it has been the advent of inexpensive, direct channels of digital communications that have allowed true customer communities to flourish.

Email can engage customers and remind them of events, as well as make personalized suggestions. Social media can allow service and support — often between members of the newly emerged customer community itself. And, a customer's relationship with a brand can go beyond the occasional transaction to a broader based partnership.

Embracing Digital Change to Change Digital Strategy

With all the fundamental changes to marketing wrought by digital tools, it's important to remember that marketing's purpose remains the same — to drive sales for the organization. As we review each of the channels and many of the new tools and strategies in the text, it's important to keep things in perspective. Marketing's goals and successes will ultimately be measured and defined by its impact on the bottom line. Digital channels provide new tools and techniques to support these goals, both in new ways, and by supporting and enhancing traditional marketing methods.

Endnotes

1 Press Release, "Unilever buys Dollar Shave Club for reported $1B value," Posted Jul 19, 2016; *https://techcrunch.com/2016/07/19/unilever-buys-dollar-shave-club-for-reported-1b-value/*.

2 Dollar Shave Club Video; *https://www.youtube.com/watch?v=ZUG9qYTJMsI*.

3 "U.S. Total Ad Share by Medium," eMarketer, March 15, 2017; *https://www.emarketer.com/Report/US-Ad-Spending-eMarketer-Forecast-2017/*2001998.

4 "Instagram More Than Doubles Advertiser Base In Six Months," *Fortune.com*, September 22, 2016; *http://fortune.com/2016/09/22/instagram-advertising-growth/*.

5 "Top Strategic Predictions for 2017 and Beyond: Surviving the Storm Winds of Digital Disruption," Gartner, 14 October 2016; *http://www.gartner.com/binaries/content/assets/events/keywords/cio/ciode5/top_strategic_predictions_fo_315910.pdf*; *https://which-50.com/seven-digital-giants-will-dominate-consumer-interactions-2021/*.

6 Chris Andersen, "The Long Tail," *Wired Magazine*, October 1, 2004; *http://www.wired.com/2004/10/tail*.

7 Ankunda R. Kiremire "The Application of the Pareto Principle in Software Engineering," 19th October, 2011. Bunkley, Nick, "Joseph Juran, Pioneer in Quality Control, Dies," *New York Times*, March 3, 2008.

8 Forrester Research Inc. "U.S. Cross-Channel Retail Forecast, 2012 to 2017."

9 "Why researching online, shopping offline is the new norm," *Retail Dive*, May 17, 2017; *https://www.retail-dive.com/news/why-researching-online-shopping-offline-is-the-new-norm/442754/.*

10 Paul Martin, UK Head of Retail, KPMG in the UK, "The Truth About Consumers," 2017 KPMG Global Online Consumer Report.

BrandYourself is the most comprehensive platform to help individuals and businesses clean up, protect and improve how they look online. This includes minimizing damaging content on the web--a bad Google result, and unfair review, an ill-advised tweet, etc--as well as building a strong online presence that enhances your brand.

www.BrandYourself.com

"Search is the backbone of everything we do as consumers. It provides answers to our important questions, helps us discover new resources, and influences our opinions about new people, places and products. That's why it's so important to understand how search engines work. Whether you're promoting a product, espousing a new idea or, simply trying to get a job, search engines hold the key to helping you get in front of the right people, and making the right first impression."

— Patrick Ambron, Co-Founder & CEO of BrandYourself

CHAPTER 2

Search Marketing: Search Engine Optimization

Search Engine Marketing (SEM) is the foundation of any digital marketing strategy. After all, the most important thing a marketer can do is ensure that the consumer can find the product you're selling. *Search engines* are the "find anything" magic that allows marketers to target consumers who are actively searching for something and present them with a solution to their problem as they are displaying the desire to purchase. *Search results* are the list of options created by the search engine that helps them complete the transaction. Search marketing is so effective it's often referred to as "harvesting intent."

Search engine marketing breaks into two broad areas: *Search Engine Optimization* (SEO) and *Search Engine Advertising* (called PPC after the pay per click method of pricing and paying for the ads). SEO is the strategic process of affecting how search engines work to make a website rank higher in the natural or *organic search* results. PPC is the use of targeted ads in the same searches to show how creative messages perform against selected target keywords. Both can appear on the same page but are very different, as you see in Figure 2.1. We'll address all these aspects of search engine optimization in this chapter and focus on the advertising aspects in Chapter 3.

■ Figure 2.1 Google PPC Results Page and General Search Results Page

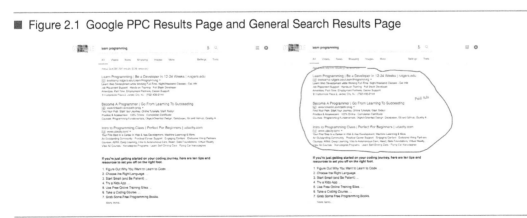

Google and the Google logo are registered trademarks of Google Inc., used with permission.

Search Marketing

Search Marketing as a whole is the single biggest category of digital marketing by revenue, accounting for roughly 40% of all dollars spent in the field. Virtually all of this spend is from the budgets of search advertisers on pay per click advertising; with only a small amount going towards SEO tools and services. Most of this advertising spend flows to the market leader, Google. Since Google has a commanding lead in market share in the U.S., and is effectively the only player in many countries of the western world, we'll approach most of the search marketing discussion from the perspective of how things work with Google. Since most search engines work similarly, these strategies and techniques are also effective against Bing rankings and other search engines with some adjustment.

Search engine optimization is the process of understanding how search engines rank and display websites on the *Search Engine Results Page* (SERP) — and is often seen as part science, part magic. There are an array of techniques and strategies that can be utilized to try and achieve a higher rank in search results, but all rely on an understanding of how search works in order to gain the best results. To truly understand SEO, it's necessary to understand a bit more about how search functions.

Search engines are focused on providing SERPs that allow users to find what they are looking for quickly, efficiently, and correctly. The most important goal here can be summed up with one word: *relevance.* If a search engine can provide the most relevant results, users will return again and again. That search engine will then have established the *search traffic* to show ads against, which generates its revenue. Without relevant results, users will seek alternatives. While other factors are important in finding what you are looking for, relevance is the most important. Google's dominance has developed from continuous innovation that led to significantly improved relevance of its search results compared to others.

The Origin of Search

Early search engines were nothing more than file search from a local computer extended across the World Wide Web. A mostly text-based hyperlinked universe was born — but how would we find anything? The file names of web pages were often uninformative as to what the page was about. Early URLs were not intuitive. Search engines needed to look at the content on the page to understand whether or not it was relevant to what the person was searching for. These "on page" signals were the key to indexing the content correctly. These signals included the content itself — the *keywords* — as well as all of the page *metadata* (structural code hiding behind the page) that could be used to further understand the context.

Initially, basic search and web directories dominated discovery on the web. File search programs were adapted to scan connected computers algorithmically, while human powered directories, most notably Yahoo!, attempted to organize the web into categories using human editors. While editors could evaluate and judge the content and its quality, the massive growth of the web made it all but impossible for the human editors to keep up. (Yahoo! was eventually forced to supplement its limited directory results — Figure 2.2 — with search results from a small new vendor named Google.)

■ Figure 2.2 Archive Yahoo Directory Page

Source: The Wayback Machine screenshot from October 10, 1996.
https://web.archive.org/web/19961020022754/http://www9.yahoo.com:80/.

The explosive growth of websites in the 90s made it clear that search engines needed to become more sophisticated than executing simple file searches across a few connected computers. To address the problem search engines broke the function into a couple of different parts: *crawlers* (also called spiders or bots) that searched the web; and *indexes* that maintained an up to date picture of the web pre-organized by relevance and proprietary ranking algorithms. These algorithms used an estimated 200 factors to determine how to order and when to display lists of results on SERPs.

Crawlers and indexes are technically complex and should not be dismissed. But simply finding web pages and storing the results were not the most differentiating of factors. Crawlers, or *bots*, are software robots that move from web page to web page, collecting all the on-page information they find. This includes keywords, key phrases and content on the page and the metadata about the page (everything from the relative placement and position of content, text formatting like bullets, bold face and italics, to page names, file names and other metadata). The content on the page — indicated by keywords and key phrases — tells the search engine what the page is about and where it belongs in the index or database. The metadata provides additional information and points to relevance and importance across the page.

Initially, it was all about what was on the page. Keywords told the search engines what your page was about, and when to show it in the search results. Naturally, website owners tried to game the system. If you were selling cameras, putting that word on the page as many times as possible could lead to higher rankings. Pages full of keywords were the result. In the arms race for relevance, search engines quickly ratcheted down the value of large numbers of keywords.

Irrelevant keywords came next. If you had a camera shop, it was great to be able to show up in searches for "camera shop" — but there weren't that many, and it was pretty competitive. What if you could show up in other places by finding ways to trick the search engines with other keywords? Soon searches for pop culture icons, for example — with their large volumes — were seeing irrelevant results due to *keyword stuffing*. Repeating "Britney Spears" over and over again on your camera store page could suddenly start driving more traffic to the web page — albeit from confused and unlikely buyers who were looking for the pop star. But since it was free, anything helped. Retailers even learned to put text at the bottom of the page with the text and background color the same, so it couldn't be seen by and confuse visitors, but could be indexed by search engines. (White on white is invisible to a person but not to a search spider!) This trick, too, was soon blocked.

Ultimately, this arms race boiled down to a big problem; search engines were determining rankings, and sending traffic based on what was on a website. But the content was controlled by the website's owners, who had strong incentives to increase visitors/traffic by gaming the system. Human-powered directories became overwhelmed and could no longer be effective. The choice seemed to be either go for decent relevance and woefully incomplete listings, or barely relevant, manipulated results from search engines.

Yahoo!, in fact, tried both of these options in its role as a leading directory and gateway for many web browsers. It added search results from a small startup called Google to supplement its directory listings. Google had innovated a new way to rank relevance, and it seemed to be working very well. (Ultimately people realized they could go direct to Google and they did!)

Google's premise was essentially to "crowdsource" the determination of relevance and *reverse link* popularity rankings. In indexing the web, search engines had a valuable piece of information — all the links on every web page. In other words, they could turn their index inside out and see who was linking to every web page. The creators of the web itself would supply the votes to determine site rankings through the act of linking to other pages.

This approach was based on a simple insight: a community of experts can be used to determine importance within their area of expertise. For example, if you wanted to know the most influential research in chemistry over the last decade, you could hire a team of expert chemists, from different points of view, and have them read and evaluate all the relevant work in the field to produce a consensus. This, like a directory, is of course labor intensive and time consuming, among other flaws. And it's not something that could be easily automated.

What if, instead, you simply took every chemistry PhD thesis for the last ten years, put their references into a database and sorted by search popularity — then viewed these by how many times each work appeared? Surely, the PhD research community is expert in the field, and their choices of reference material in their own area of expertise are independent. Thus, the works chosen by the most researchers should represent more influential or more important material. You wouldn't need to know anything about chemistry — just have access to this sorted list of materials from the experts. It turns out that this works really well.

And what is the web if not a giant reference machine? If I create a web page of my "Top 5 Favorite Funny Cat Videos" and link to them so you can enjoy, you may not agree that they are the funniest. In fact, everyone can create his or her own list. But the videos that are found on the most lists are generally thought to be the best. By ranking the ones with the most links as the "funniest," even computers (which currently don't have a sense of humor) could display a highly relevant list for "Funniest Cat Videos." In short, links — the citations of the web — become the votes for relevance.

This new way of determining relevance dramatically improved the quality of search results. Since links can't be gamed directly by the website owner, simply stuffing pop culture keywords on a page wouldn't help much since no one would vote for it with a link. (This led to the rise of *link farms* — where you can pay to add links to a page in a short-term effort to boost search ranking — but most search engines recognize these and discount them as *spammy* links.)

The small startup Google, which served up these quality links, started to see web browsers appearing directly on its simple page adorned only with a search box to get where they were going. Combined with its clean design — far different from the busy portals everywhere else — its focus on delivering relevant results to get you on your way rapidly began to win out as the launch page of the web.[1]

Search Engine Optimization

This shift in the way search engines work naturally led website owners to seek a more strategic approach to affect and improve their website rankings. Thus, SEO was born. To *optimize* for search ranking today, we start with a deeper understanding of how search engines work. All search engines:

- Follow links to a web page (from a known site).

- Index everything on the page (visible and structural, including what's new and has changed).

- Measure link popularity.

As seen in Figure 2.3 the Google system essentially uses two kinds of crawlers to accomplish this: a *deep crawl bot* that scours the entire web about once a month, and one that returns more frequently to examine rapidly changing sites — a *fresh bot.*

■ Figure 2.3 The Google Organic Crawl

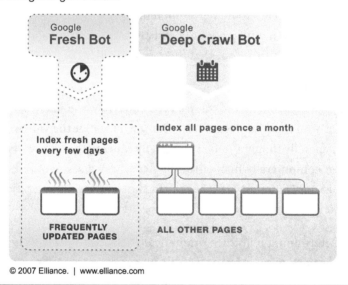

© 2007 Elliance. | www.elliance.com

Source: Elliance infographic on the Google Organic Crawl;
http://www.elliance.com/aha/infographics/google-organic-crawl.aspx.

This system evolved in response to frequently updated sites — like news organizations or blogs –needing more regular indexing in order to stay current. Google's efforts to give you complete and up to the minute results required more and more frequent visits to these sites to ensure the relevant search results reflected the most up to date material. With the rise of social media and sharing tools, it's become harder and harder for Google to keep up. Google sends it bots to re-index sites more frequently when it sees significant changes between visits.

Sites that actively change and grow by updating their content — for example by blogging or adding new pages — will see Google more often as it tries to keep things up to date. A "virtuous cycle" of content creation and search ranking begins by developing a regular content strategy. (We'll talk more about content strategy in our discussion of social media and inbound marketing later, but this is why it's so leverageable — it taps into the foundations of search and discoverability!)

One way for a website owner to handle this is to simply tell Google when something is updated. Submitting a site for indexing is fairly easy and in fact, since it's in Google's best interest to make sure it is as up to date as possible, they even have a free tool to help. Google has a suite of tools called *Google Webmaster Tools* — it's free to create an account and install on your website. One of the features is a tool that notifies Google whenever a new page is created, or an existing page is updated, so Google can send a spider to re-index the site.

Why do we care? Research proves over and over that the top listings on a search results page get proportionally more attention (results of one such study are reflected in Figure 2.4), resulting in significantly more traffic.[2] Virtually all traffic is driven from the first page of results.

■ Figure 2.4 Google Heat Wave Image of "Eye Tracking Results"

Source: Google and the Google logo are registered trademarks of Google Inc., used with permission; *http://www.traveltripper.com/blog/eye-tracking-in-2017-for-google-hotel-searches-why-the-old-rules-dont-apply/.*

Since Google limits these to ten results per page (plus ads) the difference between being a first page result and anything else can be dramatic. There's a search marketing joke that goes like this: "Where's the best place to hide a body? Page 2 of the Google search results — because no one ever goes there!" While the joke may make you groan, the truth is 95% or more of the clicks come from that first page. Two things make this less of a problem than you might think.

First, there are an enormous number of search result pages. All a business or website needs to do is try and rank as highly as possible on those that are most relevant to them. A local pizza shop shouldn't try and outrank a big brand like Domino's on the results page for 'pizza' — but it could beat the big guys in a search for "pizza in my town."

Second, with the massive amount of traffic Google gets, even a small amount of traffic from organic search can add up fast. Incorporate advertising and you can find yourself on the first page of your choice with a high enough bid — we'll review this in depth in the next chapter.

To rank highly for relevant keywords or key phrases, we have to understand how to create content and how to structure our website to indicate relevance. We do this through *On Page Optimization* (content and indexing); then work to generate links to increase the visibility of our site in relevant searches through *Off Page Optimization* or link building. By using our understanding of how Google works, we can ensure that Google knows enough to rank us properly.

SEO vs SEM (PPC Advertising)

It's important to note that while there a lot of similarities between the two methods of getting traffic to a website, there are also many differences. Which is most important? Trick question — the answer is both. SEO and SEM work best together. It's important to keep both coordinated so the two methods can reinforce each other. Generally, SEO is best for generating a steady stream of organic traffic over time, while PPC ads can generate results right away. PPC is best for short-term advertising needs in very competitive areas and is essential for new companies or websites who haven't had time to build traffic. As we see in Figure 2.5 from Prime Media Consulting, when the site is listed organically in a search result as well as having an ad appear, the combination of SEO and PPC together has been shown by some research to increase the clicks on both organic and paid links by about 20%.[3]

Search Engine Optimization and PPC ads both use keywords and can inform each other about performance. Tracking visits from organic keywords can draw attention to search volume that may be available for advertising, and converting keywords from ads can be used to drive a content strategy. It's important in this evaluation to realize both have costs. The costs associated with SEO are usually in the form of time spent, tools bought, or consultants hired by the business. SEM/PPC is based on a cost per click model which is based on a set budget approved by the business. Neither is free. However, SEO does have the benefit of compounding over time as dedicated effort and expertise yields a longer term, more permanent lift in traffic.

■ Figure 2.5 The Value of SEO and PPC Together

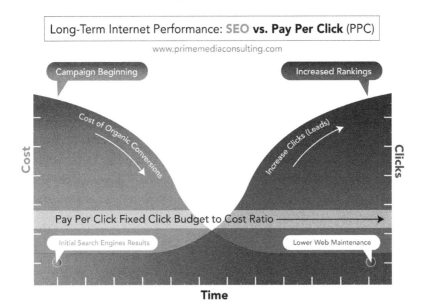

Source: Courtesy of Prime Media Consulting, 2018.

SEO Basics: On Page and Off Page

As we mentioned, Search Engine Optimization is as much an art as a science. This is a practical matter. Google and other search engines don't disclose exactly how and what their algorithms do to perform the ranking against keywords. But we do know in general which things are important: keywords, phrases, links, and lots of other factors — generally thought to be about 200 — that go into its systems. For practical purposes, if Google revealed too much, then enterprising and/or less scrupulous business owners would simply reverse engineer what they needed to attract the traffic to drive sales. Search results would become less relevant to customers, and this would hurt Google and everyone in the ecosystem around them. So, a little mystery keeps the system honest.

There's an entire industry of SEO specialists and consultants selling tools and tricks to help you successfully work the system. The "good guys" help you organize and automate the things Google encourages, deploy your website more effectively, and even help you to create and tag better content. These specialists are known as "white hat" SEO. I reference many of these firms throughout this text such as *HubSpot*, *Moz.com*, and *BrandYourself*, but there are many more quality firms out there.

However, there are also those emails we get that promise you "instant results," "front page rankings" and other "magic beans." These are from the "black hat" SEO consultants. They often maintain link farms, keyword stuff bad content, and employ a big bag of tricks to beat the system. A black hat SEO, for example, might charge clients to put links on thousands of basic websites in an effort to generate better rankings. It's important to point out that black hat is not illegal for the most part — it's simply against Google and others' stated policies (and ethics!). When Google and others discover that people are cheating, they penalize them directly or by changing the algorithm.

Algorithm changes, which reorganize the ranking factors to change the important or different factors, happen all the time — almost every day. In fact, the white hat SEO industry maintains a "weather report" which monitors these changes to the algorithm by looking at thousands of benchmark pages daily and seeing how the results change. For a retailer with millions of dollars of sales driven through organic search results, having your website's product catalog rank highly can net serious profits. Unknown or unfavorable changes can be costly so it's important to monitor these changes.

Major changes to Google's algorithm are always announced and usually involve a significant change in the importance of a ranking factor. These adjustments are given names and their impacts are described in detail to allow businesses of any size to adjust their profiles to main-

The Google Zoo—Panda, Penguin, Pigeon, Hummingbird [and others][4]

When Google began ranking websites, it used a fairly simple algorithm - the sites' relevance to what people were searching for. If you had a decent amount of traffic it ranked you high on its search results. However, as the Internet expanded, everyone wanted to be ranked. Google engineers needed a more automated logic to differentiate the rank of lower quality sites from those viewers found most compelling based on relevance. The first named algorithm release was "Panda" named after Google engineer Navneet Panda, who developed the technology that made it possible for Google to create and implement the algorithm. This supported higher rankings for dynamic news, social networking and popular consumer sites and lowered the rankings for sites containing a lot of fake words or advertising. This reportedly affected almost 12 percent of all search results.

Today, instead of having a million and one websites all trying blindly for the same ranking spot — Google shares the detail and complexity of these algorithm changes in releases with names like *Penguin*, *Pigeon*, *Hummingbird*, and others. This ensures that only the very best and relevant websites rank well and diminishes people from gaming the system. To learn more about specific changes in each update, you might go to Moz's "Google Algorithm Change History" at *https://moz.com/google-algorithm-change*, or other sources in the *Tools and Research* section at the end of this chapter.

tain their visibility (see our *Tools and Resources* section at the end of this chapter for links to some of these sources). Recent major changes — which have cute names like Penguin, Panda, and Pigeon — have changed the way Google handles things like the relative importance of backlinks, original content, and mobile and local signals.

Despite all of the money on the line and the complexity of the algorithms, the place to start is always with the basics: keywords and links.

On Page Optimization: Keywords

The best part about on page optimization — the websites' actual content and structure — is that it's totally under the control of the website's owner or webmaster. They can do whatever they want to make the site showcase the business properly to Google and other search engines. As we've discussed, this is usually done in two ways: creating relevant content tied to keywords and selecting key phrases for high rankings — then structuring the website to send the right signals to Google about its ranking factors.

Selecting the right keywords is the start of any content creation for a website. Using the appropriate keywords in creating your website is critical to ensuring that your target audience of customers, business leads, or media consumers can find you. Keyword strategy and content creation is best thought of as a *style guide* for writing, like journalism. It has guidelines designed to ensure consistency and to make things easy for the search engines.

Choosing the keywords can be an exhaustive process — there can be thousands or more in a major campaign. For this kind of heavy lifting, there are serious tools to discover and manage keyword lists. Here we'll start with a basic strategy for a typical business.

The first thing to do for any website is to understand how consumers or visitors might be looking for you. For some businesses, this is easy: a local pizzeria might focus on "pizza in my town" type of searches. It's a bit harder when a site is new or provides a product or solution that consumers aren't aware of. First and foremost, searchers are looking for something — often this means trying to solve a problem they have. For the pizza place, it could be as simple as what to have for dinner. Defining how searchers might describe the problem you solve is critical.

Next, it's about brand discovery keywords. People who you've previously reached with some form of advertising and promotion will likely search by your brand name. Making sure you appear in these searches is important; business directories, local blogs, and relevant reviews are all ways they may find you. Many businesses can run into problems here. If the business has a common name — for example "Joe's Pizza" — there might be an awful lot of them. There may be similar names as well. In this case, it's important to differentiate as much as possible. Optimizing pages for "Joe's Pizza in the Village" might be a more effective strategy than simply competing for the higher volume but less differentiated keyword.

A complicated or unusual business name might also be difficult for customers to spell. SEO needs to try and take into account all the ways businesses might be found or referred to. This includes nicknames and casual references as well. If McDonald's is doing SEO, they need to think about everything from bad spellers ("MacDonald's" anyone?) to nicknames like "the Golden Arches" and "Mickey D's."

Finally, advertising campaign related keywords also need to be considered. If your public relations or advertising is pushing a slogan or a catchy way to remember the product or service, your SEO strategy needs to have content to reflect this. If you feature a cute lizard in your ad campaigns like GEICO, someone will seek you on Google this way. A catchy song, a famous spokesperson, a funny commercial — all of these items are keywords that can be used to discover the brand. Content highlighting the new spokesperson on the brand's website will provide an avenue for discovery here.

All of this is a great start. The company now has a great list of target keywords to rank highly for. The next step is strategic. We need to decide how to trade off competitive high search volume based keywords for less competitive, lower volume, but extremely targeted keywords. Keywords that are more unique to the specific business, with unique value, local strengths, and so on. Every pizza place on the planet is going to try and rank highly for the word "pizza" and other commonly searched terms. It's unlikely that the local pizza shop would stand a chance against Domino's and Papa John's. But perhaps the hypothetical shop is the only organic brick oven pizza in town? Not as many people searching on that — but the phrase/s may be much more interesting to our potential customers and much easier to try and rank for. See Figure 2.6 on the impact of these trade-offs.

■ Figure 2.6 The Key Phrase Curve

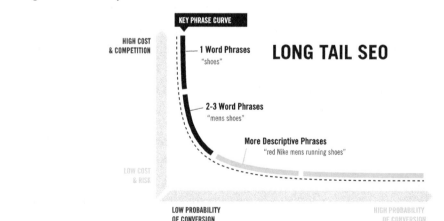

Source: Elliance Infographic; *http://www.elliance.com/aha/infographics/long-tail-seo.aspx.*

The last piece of the puzzle is ensuring the site's content reflects the keywords and key phrases appropriately.

On Page Optimization: Page Structure

More traditional search engine optimization has focused on the page structure and metadata to help make sure that content that's been created can be easily found. However, Google uses many other signals on the page that aren't the content itself to determine what the page is about and what's important. The first one has to do with the page's structure. SEO means taking advantage of every opportunity to tell Google what the page is about and what to rank it highly for. Page titles, URLs, and *metatags* are all descriptors that are used effectively to do this. Unfortunately, this opportunity is often missed. (Figure 2.7)

When a website is being created, one of the things that often happens in some form or another is there will be a team, a white board, and a diagram of the site's proposed structure. The first page — the home or main page — is depicted as a box at the top of the hierarchy. Then lines are drawn to the main sections of the site, and then pages below them. The outline comes together and is used to build the website, which gets pushed out to the world and looks great! Except... no one bothered to think about SEO early in the planning. The *file name* of the main page? "Main.html" or sometimes, my personal favorites "Untitled" or "Home." The page should be titled something like "BestPizza.html" or the like to use every opportunity to tell Google what the page is about. Always make sure the page title (including subpages) reflects the most important keywords for search engine optimization.

Another key element is the page's URL — its *web address*. Google again uses the keywords in the URL to understand more about the page. Unfortunately, as the web grew and sites themselves grew larger and larger, both content and commerce sites became very database driven. Shopping specialists and *content management systems* (CMS) use these databases to dynamically build the web pages for every piece of content or product — a catalog of 200,000 items simply can't be programmed by hand. The database gives the page a URL like *www.store.com/ SKU914hskt* — hardly memorable, and not at all useful for informing Google that the item on the page was in fact kids' sunglasses. There are many tools to overcome this, so make sure you're using them! WordPress, the most popular CMS on the planet, has free SEO plug-ins that scan a blog post or piece of content and create a keyword rich URL for Google to scan.

Formatting signals can also be used to determine which keywords to rank for Google. Google will look at the size of the text, what words are bolded or italicized, and which keywords and phrases appear in bulleted lists. The computer knows that this generally indicates importance. Much like journalism, when content and keywords are or can be important, we lead with the most important keywords first, then the second most important, etc. Don't build your content to a grand finale — it's bad for both the reader and Google.

■ Figure 2.7 Descriptors for Text Elements

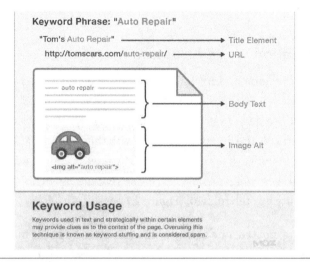

One last tip in a world of growing multimedia content: images and videos are still hard for computers to index directly. This means there are a variety of things you need to keep in mind for SEO. *Page context* is key for understanding what an image is relevant to, so make sure the page is well structured. Tell Google web browsers directly using *ALT tags* what's in an image. Use captions and transcripts that provide more keywords and key phrases for Google to index. And of course, name the image and video files something rich with keywords that tell Google what it is. Lots of pictures from iPhones end up as 'Image789' or something like it.

Of course, for the current generation of marketers, nothing speaks to them like rap music. So let's listen to the master himself — Serge the SEO rapper. While it might make you laugh, he's actually done a pretty good job of laying out the details of SEO links, and the music isn't bad (Link to YouTube video seen in Figure 2.8). And for those of you who think this is uniquely weird — there's another rapper — MC PPC. They even had a rap battle.

■ Figure 2.8 The SEO Rapper

Source: Page Rank, Charles Lewis; *https://www.youtube.com/watch?v=fnSJBpB_OKQ*.

Off Page Optimization: Links

Links are a key factor in determining how highly a site ranks. As we touched on earlier, it's the Internet's way of voting for a website — a link says "this site is relevant to a topic." When a site links to yours there are a number of factors that come into play, but the more links, the higher the site's rank will be. Unlike creating quality content for search engines to find, *link building* is an activity that isn't in the site owner's control. Other sites have to find the content that your site creates, then determine if it's worth linking to.

There are several important distinctions here because *not all links are alike.* For SEO best practices we're really talking about *inbound* links or "*backlinks.*" These are links from other sites to your site. These links vote for you as relevant and valuable. *Outbound* links are links from your site to another and tell Google you are voting for that site. *Reciprocal* links are when two sites link to each other, and much like you'd expect, it makes the value of both less as Google sees this as possible collusion. *Internal* links are links that go from one part of your site to another. This doesn't necessarily help your ranking, but it is good navigation for a visitor and makes your site profile look right to Google. Finally, *deep links* are those links to subpages or something other than the home page of your site from other sites — and can be more valuable in ranking for that page. Testimonials, case studies, recipes, "how to" tools or advice are all examples of subpage content that is valuable.

■ Figure 2.9 The Power of Anchor Text

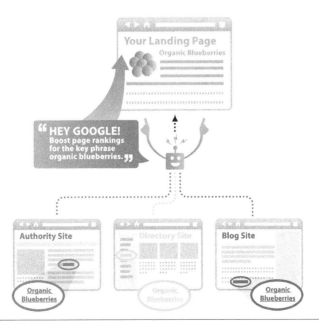

Source: "The Power of Anchor Text," Elliance Infographic;
http://www.elliance.com/aha/infographics/anchor-text-explained.aspx.

Links pass along their votes in a way that's reminiscent of high school. Hanging out with the "cool kids" (and getting links from popular, relevant sites) makes you seem cooler. The more and better sites that link to your site pass along their vote. *Quality and relevance* matter — a well trafficked highly relevant site can pass more "link juice" (yup, that's what they call it) to your site than a small blog your friend runs. The linking site shares some of its page rank with the linked site. It's also important that the site is relevant to the topic you're ranking for.

The *anchor text* of the link is also important. This is why any of your own content, from blog posts to press releases, should never use a link that says "Click here." As diagrammed in Figure 2.9 (page 39), this tells Google what the link is about. If instead it says "Best organic blueberries" than that's what information the link will pass on to rank for.

It's important to note that there is a built-in traffic quality factor that is called *PageRank*. Not named after web pages but Larry Page, who first came up with it. PageRank is a like the Richter scale for measuring earthquakes. Each level higher up is an order of magnitude more traffic. PageRank 10 (PR:10) is the highest — for the biggest sites like Google — conveying much more link power than a little PR:1 blog that has very few readers. As Google says, "PageRank works by counting the number and quality of links to a page to determine a rough estimate of how important the website is. The underlying assumption is that more important websites are likely to receive more links from other websites." SiteAndRunning, another good Internet marketing and website development company offers a clear example of this in Figure 2.10.

■ Figure 2.10 Examples of Google PageRank Scoring

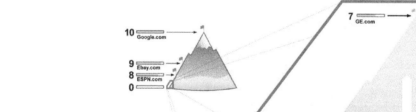

Source: "Google Page Rank Scoring Explained";
http://www.siteandrunning.com/interesting-infographics/google-pagerank-infographic.

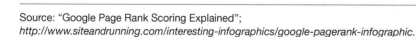

Because of this, link building to rank more highly in search is an aspect of SEO strategy that is nearly indistinguishable in many respects from online public relations (PR). Creating good content, finding other sites on the Internet that might be interested in it, and promoting it to the appropriate influencers who can help spread the word, involves time and energy to get the word out.

Content creation is an ongoing strategy in which site owners regularly create content — web pages, blog posts, infographics, pictures, videos — in the hope of not only having the content discovered on its own but that other site owners will find it valuable or entertaining enough to link to it. Generating content itself can be part of a broader strategy of engagement on social media as well. In this context it's part of *inbound marketing*, which we'll examine in more detail later on. For now, we're focusing on "*link bait*" — creating content people want to share and link to from their web pages (Figure 2.11).

■ Figure 2.11 Infographic on Link Baiting

The Power of Link Baiting

1. Link baiting starts with creating content that is highly entertaining or remarkable.

2. The content is published on the web and gains popularity.

3. A successful link bait can increase inbound links, traffic, and brand awareness.

Digg
Del.icio.us
Stumbleupon
Technorati

Source: Elliance Inc., The Power of Link Baiting;
http://www.elliance.com/aha/infographics/the-power-of-link-baiting.aspx.

Link baiting not only involves creating content but understanding where links might come from — sites that have demonstrated interest in this type of content before. Finding sites can be easy using search or tools like "Open Site Explorer" (see a link to this in our *Tools and Research* section at end of the chapter), which enables you to type in a domain name and see who's already linking to that site. This is a great way to use a well-known competitor to discover what sites are likely to link to your site, and what kind of content drives their interest.

Optimizing Content

What kind of content can a site create to generate attention? And where can a site owner go to get started with some easy links? While there are no guarantees, there are some types of content that seem to work very well at attracting links. There are also some great places to start to get some links going right away.

Content should start with the obvious basics: product information, instruction manuals, directions and the like are the first things customers will lose and seek out. Owners of a fancy television may need the owner's manual they tossed out after installing the set on the wall when they changed apartments. Other things that work well are specialized tools, customized calculators (like rent or buy calculators found on most mortgage sites), white papers, industry resources and infographics. The trick is to make your content engaging as well as functional. *Viral content* such as useful or entertaining videos (like SEO Rapper or our Cat Videos from earlier in this chapter) are always great as well.

Figure 2.12 shows a great example of a site to visit before black tie events and weddings: "Bow Brummel," how to tie a bow tie. With simple instructions and a few photos, it made my tuxedo's finishing touch a breeze. This site was created by an individual who was just trying to help others out.

■ Figure 2.12 Bow Tie Solutions

Source: Bow Tie Brummel, *https://tcf.ua.edu/bowtie/*.

This site should have been created, or co-opted, by any store selling bow ties. Brooks Brothers Men's Warehouse or someone else could have owned all that traffic.

To begin getting links, start with parent companies, suppliers and customers and other places where direct connections exist. Add in price comparison sites, product review sites, and sites that specialize in local businesses or new products. There's a whole family of sites that can provide links. Industry organizations can also be great sources — anything you're a member of, from the local Chamber of Commerce to a professional organization can help.

Next, use tools like *Open Site Explorer* to find out who's linking to your competitors or other industry players. This will reveal expert bloggers, fans, and resources that can begin the building of an outreach list — the complement to your content creation strategy. Finally, whenever you have new content, reach out and ask for links! In your invitation, explain the value or interest the blogger or website might have, or perhaps how it's related to content they have covered or commented on before.

A final way to generate content and links is to have your customers and other guests create it for you. A guest blogger will not only provide you with additional indexable content to be found, but also will spread the word and link to it himself. How far can this strategy go? Well, Yelp and TripAdvisor are two companies that are built on content generated by their users. Not surprisingly, the users have commented and written about almost everything under the sun for their respective audiences. The Yelp and TripAdvisor content generates a lot of links and traffic for the two companies.

One word of warning — don't be tempted to buy links. While it may seem like a shortcut, Google is not only fairly good at spotting these kinds of schemes, but they have been cracking down on them. Paying for a thousand links from random unknown websites might boost your ranking for a bit — but then Google will notice the unnatural increase and take action.

Even more sophisticated tricks get caught and punished. A site called RapGenius — which provided song lyrics and annotations, a highly competitive field to rank in — used a scheme where linking sites were rewarded for their links through a sketchy affiliate program. Google found out and took action to make them stop essentially buying links. As seen in Figure 2.13, for a span of 10 days, the site's traffic dropped by over 80%. It only began to return when they stopped the scheme — and then only climbing back to about half.

Last Thoughts

SEO is the strategy around understanding how search engines work to provide *relevant* sitelinks on their *search engine results pages* (SERPs.) By using that knowledge to create compelling content optimized for the keywords and key phrases most important to the business, a website can generate a lot of traffic from visitors potentially interested in the product or service they provide. *Page structure* and *metadata* are an important part of the signals Google uses to determine relevance, and also need to be optimized. One of the most important factors in determining site's relevance is the number and quality of links to the website. These add their "vote" to the site and can greatly increase its visibility in the search results.

■ Figure 2.13 Google Traffic Report

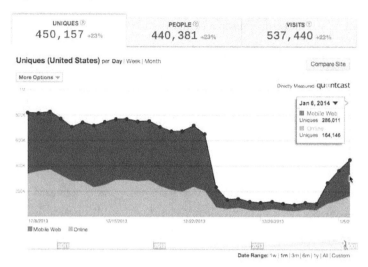

Source: "Rap Genius No SEO Genius: Lyric Site Fails to Recover Traffic After Google Penalty," *Search Engine Watch*, January 2014. *https://searchenginewatch.com/sew/news/2321516/rap-genius-no-seo-genius-lyric-site-fails-to-recover-traffic-after-google-penalty.*

Tools and Resources

■ SEO trends, data and visualizations; *https://www.google.com/trends.*

■ SEO guide; *https://moz.com/beginners-guide-to-seo.*

■ Google Web Master Console and Tools; *https://www.google.com/webmasters/tools/home?hl=en.*

■ Google development and algorithm releases: the *Search Engine Journal*; *https://www.searchenginejournal.com/seo-guide/panda-penguin-hummingbird/.*

■ Release notes on Google algorithm releases; *https://moz.com/google-algorithm-change.*

■ Google Keyword Planner; *https://adwords.google.com/KeywordPlanner.*

■ WordPress SEO Tools; *https://wordpress.org/plugins/wordpress-seo.*

■ SEO Rapper Video — great tips on design and execution of a good SEO strategy; *https://www.youtube.com/watch?v=fnSJBpB_OKQ.*

■ Inbound Link strategies; *https://moz.com/researchtools/ose.*

■ OSE link building opportunities; *https://moz.com/help/guides/research-tools/open-site explorer.*

■ Alexa Page and Traffic Rank tool; *https://www.alexa.com/siteinfo.*

Endnotes

1. General references from "The Search" by John Battelle, 2005.

2. A 2017 hotel-specific Google eye-tracking study and Heat Wave map from TravelTripper; *http://www. traveltripper.com/blog/eye-tracking-in-2017-for-google-hotel-searches-why-the-old-rules-dont-apply/*.

3. Incitrio Blog; *http://incitrio.com/amas-art-of-marketing-conference-seo-vs-ppc/*.

4. (The Google Zoo — Panda, Penguin, Pigeon, Hummingbird) Wikipedia timeline, *https://en.wikipedia.org/ wiki/Google_Panda*; and "Google Panda Has Become Part Of Google's Core Algorithm," *Forbes*, September 2016; *http://www.forbes.com/sites/johnrampton/2016/09/30/google-panda-has-become-part-of-googles-core-algorithm/#496490423f60*.

Moz believes there is a better way to do marketing. A more valuable, less invasive way where customers are earned rather than bought. They're obsessively passionate about it, with a mission to help people achieve it. Moz focuses on search engine optimization (SEO). It's one of the least understood and least transparent aspects of great marketing, and they see that as an opportunity: simplifying SEO for everyone through their software, education, and community.

Moz is a software as a service (SaaS) company based in Seattle, WA.

www.moz.com

"The trend of design toward simplicity and accessibility in software happened for a reason – simple sells, simple's usable, and simple scales."

— Co-Founder & Former CEO Rand Fishkin

CHAPTER 3

Search Marketing:
Search Advertising (PPC)

Search Engine Advertising or paid search (referred to as "PPC" because the dominant payment mechanism is the "*cost per click*" model) is the other half of *Search Marketing*. It accounts for about 40% of all digital advertising revenue in the United States — and is Google's magic money machine that drives most of their revenue, projected to be about of 80% of that $36.7B search ad segment.[1]

■ Figure 3.1 Types of Digital Marketing Activity

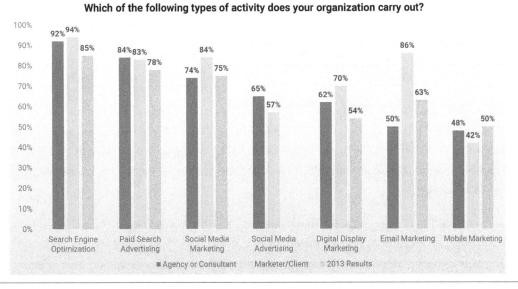

Which of the following types of activity does your organization carry out?

Source: Search Engine Marketing Professionals Organization (SEMPCO), State of the Industry Report; *http://marketingland.com/sempo-releases-state-of-the-industry-report-2015-149082*.

Paid search is very effective and one of the core activities of any marketing organization (Figure 3.1). Unlike SEO, it's also something that can have a relatively quick impact. While SEO is a strategic process that improves traffic over time (organic), paid search is more direct. One creates an account with a credit card, writes some ads, selects keywords, and you can begin seeing traffic come to your website right away.

Paid search is so important and such a significant revenue driver that even today, billions of dollars change hands simply to capture search volume needed to drive the ad revenue it generates. Google, for example, paid Apple 1 billion dollars in 2014 just to remain the default search engine on Apple devices — and is thought to be paying $3 billion each year today![2] Figure 3.2 provides data that seems to support Apple's decision.

■ Figure 3.2 And the Customer Says . . .

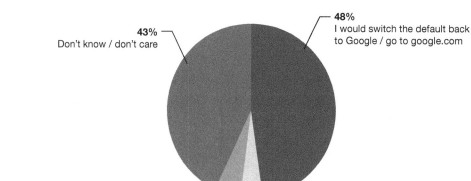

Source: Data from Goldman Sachs Survey, March 2015.

For the advertiser, paid search has many benefits. It is an amazingly effective way of reaching a large audience of potential customers. It's what we call *intent-driven* — that is, people searching for things are literally telling you what they want by typing it into the search bar. Advertisers can then target this expressed intent — "harvesting intent" — with specific messages and offers to address it.

Search is often the starting page for many users of the Internet. A search campaign on Google alone can *reach* more than 80% of unique users of the web — globally! As search is almost universally based on a CPC or *cost per click* auction model, it can be extremely cost effective — especially since ads are shown to consumers who are actively looking for something. In other words, the *timing* is usually at the decision-making part of the marketing funnel. Finally, with keyword-based targeting and well-developed tools and filters to ensure specificity in who sees the advertisement and how much is spent on a visitor (click), paid search can be an extremely flexible and responsive tool at any budget level.

Paid Search: Google and Everyone Else

In the world of Search Advertising, Google is dominant, with the largest market share on the planet. In most Western countries, they have a virtual monopoly, as seen in Figure 3.3. This search share translates into similar share on the advertising side of the business. Google's paid advertising program is called *AdWords*. It is more than a decade old, full of features and tools that help advertisers place their ads next to relevant search results in the hopes of driving sales and leads. All of the other search engines take cues from Google's features and product changes, so for purposes of our examination of search engine advertising, we'll use AdWords as our reference point.

■ Figure 3.3 Search Engine Market Share

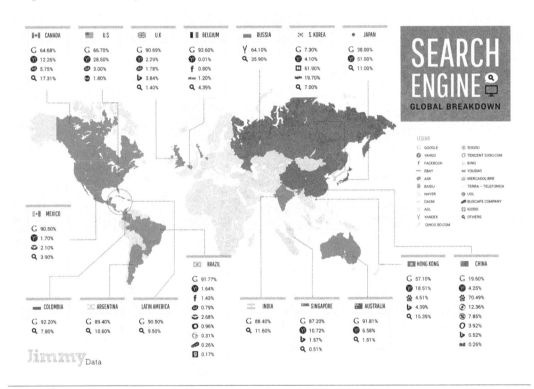

Source: *https://jimmydata.com/blog/search-engine-market-share-country-infographic.*

The AdWords program is well-developed with some terrific features, excellent tools, and lots of options. This is unfortunately reflected in its complexity. AdWords, while accessible to anyone with a credit card, can be difficult to master, which is why Google offers various levels of training and certification. For a business person trying to get help with their marketing, these distinctions help ensure the person they choose to hire has the credentials and expertise to fully take advantage of the Google platform. (Bing, of course, has a similar certification.)

Google didn't always have ads in its search results. In fact, in the late 90s, the early consensus was that the pages of search results were actually almost valueless as an advertising platform. The banner industry was blowing up with its *CPM based models* (essentially cost per thousand impressions, by viewer/audience). This concept was derived from traditional media models and its placement or contextual based targeting. Showing an ad for a mortgage when someone was reading a real estate article just seemed natural; placing a banner on a list of ten blue links seemed awkward and out of place. Google tried selling ads on a CPM basis in 2000 and for the most part didn't do very well.

Google Certification Program for AdWords

Google actually provides a certification in mastery of the AdWords program, where professionals take examinations in Fundamentals of Search and specialization exams in key areas of expertise like Advanced Search, Display, Mobile, Video, and Shopping. The foundation exam and at least one specialist exam are required to be *Google Certified*. Agencies can become badged based on their team members being certified, with the *Google Partner* title. The top 3% of global agencies are singled out as *Premier Partners*.

Here is a description of the basic AdWords exams and what is required to pass them.[3]

Exam	Description
AdWords Fundamentals	The AdWords Fundamentals exam covers basic and intermediate concepts, including the benefits of online advertising and AdWords, and best practices for managing and optimizing AdWords campaigns.
Search Advertising	The Search Advertising exam covers basic and advanced concepts, including best practices for creating, managing, measuring, and optimizing search ad campaigns across the Search Network.
Display Advertising	The Display Advertising exam covers advanced concepts and best practices for creating, managing, measuring, and optimizing Display campaigns.
Mobile Advertising	The Mobile Advertising exam covers the basic and advanced concepts of mobile advertising, including ad formats, bidding and targeting, and campaign measurement and optimization.
Video Advertising	The Video Advertising exam covers basic and advanced concepts, including best practices for creating, managing, measuring, and optimizing video advertising campaigns across YouTube and the web.
Shopping Advertising	The Shopping Advertising exam covers basic and advanced concepts, including creating a Merchant Center account and product data feed, and creating and managing Shopping campaigns.

Here is the link to the Google Certification exams for further learning: *https://support.google.com/partners/answer/3153810?hl=en*.

Here is a link to similar exams for the Bing Ads Certification: *https://advertise.bingads.microsoft.com/en-us/resources/training/bing-ads-accredited-professional-training-faq*.

However, a company called Goto.com had come up with an idea — what if you allowed people to bid on the order of search results? They could pay for the clicks generated — *Cost per Click (CPC)* — and this would create an auction-based market for the results; the highest bidder would appear first. This idea was a great revenue model, but ultimately not interesting to consumers as a destination, so the company (ultimately renamed as Overture) began to supply paid ads to show next to search results pages for other search engines. (Yahoo! ultimately acquired Overture when they discovered their initial search provider Google had become a rival.)

Google launched a similar model in 2002 placing ads next to its own search results. However, Google made one important change to the model that ultimately allowed them to create the AdWords growth engine. Google decided to use *click-through rate* (CTR) — the number of clicks an ad received over the number of times it was viewed, as a percentage — as a proxy for relevance. Google would then favor the ads receiving high CTR's in the auction for showing the ad in the first place. This meant that if an ad with a high bid was unrelated to the search, no matter how high the bid, the irrelevant ads would be dropped as their irrelevance was proven to Google.

This essentially self-regulating and market-driven measure of relevance, when added to the process, had two profound effects:

- First, it made the ads on search pages much more relevant and welcome to users, providing for a better experience.
- Secondly, by focusing on ads that consumers voted for by clicking on them, Google's CPC pricing began to ramp up revenues dramatically.

Today, this is known as a *Quality Score* — the most important factor in the auction based pricing system of CPC for AdWords, besides the bid itself. Quality Score ensures that the more relevant ads as measured by user response get shown more, get more clicks, and also make Google more money. For more detail and back story on search's beginnings — read *The Search* by John Battelle (referenced in Chapter 2).

The Economics of Search Engine Advertising

Search engine advertising is an auction-based system, making the economics of search very market-driven. Advertisers who bid higher, all things being equal, will be shown in a higher ad position and receive more clicks to their websites. This means over time, advertisers better at converting those clicks into sales should continue to be able to bid higher and claim more search clicks, and so on.

As we mentioned, search works by harvesting user intent. Let's say a user types in "Florida vacation." They might click on a link to my travel site and purchase a vacation package for

$1,000. If I make a 50% margin on this package, it's worth it to me to place ads and bid to make sure I get more clicks. Let's say I bid $5 per click, and out of every 100 people who click, 2 buy a plane ticket from me. That means $5 per click times 100 clicks = $500 for 2 sales of 2 x $1,000 = $2,000. With my profit of 50%, I make $1,000 but have only paid $500 to acquire the customer. I want to do this as much as possible. Google has made $500 and I have made $500.

Now, my archrival who has a travel company down the street and who sells the same vacation package, gets jealous of my new customers and decides to also advertise. He outbids me with an $8 bid and has the same conversion rate to sales as me, so he captures 2 sales for each 100 clicks as well. He pays $800 and generates $1000 in profit — or a $200 profit after marketing. But, Google makes $800!

The search market is very competitive, and the dynamics of the auction process mean that Google may eventually soak up all the margin available in new customer acquisition. However, Google is the single best source for new customers for most businesses. As long as the PPC cost and ultimate conversion rate keep the transaction profitable, businesses will keep advertising.

Google AdWords: How it Works

Once you are familiar with it, Google AdWords makes it easy to get started advertising on Google — all you need is a credit card. The basic elements can be created by anyone. Here are the elements you'll need to launch a campaign: *creative, keywords*, and a *destination*.

- *Creative* is the text of the ad unit itself, a compelling message for the prospective customer about your value proposition, within the space available.

- *Keywords*, as discussed in Chapter 2, are how you target the most likely potential customers — using the words they themselves type into the search engine. (Hence, harvesting intent — it's the *potential customer's* intent.) For example, back to the local pizza shop example, they might target "quick lunches nearby."

- *Destinations* are what the ad needs to send the user somewhere when they click — a *landing page*. This destination page is ideally where the prospective user can convert *interest (or intent)* into a real sale or lead.

How is all this organized? First, you create a Google AdWords Account; this is the structure by which all your advertising will be organized. The next level down is *campaigns* — unique advertising programs consisting of different kinds of creative, targeting, and so forth. Each campaign consists of one or more *ad groups*. An ad group has multiple ad units, all written to convince an interested searcher to look further. Campaigns are typically organized around a product or service. Ad groups are thematically organized by messaging, focused on a particular value proposition — one level lower in the hierarchy. The ads themselves are simple text, but writing them to attract users within the tight text constraints is a real challenge.

Google recently launched *expanded text ads* — the biggest change to AdWords since it was created. As you can see in the side by side comparison in Figures 3.4 and 3.5, these new ads provide more prominent headlines, slightly more space for descriptive text, and other changes designed to make them more effective in mobile and desktop searches.

■ Figure 3.4 Examples of Expanded Text Ads

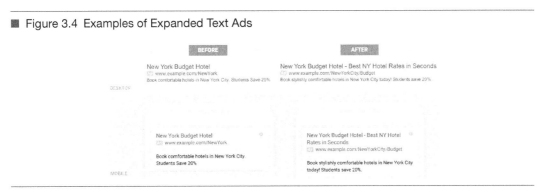

Source: WordStream Screenshot; *http://www.wordstream.com/blog/ws/2016/05/25/google-expanded-text-ads*.

Where Google used to show three ads on the top of the page and up to eight on the side, now there will be only four — two on the top and two on the bottom. Needless to say, pricing and inventory are impacted, and the full impact of this change is still being examined.

■ Figure 3.5 Expanded Text Ad Feature Matrix

Upgraded ad components	Current	Available later this year
More prominent headlines	One 25-character headline	Two 30-character headlines
Longer description line	Two 35-character description lines	One consolidated 80-character description line
Relevant display URL	Manually entered display URL. Any mismatch between your display, final, and landing page URLs will cause your ad to be disapproved.	Domain automatically extracted from your final URL to ensure accuracy. You can customize the URL path.

Source: WordStream, *http://www.wordstream.com/blog/ws/2016/05/25/google-expanded-text-ads*.

Setting up a campaign is fairly simple: generate an ad group and select keywords and key phrases — the things users' type in — to show your ads against. Then, create ads that express your value proposition and encourage the searcher to see your product as the solution to the problem they have. It usually is a good idea to create a dedicated landing page (destination where users will "land" when they click the ad). This page should specifically reinforce the messaging of the ad group to enhance the chances the user will convert.

Your ad will show as a function of your bid. Google searches function as a "reverse Dutch auction" format, where the bid you place determines your chance of winning, but the clearing price is one increment higher than the bid below you. Thus a bid of $2 per click might rank you first, but if the second place bid is $1.70, you would only pay $1.71 for any clicks you receive. Google provides excellent budgeting tools to ensure you spend appropriately and can bid more or less for certain situations.

One other factor in the bidding process is the Quality Score mentioned earlier. Quality Score is 30% of the bid in an auction and represents a relevance factor to ensure that advertisers don't simply bid on every keyword imaginable in a search for volume (as well as ensure they put the effort into making their ads as good as they can be). As seen in Figure 3.6, roughly two thirds of the Quality Score is the relevance and expected CTR of the ad itself, but the remaining amount is also important. This portion factors in landing page experience, including relevance of the landing page keywords. Lastly, accounts with a history and past success get a slight benefit.

■ Figure 3.6 AdWords Quality Score

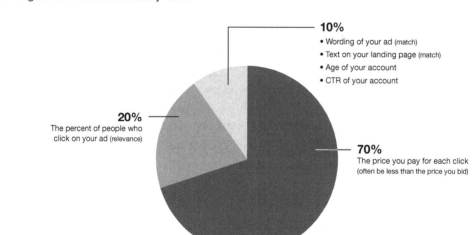

Source: SearchEngineLand; *https://searchengineland.com/reverse-engineering-adwords-quality-score-factors-244192.*

Quality score depends primarily on click-through rate, which is Google's way of verifying that users think your ad is worthwhile. A high click-through rate and the resultant high-quality score can have the impact of reducing your cost per click as you won't need to bid as high to achieve high rankings in an auction. This is a market-driven way for Google to ensure relevant and high-quality ads for its users, and reward better advertisers. (Of course, Google makes its money on clicks, so this is good business too.)

Beyond Search: Additional AdWords

Google search ads are shown against user searches, and are necessarily limited to the number of searches seen through Google and its partners (other search engines that Google powers). However, Google also has a program to allow them to share revenue from the demand generated by the AdWords program.

Google Display Network

Sites that participate in the *Google Display Network* (GDN) can show ads from the AdWords program on their websites and Google shares some of the revenue with them.

■ Figure 3.7 Sample of Where Ads Might Appear in the GDN

| Beethoven.com | BroadwayWorld.com | Poetry.com | rides-mag.com |
| www.beethoven.com | www.broadwayworld.com | www.poetry.com | www.rides-mag.com |

| RSportscars.com | Quote.com | Seeking Alpha | cdkitchen.com |
| www.rsportscars.com | www.quote.com | www.seekingalpha.com | www.cdkitchen.com |

Google and the Google logo are registered trademarks of Google Inc., used with permission.

This can be a great way to get added volume of placements to show your ads already developed for search, but there are pros and cons. The main benefit is the huge increase in volume and reach of potential customers — the GDN reaches 92% of consumers. The cons, can be a varied quality of sites and placements (although you can work around this) and the targeting itself. While GDN placements can also be keyword based, these keywords are taken from the *context of what the site says, not what a user types*. Thus, the intent is missing from the targeting, resulting in a hugely lower click-through rate on an order of magnitude.

A decent search ad might see a 2% CTR where the same ad would be lucky with a .2% CTR in the GDN. Since we often pay by the click, this isn't always a bad thing, but the lower revenue potential should be considered. It's advised to create separate ad groups for targeting searches versus the GDN — the messaging and impact may be very different.

Google Shopping and Product Listing Ads

Another kind of ad very important for e-commerce is the *product listing ad* (PLA). These ads are very different than regular search ads but appear in the results in an image filled "carousel." When Google determines a search might be for a product, it can display a PLA — comprised of a picture, short description, price, and the store name. These ads are driven from data feeds from the business (product owner) and involve no creation of text ads, nor targeting. Google determines when to display the ads based on query. However, since the searches the PLA's are shown against have displayed clear commercial intent (Figure 3.8), they are very high converting — more likely to lead from conversion to a purchase. It also shows all the information a potential customer would need, so by the time they click through many of their typical questions have been answered.

■ Figure 3.8 Examples of PLA Ads

A product listing page on Google demonstrating PLA Ads for sneakers. Google and the Google logo are registered trademarks of Google Inc., used with permission.

Amazon, the largest e-commerce platform in the world, also has a presence in product listing ads, capturing its huge customer base when they are searching for products. Whereas Google uses its position as a start page for discovery, and to separate out commercial searches for PLA units, Amazon is already a commercial platform. Naturally, Amazon has a very large number of searches that have commercial intent: people are directly searching for products on Amazon's site! Amazon's ad business and data feed business are quite large, estimated at over $1 billion per quarter.[4] (Although of course both are dwarfed by its e-commerce business, expected to account for up to 50% of all U.S. e-commerce by 2021.)

YouTube: Text Overlays

While YouTube is primarily a place where video ad placements are used, it's worth noting that it is easy to use the GDN to place text ads as overlays on the bottom of YouTube videos. This combines contextually relevant advertising with the power and impact of video with the accessibility of simply reusing an easy to create (compared to a high-quality video) text ad. The same ads being used for search can be shown here with contextual targeting or by selecting relevant placements. For example, In Figure 3.9 we see a video on dog grooming could be a great place for a text ad from the local pet store.

■ Figure 3.9 eHow Dog Grooming Video

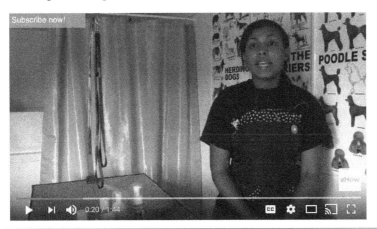

Source: How to video by eHow; *https://www.youtube.com/watch?v=LFtdPtnghm4*. Standard YouTube License.

The Future of Search: Mobile and Local

With search engines driving such a substantial part of the revenue in digital advertising, it's natural that innovation and change are fast and furious. There are many, many areas that are hotbeds of innovation today — it's worth mentioning just a few.

Mobile and Local

By some measures, mobile accounts for more than 50% of all searches and is rising. Reacting to the implications of this trend has meant a major shift in Google's output. The recent change to extended text ads, with two on top and two on the bottom of the search results page, is a direct result of this — providing a more mobile friendly ad unit and a more "mobile first" design to the search engine results pages.

Also important is that ranking factors themselves are impacted by the rise of mobile. Mobile searches are more local and often imply immediate consumption of information, shopping or services in the area (Figure 3.10). "Pizza places near me" is a great example. The searcher wants lunch, not the pizza website with the most traffic or most links.

■ Figure 3.10 Local Search: Mobile versus Desktop

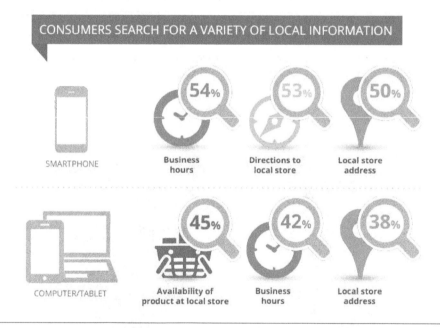

Source: *https://mobilemarketing.com/websites/stats/m-commerce-stats-2013-2014*.

Voice Interfaces

One area greatly impacted by mobile devices themselves is the growth of voice interfaces for accessing searches. Apple's Siri, Amazon's Alexa, Microsoft Cortana, Samsung's Bixby, Google's voice interface for Android, and others are all vying to be the starting point for searches as more and more people try and use their mobile devices on the go, without use of keyboards.

Currently the capabilities of each of these assistants vary. A recent *Fast Company* article predicted that as long as people have to learn how to use, ask questions or make requests of assistants differently, or feel like they must buy or use more than one, it will slow broader adoption.[5] But, assuredly as consumer confidence grows, so will the use of voice interfaces for search.

Multimedia: Video and Pictures

Another thing traditional search has struggled with is to simply and effectively index multimedia results. It's often hard for search engines to know what a picture or video is relevant to since there's no easy way to parse the content as there is with a text file. Most rely on contextual clues from the page's metadata, the titles, caption and so on. But the demand for multimedia is so huge that YouTube is actually the second largest search engine by volume after Google itself.

New specialist search engines like GIPHY, have arisen to address this challenge and capture the demand. The company is said to *serve over two billion "GIFs"* every day to over 300 million active users, and are seen by hundreds of million people searching on both YouTube and the Web. The implication is that because GIPHY understands how this works for micro-form content, it will also be able to distribute micro-versions of advertising messages as well.[6]

Other new engines like TinEye conduct a reverse image search to get more information on where that image originated from. Vevo, Tumbler, and Soungle provide easy search for specialized media such as music, sounds, or video through advanced methods of digital identification.

Privacy

New search engines are always entering the fray in an attempt to capture some of the lucrative market share. Their price of entry? Solving the problems of search in a better way. One such contender is DuckDuckGo, whose main claim to fame is that it does not track its users search queries. By providing privacy, DuckDuckGo forgoes learning about its users and personalizing results and ads, in the hopes that users concerned about privacy and tracking will turn to its service for private results.

DuckDuckGo, founded in 2008 and first funded in 2011, differentiates itself from its behemoth competitor Google by claiming to be the only search engine not to capture user tracking and customized search results. It also says it delivers fewer spam results.

By June of 2013, the website had 1.6 million direct visits and 14 billion users of its search API. That number ticked up dramatically after the website was mentioned in mainstream media reports on how users could avoid the NSA's wide-reaching digital dragnet of personal communications. It hit 5 billion searches in 2017 with no signs of slowing down.

DuckDuckGo is private in two ways. First, the company doesn't track you directly. This means no personalized results, but that's a fair tradeoff for most. The second way is that DDG doesn't pass through information on what you searched on or other user identifiers as it sends you on your way through the search results. Sites you visit have to figure that out for themselves.

Today DDG additionally offers an encrypted version that automatically changes links from a number of major sites to point to the encrypted versions, including Wikipedia, Facebook, Twitter, and Amazon. With concerns about everything from intrusive advertising tracking, to warrants for digital information, to government spying, as well as personal information being hacked constantly, each new report sends DuckDuckGo more users. While hardly a giant, it appears to be addressing a true niche.

Source: "Government Spying Sends Users to Private Search Engine DuckDuckGo"; *http://www.adweek.com/socialtimes/ government-spying-sends-users-to-private-search-engine-duckduckgo/130640*. "DuckDuckGo: what is it and how does it work?" *Wired UK*, February 2017; *http://www.wired.co.uk/article/duckduckgo-anonymous-privacy* 2017 review.

Social Media

Last but not least is the rise of social media. Social networks offer interesting options for advertisers because of the ability to refine targeting, build strong customer affinity and engagement to specific sites and offerings, leverage popularity of mobile and deliver reliable conversion tracking. Two thirds of social media advertising spend is expected to go to mobile in the next three years. Sharing of links on social media is one of the main reasons for its success to date; and yet "social popularity" is still difficult for search engines to track and factor into their search results. Showing the results most important to your friends, and the ads for places they patronize, is one way search engines can try to improve results relevance with social signals.

We will delve much deeper into this, and other varied strategies for social media search and advertising in Chapter 6.

Tools and Resources

■ Here are links to the Google Certification exams for further learning: *https://support.google.com/partners/answer/3153810?hl=en.*

■ Here is a link to similar exams for the Bing Ads Certification: *https://advertise.bingads.microsoft.com/en-us/resources/training/bing-ads-accredited-professional-training-faq.*

■ Google AdWords Planner: *http://adwords.google.com/start/te/how-it-works/#?modal_active=none.*

Endnotes

1. "Report: Google earns 78% of $36.7B U.S. search ad revenues, soon to be 80%," *Search Engine Land*, March 14, 2017; *http://searchengineland.com/google-search-ad-revenues-271188.*

2. "Google may have paid Apple $3 billion to remain the iPhone's default search engine," *Business Insider*, August 14, 2017; *www.businessinsider.com google-paid-apple-3-billion-remain-iphone-default-search-engine-analyst-estimate-2017.*

3. Google Ad Words Program Exam; *https://support.google.com/partners/answer/3153810?hl=en.*

4. "Amazon's ad business is a key part of its future profit growth," *Motley Fool*, October 30, 2017; *https://www.fool.com/investing/2017/10/30/amazons-advertising-business-just-had-its-best-qua.aspx.*

5. "Keeping Track Of All These Voice Assistants Is Becoming A Problem," *Fast Company*, July 10, 2017; *https://www.fastcompany.com/40437293/so-many-digital-assistants.*

6. "In Six Seconds, Giphy Could Make Billions," *Fast Company*, October 3, 2017; *https://www.fastcompany.com/40474454/in-six-seconds-giphy-could-make-billions.*

Movable Ink is one of the fastest-growing technology companies in New York City. We believe that content is at the heart of great marketing experiences. Our software enables email marketers to personalize content at the moment of open, creating better customer experiences and driving stronger results.

New York, NY, USA
www.movableink.com

"Email drives the highest ROI within digital marketing, generating $38 for every $1 spent. It's the preferred medium for consumers to receive communications from a brand. Every person on a brand's email list is a potential or repeat customer that has opted in to hear from that brand. Modern technologies enable marketers to provide consumers with personalized and contextual experiences like never before, and to test and optimize their way to pitch-perfect messages for every inbox."

— Vivek Sharma, Co-Founder & CEO of Movable Ink

CHAPTER 4
Email Marketing

Email Marketing is one of the most foundational of all the digital channels. It can be used for almost any marketing purpose, from customer acquisition to retention and loyalty, and is the core of modern customer relationship management (CRM). Email is also incredibly cost effective, with the Direct Marketing Association (DMA) saying email (marketing email) brings in $44 for every $1 spent.[1] Yet as one of the oldest forms of digital, email also seems quite tired in many ways. As consumers, we get too much email and are deluged with unwanted and unsolicited email in the form of spam. Email just doesn't have that "sexy" factor that newer and more multi-faceted digital channels do.

However, email's usefulness to marketers is undisputed. Most marketers say they will be increasing their use of email as much as possible, because, despite its age lines, it remains a critical element in the digital marketing world. Email is the de facto "username" when we register for new accounts and the primary way we receive everything from shipping notices to receipts. While social and mobile channels garner much of a marketers' attention, email is there too. Email is the source of our identity on all social networks, and these days most email is now opened on mobile devices! Facebook, for example, originally used the ".edu" email suffix when registering users to ensure it was a network of college kids.

Email Effectiveness or Why We Still Love Email

The advent of smartphones and their "always on" ubiquity makes email even more important and a great way to reach consumers on the go. Research shows most people now check their email the first thing in the morning, the last thing at night, and many places in between.

Source: TechCrunch Screenshot, Aug 27, 2015, *https://techcrunch.com/2015/08/27/study-42-of-americans-check-their-email-in-the-loo/*.

Source: Email, We Just Can't Get Enough, Adobe News, August 26, 2015, *https://blogs.adobe.com/conversations/2015/08/email.html*.

One explanation for the email's "unsung hero" status is that when measured by spend, email only accounts for a few billion dollars out of all the digital channels (Figure 4.1), compared to the tens of billions spent on search and display advertising. Given its significance, that hardly seems appropriate. Yet email dollars are consumed primarily by the purchase of the tools and systems needed for bulk email deployment and tracking. Valuing email's impact in digital marketing by its revenue would be as wrong as valuing a house by the cost of its lumber. Email is the backbone of digital identity and ties together customers and their cross-channel profiles.

■ Figure 4.1 U.S. Email Marketing

U.S. Digital Marketing Forecast, 2014–2019						
	2014	2015	2016	2017	2018	2019
Strategy	$149	$175	$203	$233	$266	$300
Analytics	$276	$354	$442	$539	$645	$760
Data	$327	$355	$382	$409	$434	$460
Creative	$334	$374	$416	$458	$503	$549
Integration	$337	$379	$422	$466	$513	$561
Delivery	$640	$626	$598	$557	$503	$435
Total	$2,067	$2,266	$2,466	$2,665	$2,865	$3,067

Source: Data from Forrester Research, Inc.

Email's direct, one-to-one relationship with a customer makes it a very robust channel for successful direct marketing — and by its nature, is fairly tactical. It requires a great deal of experience and testing to create successful email campaigns; from creative and content marketing expertise to the technical aspects of launch and measurement of digital communications. But "success" is also grounded in good marketing principles and strategy, the aspects of which we will address as we move through the chapter.

This one-to-one relationship with a customer or prospect makes executing email-based marketing campaigns a very personal form of direct marketing. From simple personalization of an email newsletter, to using email addresses as an identity marker to tie together a range of marketing efforts, the message can be refined with almost surgical precision. As a high-volume marketing channel, the tools and techniques from developing creative to tracking and delivery have evolved far beyond simply crafting a personal email for a prospect met at a conference. Now, successful campaigns are grounded in sophisticated tool kits and strategies that enable mass deployment of this most personal messaging channel.

Email Strategies and Execution

With email's effectiveness in meeting so many marketing goals it's no surprise marketers desire to expand its use and realize its full potential. It is important that any aspiring digital marketer understand the best practices of email marketing and how to best design an effective email strategy. In this chapter, we'll review:

- Building a list
- Designing an email
- Creating an email
- Deploying email campaigns
- Measuring success

Email marketing is essentially about sending large numbers of emails to potential customers, in the hopes of generating leads or sales. There are many different strategies and approaches to achieve this, but for legitimate marketers the ground rules are pretty straight forward: You must send the right message to the right audience at the right time. The challenges in doing so require thoughtful strategies for leveraging data to create, design, and deploy compelling content at scale for each individual customer.

First, email at scale is difficult and very different than sending an email as follow up to an individual. *Email campaigns* are designed communications that can go out to thousands or even millions of people at a time and generate large-scale impact. To be effective requires understanding a few important ground rules — especially when all of these thousands of emails are personalized to each individual customer. First, one must have the technical capability to efficiently create and source content for the email; second is the ability to send these personalized emails at scale; and third and most important, the legal and ethical grounds to ensure customer acceptance of the email being sent.

How Email Works

Sending email for marketing almost always requires specialized tools and services. For most marketers, this means an *Email Service Provider* (ESP). What's an ESP? A company that provides the scalable infrastructure to create, deploy, and track large volumes of email, as well as ensuring compliance and deliverability in the face of changing laws, regulations, and technical challenges. Among other things, they usually provide:

- Templates for creating emails

- Tracking of "opens," clicked links, and other key data points

- Specialized infrastructure for delivering mass emails

- List management and compliance features

While it's possible to contract with a vendor directly to manage your email marketing or even build an internal system with hardware and software, more and more companies use *Software as a Service (SaaS)* models. This is when a company pays a monthly fee, usually based on list volume or send volume, for cloud-based managed services. Email Service Providers are specialists, with dedicated hardware and management software that allow even small firms to utilize sophisticated tools for creation, deployment, tracking, and compliance, all available as part of a monthly cloud-based subscription. Exceptions to this include selected communications from firms in finance, pharmaceuticals, energy, and other industries with heavy regulatory requirements who may require more control.

ESPs handle a large array of specialized tasks that make it easy for marketers to focus on creating and deploying email campaigns to reach their goals. Sending high volumes of email requires the functionality found in these proprietary marketing automation platforms to push out these campaigns. The scale is sometimes hard to imagine but remember that some companies have tens of millions of customers. A company sending out an email a second (perhaps through a team of very unlucky interns) would need almost a year to reach 30 million customers. Scaled infrastructure is key to making sure that the email about "This Week's Specials" reaches your customers this week , and that the content is relevant to the customer's current interests and context.

Having an Email Service Provider also simplifies tracking and compliance. With a system in place to manage lists through a trusted third party, it's easier to ensure that customers can and will unsubscribe to a list instead of reporting it as spam. ESPs ensure that emails contain the legal necessities such as business information and unsubscribe instructions to make sure companies don't trip on laws that protect the consumer. Many ESP plans used by small businesses or those starting out in the market have affordable price points or even offer a free tier to get started, sometimes known as a "freemium model." Two popular ESPs used by small and medium businesses are MailChimp, which provides a "forever free" tier for those starting out with small lists (under 12,000 emails at last check) and limited sending needs, and Constant Contact, which provides a free trial. Both provide excellent educational material and support for those getting started.

Who to Send To: List Building

The first thing an email marketing campaign requires, of course, is someone to send an email to. While some businesses see *list building* as a "chicken and egg" type of problem, most start very simply: collecting emails from existing customers. Local businesses might have a signup sheet on a clipboard at the cash register or a comment card at the table in a restaurant — this begins the tradeoff of email marketing with existing customers. Customers and those interested in the product or service will be the first to sign up, allowing the marketer to begin building a list to market to. Larger retailers and companies with bigger budgets list build by requiring cashiers and other personnel to collect email addresses as part of their checkout process. Whether it's an offer to join a loyalty program, receive receipts by email, or simply to get a coupon, there's an exchange being made to build the email list — a valuable long term, *permission-based* asset for communicating with customers.

While most marketers focus on building their lists organically, many businesses are tempted to speed up the process by renting or buying an email list. Renting a list is simply a form of advertising and promotion. A marketer might locate someone who has an email list that may have potential target customers in it, and contract with the owner of the list to send these people an email. When done properly, this type of *qualified list* represents high value leads, and the trusted third party sending the email on the behalf of the marketer provides an implicit endorsement, often written in the style of the owner and their newsletter. The downside of renting is that the marketer never takes possession of the actual email contacts, so they can't follow-up. One might receive some basic metrics on reach and who opened, but usually not enough data to track the effectiveness of the campaign. One of the best uses for this kind of promotion is a branding or awareness campaign for a new product, where it's necessary to expose people to the new message in order to kick off longer term marketing plans. A strong offer or promotion can often get people on this list to offer their email on their own and start a relationship.

Buying a list is another option but one that is rarely effective and often associated with low quality bad actors. Owners of high quality lists are generally protective and send only their own emails or those from chosen and vetted sponsors for a fair market price. Emails bought through list vendors ("5 million addresses for only $99") are often harvested or even stolen. Email list vendors can acquire emails through a variety of methods: scraping posts on websites and social networks that contain them, hackers who break into databases, so-called "dictionary attacks" whereby they simply string together names and company domains (e.g. first initial, last name @ company.com such as *msmith@bankofamerica.com*).

Newer methods include misleading collection efforts and list resale, often called "co-registration." Co-registration provides some value — a coupon or white paper or something — in return for an email. The fine print allows for "partner resale."

These last scenarios fall between slightly unethical to downright illegal. From a practical perspective, it simply isn't worth it. A legitimate marketer might pay to make a short speech in front of a group of relevant executives, but they would never hand over their wallet to jump on a soapbox in a train station. These types of lists usually represent unqualified people who likely have no interest in the brand or message and may even be actively hostile. A legitimate brand may run the risk of being labeled *spam* — both bad for their reputation and potentially open them up to large fines or other legal repercussions.

Building a list, then, is the way to go. All major ESPs provide simple sign up forms as part of their list management services. To induce prospective customers to share their emails, most marketers provide a value exchange: discounts and coupons (hard $$ always works), early or proprietary information (VIP status), and perhaps most popular, useful or timely information. This approach can look and feel very commercial — a clothing retailer providing fashion trends information, or a ticket reseller providing concert alerts and information — but it's a tradeoff consumers are willing to make.

There are three levels of receiver activity that are inversely proportional to the ultimate quality of the list created. That is, the harder it is to sign up, the more likely the list represents truly engaged and interested people. (This isn't simply theory — the open rates and other key metrics of email lists demonstrate this.)

These three levels are:

- *Opt out* means that you are automatically added to the marketing list unless you expressly uncheck the option and say no. We've all seen "would you like to receive…" This provides the highest volume of emails, but lower receiver engagement — users trade their email for something but don't open future marketing messages.

- *Opt-in* requires the user to take an action to sign up. These users clearly know the value of what they are asking for and are more apt to open and engage with subsequent messaging.

- *Double opt-in* is the strongest form of list building. This means the user affirms they want their email added to the list — and then confirms this again by interacting with an email confirmation sent to them. As seen in Figure 4.2, this avoids users gaming the system by using other people's legitimate emails to claim value, and ensures a high quality list of truly interested recipients for the marketer.

■ Figure 4.2 The "Double Opt-In" Process

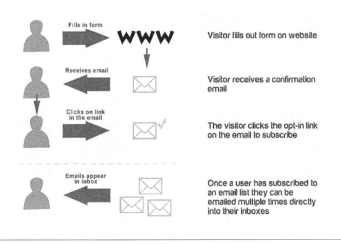

Source: Juno Web Design, a brand of United Online, offering reliable, value-priced Internet access. *http://www. junowebdesign.com/email-marketing-double-opt-in*.

Spam — Unsolicited Bulk Email

As consumers, we know that one of our biggest pet peeves is simply receiving too much email. It's an overwhelming firehose of necessary information but a large portion of it is *spam — unsolicited bulk email.* From a consumer's perspective, spam is easy to define: Email I don't want, that comes too frequently, or that I didn't ask for. This has raised some challenges for legitimate marketers as qualitative filters built to catch spam sometimes make it difficult to get our communication through to recipients. What is too frequent for one person may be fine for another.

Spam, in its basic definition, is *unsolicited bulk email*. There are legal specifics, but each term is essential. *Unsolicited* means it wasn't requested—the user didn't "sign up" as we described earlier. It also means that no business relationship currently exists between the sender and recipient. *Bulk* means that 200 or more of essentially the same message (customization doesn't count as different) are sent "en masse." An individual person can send as many emails as they want until they get tired of clicking send, one at a time, but bulk email is mass email. (Note: this area has legal specifics and varies from country to country—consult a professional or your ERP with a specific question.[2])

The CAN-SPAM Act is a United States law that was enacted to govern spam. It sets the rules for commercial email, establishes requirements for commercial messages, gives recipients the right to have you stop emailing them, and spells out tough penalties, large fines, and legal action to spammers who violate the rules. High profile cases often shut down the worst offenders, sometimes only temporarily, but sadly, the true bad guys simply move to jurisdictions with no legal problems. Email is international after all.

Legitimate companies too can face business challenges due to spam. You'd be surprised to hear the brand name companies that made the list of "spammers" in the past few years (see link in the Tools and Resources section at the end of this chapter). Spam blocking tools are also problematic. It's tough to generate sales from your beautifully designed marketing email if it's never seen because it goes into an individual's spam folder or company firewall. Best practices dictate that to send valuable email, you must set clear expectations of the content and amount of email to be received, provide simple ways for receivers to unsubscribe, and be careful not to *over-communicate* and upset your subscribers. Legitimate ESPs will actually shut down marketers whose complaints get too high to avoid problems for their other clients. Getting blocked could be the least of your worries!

Assuming you're planning on executing email campaigns the correct way, and have selected a reputable ESP partner to assist you with compliance and deployment, a digital marketer's decisions then come down to three strategic questions which will drive our next round of tactics:

- What to send in the email (the content)?

- How to design it for deliverability and appeal (the "envelope")?

- When to send (the deployment strategy)?

Good representation of top subjects and purposes of email campaigns can be seen in Figure 4.3.

■ Figure 4.3 Marketers Top Email Initiatives

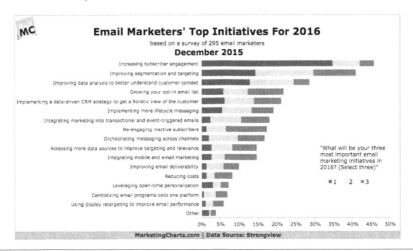

Source: http://www.marketingcharts.com/featured-63933.

What to Send: Content Considerations

Content is the core building block of all marketing, and email is no exception. Designing the creative content (message, image) in a marketing email is like any other form of communication; effectiveness will depend on having a larger content strategy. Email content consists of both text and images. While it's important to provide customers with the right message or offer, marketers should also take advantage of visual content. Images work so well because humans are evolved to be visual. Our brains can process and respond to images 60,000 times faster than text, therefore visual content provides a powerful and effective way to tell a brand story. A complete content strategy must consider how images, the offer, audience, industry, the relationship of the sender to the recipient, timing, and other factors come together to create the best possible customer experience. However, there are some basic principles that help us understand what people expect when interacting with digital commercial messaging. The most basic questions to answer are: "What's in it for them?" and "Why would I want to open this message?"

The first important principle to remember is that the initial and ongoing value a customer receives will determine their willingness to open and *continue to engage* with emails over the lifetime of the relationship. Building a sense of value exchange and trust is critical. Email communications should support the brand, its core values and messaging, and be a synergistic element of the overall integrated communication strategy. If a brand has a heavy focus on visuals and imagery, it makes sense to continue that style in email communications to create a consistent experience. Email images, text, colors, appearance, and layout should match the brand's site structure to the extent possible. Email marketing should reinforce the brand experience.

From Good to Great:
Some Fun Email Campaign Ideas

There are many "best of" lists out there profiling wonderful email campaigns, from humorous to stylish to simply effective. Companies like HubSpot, Marketo, Moz, and others offer lots of great campaigns that you can get ideas from. Here are just a few of our favorites paraphrased from HubSpot's "Best" of 2017 list.

Birchbox. The subject line of this email from beauty product subscription service Birchbox got one of the HubSpot colleagues clicking when it read: "We Forgot Something in Your February Box!" Of course, if you read the email copy, Birchbox didn't actually forget to put that discount code in your box—but it was certainly a clever way to get your attention.

As it turned out, the discount code was actually a bonus promo for Rent the Runway, a dress rental company that likely fits the interest profile of most Birchbox customers—which certainly didn't disappoint. That's a great co-marketing partnership right there.

Uber. The beauty of Uber's emails is in their simplicity. Subscribers are alerted to deals and promotions with emails like the one you see below—a brief initial description, paired with a very clear call-to-action. HubSpot noted how consistent the design of Uber's emails are with its brand. All of its communications and marketing assets tell the brand's story—and *brand consistency* is one tactic Uber's nailed in order to gain brand loyalty.

HireVue. This is great example of list management with humor. "Saying goodbye is never easy to do… So, we thought we'd give you a chance to rethink things." That was the subject of this automated unsubscribe email from HireVue. HubSpot editors loved the flow, from simple, guilt-free messaging to the great call-to-action button copy. It's a clever way to purge subscriber lists of folks who aren't opening your email lists, because low open rates can seriously hurt email deliverability.

We also encourage you to read HubSpot's "104 Email Marketing Myths, Experiments and Inspiration" for other ideas (link at the end of this chapter in Tools and Resources).

Source: "15 of the Best Email Marketing Campaign Examples You've Ever Seen." Originally published July 20 2017, updated October 11 2017; *https://blog.hubspot.com/marketing/email-marketing-examples-list*.

Email marketing also calls for a balance between creativity and practicality, creating a sense of comfort and relevance at each stage of the relationship. Too mysterious and customers won't trust or understand who it's from or why to open; too mundane a message won't grab their attention. Marketers call this "clarity with a hook," which usually involves value, urgency, exclusivity, or timeliness. All of these "hooks" help, but are not that easy to do!

Another essential principle of email marketing is to make sure the key message points in the sent email are always *above the fold*. This term, derived from the top stories being on the top half of a folded newspaper to catch the eye, means that the core message can be read as the email opens, without scrolling. In these days of fragmented platforms and devices it's important to understand who and how people are accessing email. Globally, the breakdown is roughly desktops (37%), laptops and tablets using webmail (30%) and smartphones (33%).[3] Marketers must also test multiple platforms to ensure the email views properly. Any reputable ESP will have a responsive design function or capability that ensures email design is optimized for various devices. (See more statistics in our Tools and Resources section at the end of this chapter.)

Lastly, email is often opened where elements like images, multimedia, or active code are disabled by default to prevent unwanted tracking and malware when activated. When designing, it's important to consider what the "text only" version might look like and how it will read without these elements. This is particularly difficult for visual brands, but the main hurdle is — can the reader complete the desired goal or "action" of the email if the images aren't present? If the special sale information or promo code is only visible in an image that isn't displayed, this will drastically reduce effectiveness. Providing a text alternative to explain your offer and perhaps even entice the user to turn on images for the full effect are common work arounds.

How to Send: Design Considerations

Just as a beautifully written direct mail offer will never be seen if the envelope and other materials fail to make it appealing and compelling to open, so to for the components of an email campaign. Things like subject lines, email design, and even the sender designation can positively affect your email campaign open rates. Here are a few key pointers to entice the user to open the email and help them to easily find the content:

- **The subject line** is perhaps the most important (and overlooked) element of the email. Most ESP services allow testing of subject lines to maximize open rate. Subject lines should be between 25-40 characters, according to most research, and provide a clear and compelling reason to open the email. Discounts, sneak previews, or highlighting "special" compelling information are all proven ways to encourage users to open. However, words like "free," "clearance," "alert," or anything with dollar signs are among hundreds of words or phrases spam filters reject. Sites like HubSpot Trigger Words are a great source for the full list. (Yes, this is in Tools and Resources too!)

- **The sender line** is equally important. It's critical that it communicates the brand message but also feels personal. Many brands adopt the "First name, Last name from Company name" approach which is a personal approach but retains brand equity as well.

- **Design and layout** involve the finer points of structuring the email itself. This may seem like more of a digital design challenge, so most major ESPs provide a variety of *customizable templates* to help non-designers achieve their goals. These are easy to update with brand messaging but designed with best practices in mind. These types of templates allow marketers to begin their email marketing standing on the successes of previous and proven brand experiments. Of course, with in-house design expertise, you can accomplish the same thing with your own custom designs. MailChimp has a large variety of templates to get you started. Examples in Figure 4.4.

■ Figure 4.4 Sample Email Templates

Source: Courtesy of MailChimp *https://inspiration.mailchimp.com/#all*. © 2001-2018 MailChimp®. All rights reserved.

When to Send: Strategy Considerations

Experienced email marketers often respond to questions about how often to send emails by saying "as often as possible." Frequency is proven to be effective when coupled with a good list and compelling content. However, email marketing is about strategizing ways to support more frequent outreach by finding new ways to provide welcome value. In fact, whether a marketer sends more emails or fewer emails that are more finely targeted, they are still required to come up with a greater amount of compelling content. A compelling message doesn't have to necessarily be sales driven. Providing valuable information — themes or staggered offers — and occasional entertainment ensures that the recipient remains engaged and intrigued enough with the brand to continue to be open to more sales or conversion-oriented messages in the future.

The first place to begin from a marketing perspective is to define what are considered "necessary" brand communications. Receipts, shipping notices, and other logistical updates all provide opportunities to send valuable information and earn trust. While overt marketing can sometimes miss the point here, this approach can institute the basis for recipients to welcome the brand into their inbox, even look forward to the company's messages. This establishes you (the brand) as a sender whose messages deliver high value — everyone wants to know where their packages or travel updates are! This also lays the groundwork for additional appropriate touch points for future marketing.

Communications like these are ideal for targeted *cross-selling* messages. Just bought a sweater? The confirmation email could offer a link to select a pair of pants to go with it. Purchased a plane ticket? An array of hotels and rental cars await. Sometimes *upsells* like upgrades or additional product enhancements can be a positive addition when crafted appropriately.

Newsletters and informational emails can also be a welcome inbox addition. Fashion trends or on site reporting from events ("what did they wear?" type of messages), interviews with industry figures, even case studies about how other customers gain value are good examples. This type of content is easy to create for newsletters or other regular communications. The content supports the brand and the sales messaging can support the content.

More sophisticated strategies involve developing communications that are based not on the schedule of the marketer, but on the schedule of the customer. These are called *Trigger-based emails.* They allow an optimized, and customized but standard email to be sent out based on an action or "trigger" point reached by a consumer or groups of consumers. Many trigger-based emails are calendar- or event-based; for example, Mother's Day, the holidays, or even spring planting season for a garden store. Others can be based on a customers' unique journey through a website or a known and planned behavior like renewals, reorders, or events — like watching a video or downloading something, for example. See Figure 4.5 for examples of email marketing triggers that are easy to find and adapt to your business.

Additionally, sophisticated uses of essential communications, cross-selling and upselling, triggers, and behavioral marketing require the ability to manage and activate all kinds of data and content across multiple sources from web, social media, CSV files, blog, CRM data, APIs, and more. The email campaigns that provide the best possible customer experience require content that goes beyond the basic product offer, and email marketers should consider multiple sources to pull and repurpose existing content that's often scattered across the entire enterprise. Behavioral marketing is also becoming more important with email and is allowing marketers to go beyond the basic cross-sell of suggesting a pair of pants with a sweater, but suggesting pants based on the customer's browsing history, product preferences, lifestyle preferences all the way down to what's actually in stock online and in store at the nearest location. Much of this is being enabled by technology, and increasingly, AI and machine learning will play a larger role in email content.

One common trigger-based email that has a very high ROI is an *abandoned shopping cart reminder* — as seen in Figure 4.5. This is the scenario where a customer has created an account, shops, drops an item into the online shopping cart, but fails to complete the purchase. This can trigger an automated email to them in a few hours or days later with an easy clickable button that drops them right back into the purchase process — even providing a new offer or incentive to complete the purchase, like free shipping or credit towards the next purchase.

■ Figure 4.5 Trigger-Based Email

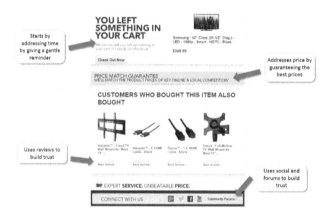

Abandoned shopping cart reminder.

An example of a great trigger occurs in *lead generation.* A prospect completing a form triggers an email full of marketing information on the product, along with the desired PDF or white paper that the prospective customer signed up for. One client of mine, a 3-D printer company, needed to find leads among teachers who might purchase printers for the classroom. They collected emails by offering a valuable "Teacher's Guide" with many ways to incorporate 3-D printing into classroom learning. Naturally, the teachers began to receive regular follow-up tips and offers.

Cadence-based emails take the strategy of messaging on the customer's timeframe to its logical conclusion. In the online travel space, purchasing an airplane ticket puts you on a sequence of timed emails leading up to and after your flight: reminders, checklists, offers of hotel and rental cars before the flight. An informational email a week ahead with tips to prepare for your flight, destination-based weather updates and suggestions, and finally "day of" reminders with travel tips are all welcome — and all on a logical pattern designed to maximize the brand's utility and value.

Perhaps the best example of a cadence campaign for true "life cycle" marketing is the example of a client marketing baby formula to expectant mothers, illustrated in Figure 4.6. By collecting just two pieces of information from a potential customer — email and the due date of the baby — this brand was able to construct a sophisticated and effective cadence of emails to the moms to be. Signing up launched a weekly delivery of a "what to expect when you're expecting" email for the user. Carefully selected emails — and the resultant clicks — allowed for further segmentation and targeting. Early on, the emails provide information and support. As time goes on brand messaging on the uses of formula as part of bringing up baby are highlighted, segmented for different personas of "Moms" (working moms, etc.). Finally, as the big day draws near, coupons and free offers — or even gift bags mailed to them if they provided their address — become timely.

■ Figure 4.6 A "Life Cycle" Email Marketing Campaign

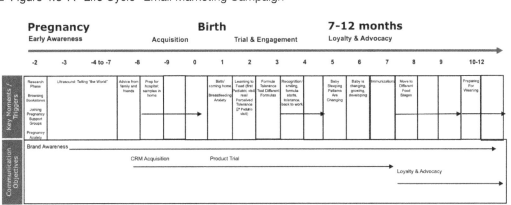

Source: Kagan, 2018

After the due date is reached, follow-up emails continue with tips and parenting advice, as well as how to coordinate formula into the process. Finally, as the child exits the target age for consumption, the messaging fades away as well. Truly "life cycle" at its best.

Measuring Success

All of digital marketing can be very data driven, and email, with its roots in direct mail, is no exception. Key metrics like delivery rates, open rates, click rates and the like, can be used to compare and test better messaging and design, modeling the impact of one area or another for future improvement. The bottom line, as always, is the bottom line — how much revenue did the email campaign generate is always the ultimate metric.

At the highest level, marketers monitor how many people are on an email list as an important baseline to track growth. This is referred to as *reach.* Email list growth, *reach,* is a measure of current list size, plus new additions, minus unsubscribes. This is a metric that speaks to the viability and engagement with the brand or campaign. Most marketers focus on getting new emails — but managing (and interpreting) the churn off the list can be a critical factor in keeping a list growing and healthy. One good way to do this is to allow those trying to unsubscribe to instead reduce the frequency of emails they receive (weekly digests instead of daily, for example). Another is to allow them to "pause" for a while as shown in this example in Figure 4.7 from Gatwick Airport.

■ Figure 4.7 Example of Alternate Unsubscribe Communication

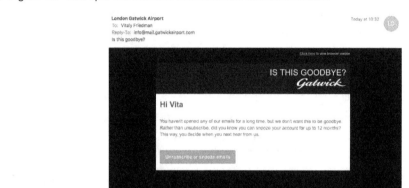

Source: Gatwick Airport Communications. *https://econsultancy.com/blog/69181-10-rules-for-getting-email-unsubscribes-right*.

The *delivery rate* of an email list is another important factor to understand. Emails sent don't always arrive successfully; some of the emails *bounce* from a bad address, others may be blocked by spam filters. A high bounce rate of emails, the percent rejected per emails sent, may indicate that the subject line, size, or content is triggering firewall or spam filters.

Once you have a good understanding of *list performance*, other significant metrics representing email success are the *open rate* — percentage of emails opened by the end user over successful deliveries — and the *click-through* rate — clicks within an email to another digital destination. The open rate is a *direct indicator* of interest in seeing what's inside, attributable to the success of the subject line and its value proposition. It is also a *broad indicator* of the strength of the brand and its perceived value. If reading the message inside is the ultimate goal, success is getting as many people to see it as possible.

The click-through rate on internal email links is more important if the emails are intended to drive sales, for example from an e-commerce site. Compelling offers or appealing products can influence this. Finally, the most important metric is the ultimate *conversion rate* and the dollars generated by the email.

Figure 4.8 offers an example of email marketing statistics that MailChimp tracks for various industries in their "Email Marketing Benchmarks Report."[4] It contains lots of data and guidance on metrics to help marketers evaluate and differentiate email marketing opportunity across industries. We've selected just a few here to illustrate the variance between different audiences.

■ Figure 4.8 Email Metrics by Industry

Industry	Open	Click	Soft Bounce	Hard Bounce	Abuse	Unsub
Agriculture and Food Services	24.71%	2.98%	0.58%	0.43%	0.02%	0.29%
Beauty and Personal Care	18.48%	1.96%	0.38%	0.38%	0.03%	0.32%
Business and Finance	20.97%	2.73%	0.66%	0.55%	0.02%	0.23%
Computers and Electronics	20.87%	2.16%	1.02%	0.70%	0.02%	0.31%
Construction	22.10%	1.95%	1.56%	1.20%	0.04%	0.43%
Health and Fitness	21.93%	2.57%	0.43%	0.44%	0.03%	0.39%
Manufacturing	21.74%	2.33%	1.41%	0.99%	0.03%	0.36%
Media and Publishing	22.14%	4.70%	0.28%	0.18%	0.01%	0.12%
Pharmaceuticals	20.02%	2.51%	0.79%	0.74%	0.02%	0.22%
Retail	20.96%	2.50%	0.35%	0.30%	0.02%	0.28%

Source: MailChimp, Email Marketing Benchmarks, 2017; *https://mailchimp.com/resources/research/email-marketing-benchmarks/?_ga=2.38332707.1201754590.1506346160-1673647173.1499819357.* © 2001-2018 MailChimp®. All rights reserved.

Integrating Email with Other Channels

As previously noted, an email address has become the de facto form of identity online. This has led to some interesting effects where email is being used beyond the inbox. While communications for many casual topics and personal reasons have moved to social media or chat and messaging apps, email is still the primary method of commercial messaging, ecommerce confirmation, customer relationship management, and support. Due to its flexibility and the clear canvas it presents, email also can serve as a great hub for content from other channels such as social media, pulling in live feeds and images like user-generated content (UGC).

Beyond its growing use as a registration gate for social media, email is also being used in search and display advertising. It helps provide both a better targeted audience in advertising and allows better messaging in advertising targeted at known users and customers versus new acquisition. Google, for example, allows *remarketing lists in search advertising* (RLSA), where an advertiser can upload a list of emails. When Google can match the email to a current search, the advertiser can bid more or less on ads to reach that user, even modifying the message they see. (From "Try Us!" to "Come Back!" for example.)

■ Figure 4.9 Mobile App Usage by Age

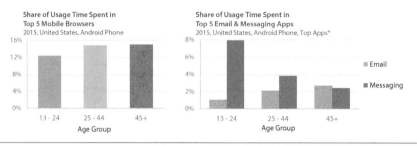

Source: *https://techcrunch.com/2016/03/24/email-is-dying-among-mobiles-youngest-users/*.
Original: *https://www.appannie.com/en/insights/adapting-your-strategy-user-engagement-patterns/*.

Social media allow for similar if not even more powerful targeting. Custom audiences on Facebook and Instagram, and tailored audiences on Twitter, allow advertisers to upload email lists and match them to known and existing user profiles. Facebook will often match more than half of an email list due to its ubiquity. These users can then be organized into a custom audience that can be targeted for more specific messaging and activation — even matched to their known preferences. Finally, these profiles can be used to generate "lookalike" audiences — potential new users and customers who have similar demographics and interests based on the same characteristics as the original list. All of this enabled from the baseline of the lowly, reliable email newsletter, as shown in Figure 4.10.

■ Figure 4.10 Custom Email Audiences

Source: *http://www.emailvendorselection.com/featurewatch/ontraport-integrates-facebook-custom-audiences/*.

Final Thoughts on Email Marketing

Email Marketing is one of the cornerstones of all the digital channels. It can be used for almost any marketing purpose, from customer acquisition to retention and loyalty, to managing passwords and communication for commercial purposes. It is the core of modern customer relationship management. With the rising use of mobile, email is now ubiquitous, allowing users to view and access information and offers by email anywhere, anytime.

The email address is used almost universally by websites to confirm one's *identity*. A confirmed email address plus related user data allows for targeting, segmentation, and *dynamic message personalization*. Email promotions and offers most effectively *generate actions*: sales, downloads, inquiries, registrations, etc. Email newsletters and other coordinated messaging helps *build awareness, contribute to branding, strengthen relationships*, encourage trust, and cement *loyalty*. Email is also frequently used to support sales through other online and offline channels such as social media activity as well as in-store sales and events. We will revisit email consistently throughout the rest of this book.

Tools and Resources

- "More on Spam," *Business Insider*: *http://www.businessinsider.com/the-companies-who-send-the-most-email-spam-2016-2.*

- HubSpot's "104 Email Marketing Myths, Experiments and Inspiration" at *https://offers.hubspot.com/email-marketing-myths-experiments-inspiration?hsCtaTracking=479b0e82-5f3a-4247-92c6-cd005ff8fb0c%7C1f677a8c-f4dc-4eb1-8f39-627e8a45e087.*

- Other sources of email statistics to understand how users receive and engage with email: *https://www.hubspot.com/marketing-statistics, http://www.wordstream.com/blog/ws/2017/06/29/email-marketing-statistics.*

- MailChimp Email Templates: *https://kb.mailchimp.com/templates/layouts-and-themes/create-a-template-with-the-template-builder.*

- HubSpot Trigger Words: *https://blog.hubspot.com/sales/crazy-persuasive-words-thatll-immediately-motivate-your-prospects-to-take-action-infographic.*

- MailChimp Email Benchmarks and Factbooks: *https://mailchimp.com/resources/research/email-marketing-benchmarks/?_ga=2.38332707.1201754590.1506346160-1673647173.1499819357.*

Endnotes

1. "70 Email Marketing Stats Every Marketer Should Know," January 2016: *https://www.campaignmonitor.com/blog/email-marketing/2016/01/70-email-marketing-stats-you-need-to-know/?utm_source=rss&utm_medium=rss.*

2. Wikipedia; *https://en.wikipedia.org/wiki/Email_spam.*

3. Emailmonday, Ultimate mobile email statistics; *http://www.emailmonday.com/mobile-email-usage-statistics#time.*

4. "MailChimp Email Benchmarks;" *https://mailchimp.com/resources/research/email-marketing-benchmarks/.*

The Interactive Advertising Bureau (IAB) empowers the media and marketing industries to thrive in the digital economy. Its membership is comprised of more than 650 leading media and technology companies that are responsible for selling, delivering, and optimizing digital advertising or marketing campaigns. The trade group fields critical research on interactive advertising, while also educating brands, agencies, and the wider business community on the importance of digital marketing. In affiliation with the IAB Tech Lab, it develops technical standards and best practices. IAB and the IAB Education Foundation are committed to professional development and elevating the knowledge, skills, expertise, and diversity of the workforce across the industry.

IAB is headquartered in New York City.

www.iab.com

"Big marketers are facing a crisis. Small and mid-sized brands, driven by data and digital marketing, are throttling growth for nearly every major consumer category."

— Randall Rothenberg, President & CEO, IAB

CHAPTER 5
Display Advertising: The Basics

Display Advertising is the second largest channel by revenue (after search) and has become somewhat revitalized by recent growth and innovation in the space, including video, enhancements in targeting and tracking, and programmatic ad sales (which we will explore in the next chapter). Display is an extremely versatile channel that can be used for branding and awareness as well as to impact goals related to performance and conversion. With best practices and creative techniques, even the humble banner ad can break through the clutter, becoming a very cost-effective way to reach one's marketing objectives.

One key area of innovation we will review in depth in this chapter are the nuances behind better use of targeting, moving from simple demographic and contextual targeting, to more sophisticated behavioral targeting. Better tracking allows for techniques like *retargeting* to bring visitors back with customized offers and messaging, using methods that have a demonstrably high return on marketing dollars. As we revisit a graphic from Chapter 1, Figure 5.1 demonstrates again the impressive growth of display advertising as a preferred mode of digital marketing.

◼ Figure 5.1 Growth Projections for Digital Marketing

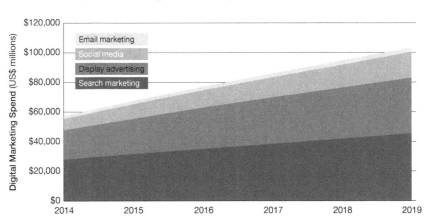

Source: Kagan 2018, based on data from Forrester Research and eMarketer 2017.

Industry analysts like Forrester Research, IAB, and others, project display to continue to grow at an impressive clip, fueled by advances in rich media and the incredible rise of programmatic buying for display advertisements. *Programmatic* advertising is the process of *automating media buying* by targeting audiences and demographics. It has grown tremendously, but if anything is underestimated as enormous amounts of ad inventory are cleared at low prices. We will delve deeper into these concepts when we cover advanced topics in the next chapter.

In this chapter, we will focus on the workhorse of display advertising, the *banner ad*. Although much maligned, it is undergoing somewhat of a renaissance. New forms of targeting, new sizes and multimedia ad units, and new ways of buying have all combined to make the second largest digital marketing channel one of the most exciting and fastest growing. While most people associate display advertising only with the standard banner ad, display comes in a wide variety of shapes and sizes, featuring rich media and video as seen here in Figure 5.2. This evolution has made the display channel more and more powerful as a tool to reach the broader market with brand messaging.

■ Figure 5.2 Market Sizing Ad Formats

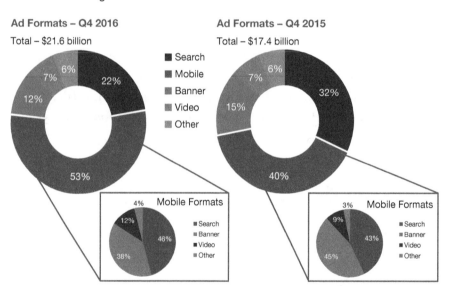

Perhaps paradoxically, the display ad often seems to be the most mundane of the ad units. It strongly resembles the magazine ad model it is nominally derived from — space on a page, paid for by estimated audience size. However, comparison stops here. Old media comparisons neglect the richness of multimedia, the specificity of new ways of targeting and segmentation, and the cost efficiencies of programmatic and exchange-based buying of audiences at scale that is the very essence of digital display.

The Evolution of Display Advertising

The first-ever banner ad, seen in Figure 5.3, appeared on *Wired* magazine's website *hotwired.com* on October 27, 1994. The size was chosen based on what "looked good" in the standard browser window at the time.

■ Figure 5.3 The First Online Banner

Source: *https://blog.hubspot.com/marketing/history-of-online-advertising*.

It was an ad for AT&T that asked users "Have you ever clicked your mouse right HERE?," with an arrow pointing to text that read "YOU WILL." Once viewers clicked on the banner ad, they were directed to a virtual tour of seven of the world's great museums.

Three years ago, in the *Harvard Business Review*, Joe McCambley, who helped create the ad, said:

> *"That first banner that Modem Media, the fledgling digital agency where I worked, built for AT&T, was helpful, and it was useful. At a time when people wondered what the Web was all about, it connected visitors of hotwired.com to a tour of seven of the world's finest art museums. It demonstrated how AT&T could transport people through space and time via the Internet — just as AT&T had done 100 years earlier with the first long distance network. Of those who saw the ad, 44% clicked."*[1]

The model for the banner ad was simple; if a website was sort of like an online magazine, then why not include an online magazine ad? Much like print ads, the size and placement of the ad determined the rate, and the size of the audience viewing the ad could be multiplied by this rate to get a price based on the CPM (cost per thousand). Easy to transfer and understand.

Another display ad milestone occurred with the launch of *DoubleClick*. DoubleClick was the first company to embody what we now call *ad operations*, conducting all the mundane but important functions around deploying and tracking ad campaigns across the Internet — not just one site at a time.

Before the end of the year 1996, DoubleClick developed a technology called DART (Dynamic Advertising Reporting and Targeting) which helped advertisers to track all the clicks and optimize their ads during the life of the campaign. Because of its huge network, Double-Click allowed its advertisers to advertise in a plethora of websites, and unlike print and radio, DoubleClick provided the advertiser a chance to customize their ad campaign depending on its performance. For example, if an ad was not doing well on one website, the advertiser had the option to take the ad down from that website and focus on another one that was producing better results. DoubleClick made its revenue by brokering ads and offering premium tracking & analytics services to their advertisers. The price for advertising on their network was based on a cost per thousand impressions (CPM) model. DoubleClick also generated CPM revenue from the email marketing services it provided.[2]

Standardization: the Building Block to Growth

At first, ad deals were contracted website by website, and handled more like a sponsorship. But with the explosive growth of websites and content, and the accompanying need to monetize, more and more advertisers wanted to advertise across multiple websites. They needed a service like DoubleClick's. With the birth of ad operations also came the *standardization of ad sizes*. 468X60 was the first and basic standard size, based on that first AT&T ad. Other sizes that became popular among advertisers were 125×125 *cubes*, 120×600 *skyscrapers* and 728×90 *leaderboards*. Now, with standard ad units, advertisers could create an ad once and show it on websites across the web.

With the explosion of online ads, of course, click-through rates (CTR) dropped drastically as the novelty wore off. Today display ads routinely have CTRs of less than 0.1%. Of course, this doesn't begin to capture the value of their branding impact.

Another difference from traditional media, display banners can be upgraded to grab the viewer's attention with video, rich media, sound and motion. One of the first interactive ads appeared in 1996 from HP. It enabled the user to play a simple game of "Pong" associated with the HP brand.

This was a major breakthrough to the concept of display ads — now the user was being invited to actually engage with the ad in a way very different than just clicking through to a destination. This *engagement value* for brands persists to this day.

Display as a channel has significant strengths. Its roots in traditional media makes it easy to understand and banner ads can be used to tie together and support other traditional and digital advertising activity. The standardization of banner sizes and formats (mostly by the *Interactive Advertising Bureau* — IAB.com) allowed for a "build once, deploy anywhere" approach escalating availability of unprecedented inventory with reach and scope.

Even with advances in targeting helping marketers hone in on key audience segments and improve performance, banners have their weaknesses. With the proliferation of banners and predictability of their page locations, the format can seem tired and unexciting. Consumers have even developed a "banner blindness" condition — in that they are simply ignoring the ads.

The growth of non-standard, native, and interruptive ads has attempted to address this problem with mixed success. Despite the ubiquity and creativity of banner ads, it's often hard to track their effectiveness and impact, especially for brand goals. Finally, the enormous inventory and reach of ad networks and exchanges has resulted in both low prices and an increased complexity of the display ad ecosystem, seen here in Figure 5.4, making it very difficult to navigate. This often creates problems in attribution and trackability that in the worst-case scenarios can lead to outright fraud.

■ Figure 5.4 The Complexity of the Display Ad Ecosystem

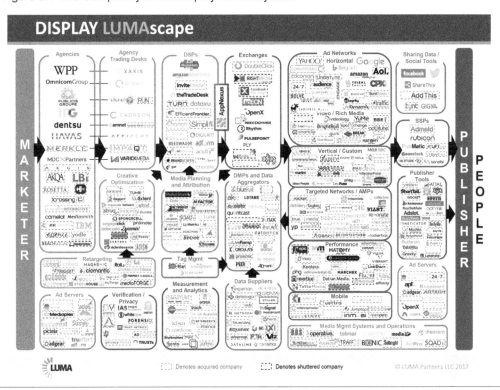

Source: Courtesy of Lumascape; *https://www.slideshare.net/tkawaja/luma-display-ad-tech-landscape-2010-1231*.

Display Measurement

One of the great challenges for any form of advertising is defining success. Ideally, the goal is to make money. However, it's often quite difficult to tie an advertisement to the cash register ringing in a store. Traditional media often use surveys and focus groups to determine key metrics like brand awareness, brand favourability, message association, and purchase intent. These are useful and healthy proxies. With digital media, we have become so focused on measuring things like clicks and impressions, we sometimes miss the bigger picture.

Measurement: the Viewthrough

Let's consider the click, a core measure of success in search and other digital marketing channels. Not only is it a decent measure of interest in an ad, it's often the action that we're charged for — so this is indeed becomes an important metric. As with search, where the goal is to find something, the click is a solid indication of engagement or interaction. The situation changes, however, when display advertising enters the picture. Display doesn't target intent as much as search — it's more contextual in nature. Banner ads are shown almost by definition when a person is reading or consuming other information. A click, while still valuable, simply doesn't gauge a person's true level of interest in a product or service, does not always capture the whole picture. That's where the *viewthrough* comes in.

A viewthrough is when a person sees an ad, does NOT click on it, but then proceeds to the desired destination soon after. (The industry standard attribution period is 30 days, but this often happens within 48 hours.) The logic is that someone may have received the ad's message and chosen to act on it later. In fact, research shows this is exactly what happens. A good "guesstimate" of the viewthrough factor for display can be up to 50%! While the complexity of the display ad ecosystem and the multitude of other factors that can influence the journey make this an imperfect science, it's clear from controlled research that the viewthrough is real.

One large travel company conducted a test to try and quantify this effect. The company showed two groups of consumers 500,000 ad impressions. One group of viewers saw a generic ad for the company. The other saw an ad for the charity the American Red Cross.

The group shown the ad for the travel company clicked about 1,250 times. Of the group shown the charity ad, 130 turned up at their website in the next 48 hours (presumably the "natural rate"). During the same time, an additional 600 plus showed up from the group that was exposed to the travel ad. In other words, even when controlling for people who might have come on their own, the clicks alone underestimated the ad's traffic impact by more than 40%! Display ads then can count on an impact beyond the direct traffic they send — the viewthrough.

This also demonstrates the challenge of *attribution.* Since it's the easiest to track, most of the credit for success (sales or conversions) goes to the ad with the last click. Yet in many cases, there's a multifaceted marketing effort with many touchpoints for a consumer — both online and offline. For example, what if a billboard inspired someone to search for a brand? The search engine would get the credit for the actions that followed and the billboard would not — yet it was the marketer's investment in a billboard that began the chain of events. This is especially relevant if the goal of an ad is visitors and traffic. But what if the goal is not performance oriented (trying to get someone to take an action) but about communicating a message and branding around a product?

Measurement: Engagement and Other Success Metrics

For nonperformance-based success metrics, tracking and "success" can be more difficult. But it's critical to at least understand the true goals when launching a digital display campaign. Clicks and online sales are easy to measure and are often simple yes or no questions. Brand metrics, such as awareness, favorability, and purchase intent in the real world, are much harder. There are many companies trying to solve this problem, as well as the "last mile" of connecting digital to in-store sales — all with varying degrees of success. For our purposes, it's important just to be aware it exists, and metrics associated with it (as seen in Figure 5.5).

■ Figure 5.5 Measuring Impressions and Interactions

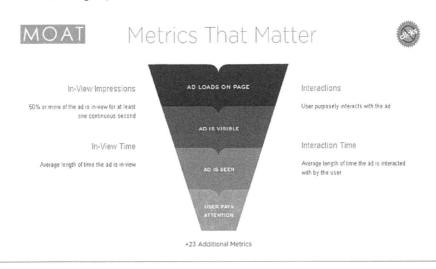

Source: MOAT Analytics.

How Display Works

Display advertising is a highly complex ecosystem of deployment, tracking, and optimization. At a high level it's fairly simple. Publishers have *supply* — spaces to show ad units to their visitors to generate revenue. Advertisers bring *demand* — creative messages they want to share with their target audiences. The entire ecosystem in between is about deploying the best creative, to the best audience, at the best price. Tracking and verification, standardization of ad unit sizes, and optimization opportunities all derive from this challenge.

The Interactive Advertising Bureau (IAB), is the industry's organization for collaborative efforts on standards, training and research. As we discussed earlier, long ago (in Internet time) the IAB helped set standard ad unit sizes to establish a common set of formats. This was and is critical to the development of an industry. By having standard banner sizes, inventory can be compared and priced properly, and creative need only be made once and deployed anywhere. Access to current IAB standards can be found at the end of this chapter in the *Tools and Resources* section.

These standards are not always adhered to, and often new units are proposed that fail to get traction. Demand remains most robust in the more standard unit sizes. This however, is a very good thing. Imagine if to advertise on television, you needed a 45 second commercial for one channel, a 20 second commercial for another, and so on. It would be too difficult and too expensive to launch mass media campaigns for most advertisers as the cost to participate would rise significantly. Banner standards serve the same function as the 30 second commercial in the digital world; they make it easier to buy and deploy ad budgets, and compare and optimize results.

This standard setting process continues to evolve today helping new channels and formats take off — mobile, video, gaming, even native advertising and virtual reality all have efforts underway.

Deploying the Ad

Once creative is designed, it's deployed by specialized ad servers through third party ad operations like DoubleClick, now part of Google. These ad servers provide a lot of benefits in the highly fragmented world of the Internet. First, they allow a single point for upload and deployment of creative units. When an advertiser creates many different sizes and messages for a variety of ad units for an ad campaign, they can simply upload them once to an ad server, which then deploys them to publishers via a *snippet of code* on their website using a process known as *ad trafficking*. By using a centralized store to deploy the ads around the web, other benefits are gained. Rules about deployment times and audiences can be created once and leveraged across entire campaigns.

A broader view of the audience offered by the ad server allows them to avoid showing the same ads to the same people even though they are on different websites, and ensures that the campaign optimizes on the best performing ads more quickly. Verification and reporting are much easier and provide comparable data across the campaign from whatever sites the ads are deployed to.

■ Figure 5.6 Media Buying Model

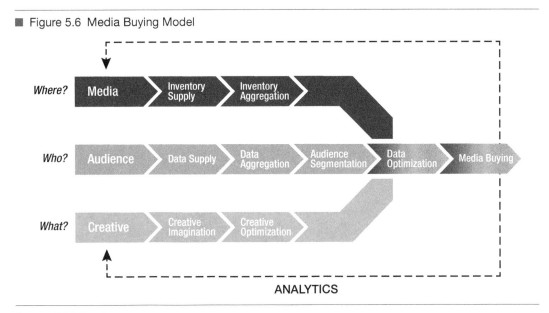

Source: GCA Savvian.

This centralization was initially part of a simple process of inserting a trusted middleman into the advertiser and publisher relationship. The process of deciding which ad units to fill with which creative to show to what target audience provided plenty of opportunities to optimize performance. Many new players have sprung up attempting to improve each piece of the process. The complex landscape we have now has developed from this innovation. *Demand Side Platforms* attempt to optimize the buyer's process by getting the best audience at the cheapest prices. Meanwhile *yield optimizers* try and ensure that inventory on a publisher's site generates as much revenue as possible in a world of competing networks, exchanges, as well as direct sales. Various *creative optimizers* and data suppliers try to ensure that each step of the process gets optimized a bit further. (Figure 5.6)

Ad Networks, Exchanges, and the Long Tail of Inventory

One benefit of standardization and systemization of the display ad ecosystem has been the ability of smaller and smaller publishers to participate in and harvest demand from the advertisers on the Internet. The IAB maintains a chart that shows the percentage of total revenues that go to the top publishers. While the top 10 (72%) and next 15 (11%) still command the lion's share of ad revenue (percentages sound familiar?), what's fascinating is that the revenue going to the bottom tier has more than doubled over the last decade, to 11%. As seen in Figures 5.7 and 5.8, more and more revenue is being driven to the "Long Tail" of publishers as advertisers seek to deploy their budgets more efficiently and find their desired audience wherever they may be, not just on the top sites.

■ Figure 5.7 Ad Revenue Chart

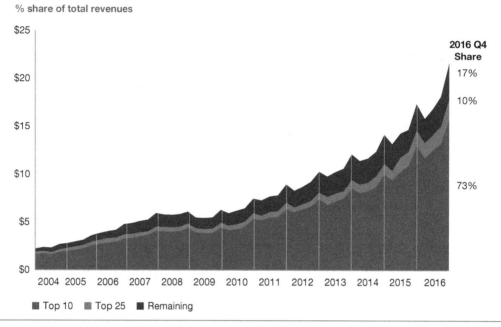

% share of total revenues

2016 Q4 Share

17%

10%

73%

■ Top 10   ■ Top 25   ■ Remaining

■ Figure 5.8 Display Pricing Models

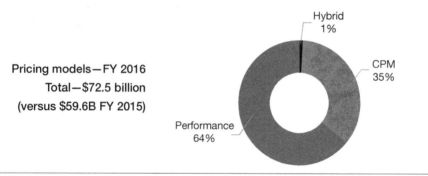

Pricing models—FY 2016
Total—$72.5 billion
(versus $59.6B FY 2015)

Hybrid
1%

CPM
35%

Performance
64%

It's important to remember that this revenue based measure underestimates the impact of the long tail. The lower priced inventory of the smaller websites, who lack a sales force of their own, is often sold at bargain basement prices in auctions. Also, more and more of it is sold on a performance basis, which can hide the enormous volume that the combined inventory of the smaller sites actually represents.

Below the top tier of web properties, *Ad networks* often harvest inventory from the best sites in a variety of verticals. Sports sites, mommy bloggers, gadget sites, foodies and many more can be aggregated up to create easy buying opportunities for advertisers. By gathering enough inventory to make it easy to deploy budget against their goals of reach and frequency, networks can generate premium revenue for sites that may be too small to sell their inventory on their own. Ad Networks generally represent the inventory of top sites exclusively through a sales force of their own who receive commissions. They are incentivized to get good prices for their clients. (Many top sites will get minimum guantees on their inventory in exchange for this.)

■ Figure 5.9 Double Click Ad Exchange Model

Source: Search Engine Journal, *www.searchenginejournal.com/google-launches-the-doubleclick-ad-exchange/13348/*.

Ad Exchanges, on the other hand, do not take possesion of the ad inventory. As we see in Figure 5.9, exchanges exist to facilitate transactions — primarily creating a market of buyers and sellers, usually profiting by creating transactions — not from the sale itself. (We'll talk about real time bidding in these marketplaces in the next chapter.)

By providing representation and a market for smaller publishers, networks and exchanges have brought the "long tail" of ad inventory into the ecosystem for advertisers to take advantage of. While the prices are often low, this does provide needed revenue to publishers beyond some of the basic systems for revenue sharing.

Advertisers benefit from ad networks as well. They can leverage the reach and frequency to get a high volume audience with a single buy — instead of the impossible task of negotiating ad deals with hundreds of smaller sites. They can narrow the focus of their campaign with explicit demographic data to make sure they reach the right audience, often through a vertical network, and then use the campaign data to narrow the focus to the best performing segments. Follow the link in Figure 5.10 to a great IAB video that talks about the display trading ecosystem.

■ Figure 5.10 Video Explanation of Ad Networks and Exchanges

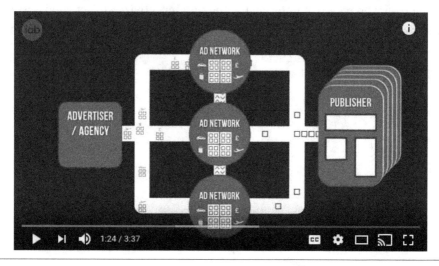

An IAB video that explains the increasingly complex environment with data now powering real time bidding and selling. This video aims to demystify the display landscape in 3 minutes!

Source: IABUK, *https://www.youtube.com/watch?v=1C0n_9DOlwE*. © 2018 Interactive Advertising Bureau. All rights reserved.

Digital Display Options

As we mentioned, early on there were quite a few ad sizes. However, the market had the most inventory in and interest from advertisers in what is sometimes known as the *Universal Advertising Package* (UAP). The "package" with the four basic units we talked about earlier — the banner, the skyscraper, the square, and the rectangle — allowed advertisers to create ad sets in these sizes increasing their chance of finding well-priced inventory wherever they wanted to deploy campaigns. See Figure 5.11 for a description of all IAB ad sizes, and examples of the four UAP ad units.

As we stated at the top of the chapter, the standard banner is still the workhorse of display campaigns. Despite declines in click-through rates, and questions surrounding proving effectiveness, banners in all their shapes and sizes remain effective and useful advertiser tools. There are many case studies on how and what has worked best, and galleries full of the most innovative, award winning banners. Aside from these being great sources of inspiration, the basic principles are simple and still useful to keep in mind.

■ Figure 5.11 Universal Ad Package and Ad Sizes

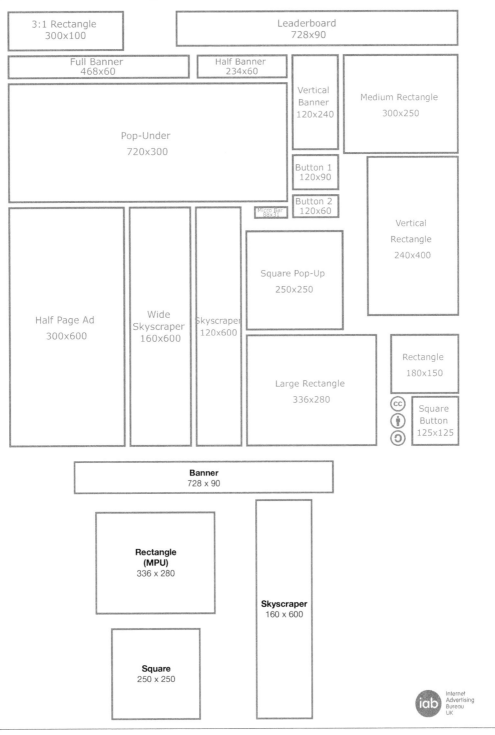

Source: IAB UK.

Research has shown that there are some basic strategies and tactics that help cut through the clutter and draw attention to an advertiser's messaging. One of these basics is that *incentives* or an offer of some kind are usually necessary to grab attention and break through to engagement. Incentives tend to fall into a few categories:

- Synergy with content or context on the publisher's website
- Use of rich or interactive media
- Interruptive creative and messaging

Content. Messaging that integrates well with the content and context of a website is always a positive. For example, an ad for a digital camera or discounted printing on a photography website would be very appealing to that audience. Adobe has had great success by offering free stock images with its ads for the Adobe Creative Cloud Photography plan. For offers to work successfully, it's important that the creative message itself is perceived as relevant.

Rich Media. The data shows that another way to rise above the noise in display is the use of rich media. Sound and motion, video and animation, or even games all serve to make an ad, and its incentive, more noticeable, memorable, and often actionable. A recent article on Quora, found in a study that 91 percent of those that interact with incentivized advertising actively look for or pay attention to the message of the brand behind it.[3] Of course, there are additional costs in the production in both the creation and the deployment of rich media ads, so this is a tradeoff.

Disruption. Finally, one additional factor that makes ads get noticed: The annoyance factor. We've all seen the interruptive placements, pop-ups and pushdowns, expandables, and other types of "in your face" ad units; but they get results. This despite that they are widely reviled by consumers and can often create a negative brand impression. What's an advertiser to do? Is it possible to be clever and impactful without being irritating?

The answer, thankfully, is yes. What consumers really desire is *control*. This means no "auto play," automatic expansion, or unrequested action from the ad unit. Research shows that it is very possible to offer a high impact ad with *low intrusion* (annoyance factor) by simply enabling user control. When the user has the option to expand, hear, view, or engage with an ad, rather than have it playing automatically, this can make a key difference in receptivity as shown in Figures 5.12 and 5.13. *User initiation* also makes these high impact ads acceptable; avoiding the "rage clicks" we've all experienced when we encounter sudden non-user-initiated ads in a desperate search to shut them off. How many times have we waited for an ad to finish in order to read an article or view a video? The one exception, ironically, seems to be young men in entertainment environments, who seem to accept the intrusion as part of the experience.

■ Figure 5.12 Impact Intrusion Matrix

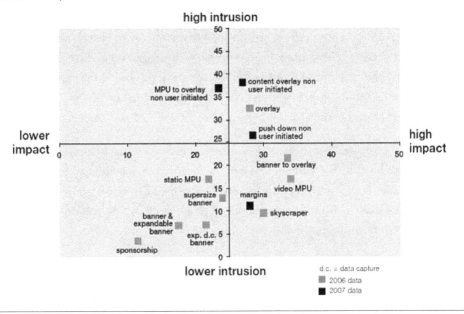

Source: IAB UK. From an Orange telecom Study.

■ Figure 5.13 Survey Data on Intrusive Ad Types

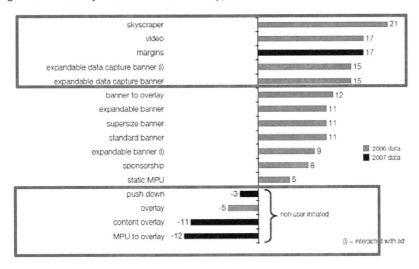

More intrusive ads tend to be better favoured amongst youth and in entertainment environments, for example overlays have a positive acceptability score of 7 for men under age 35 in entertainment environments.

Source: IAB UK, From an Orange telecom study.

Getting the Most Out of Display Creative

It is important when designing successful ads to take advantage of all the features available for *creative execution*; understanding the many options to ensure an ad is seen and engaged with. Another key part of this is to execute a proper *targeting strategy*. This ensures that the creative message is seen by the appropriate audiences. Fortunately, not only are there guidelines and best practices to follow, but like everything in digital, all of this can be tested and optimized on when the real world results come in.

The first step to an advertisement's success is simple: it must be seen! Recent studies published by Google support the industry-wide discussion on the topic of *viewability*. Viewability is a digital ad metric that aims to track only impressions that can actually be seen by users. For example, if an ad is loaded at the bottom of a webpage but a user doesn't scroll down far enough to see it, that impression would not be deemed viewable.

Viewability is a challenge that can be solved in a couple of ways. For many advertisers, the simplest solutions are to pay a premium for an "above the fold" position — an ad that loads on the top of the page in the browser window, as seen in Figure 5.14 below. For others, it's best to pay on a performance basis only for those ads that are clicked on. Larger advertisers can afford to spend money on *ad verification services* to make sure their ads are seen, or before they pay a premium for guarantees.

■ Figure 5.14 Most Viewable Ad Positions

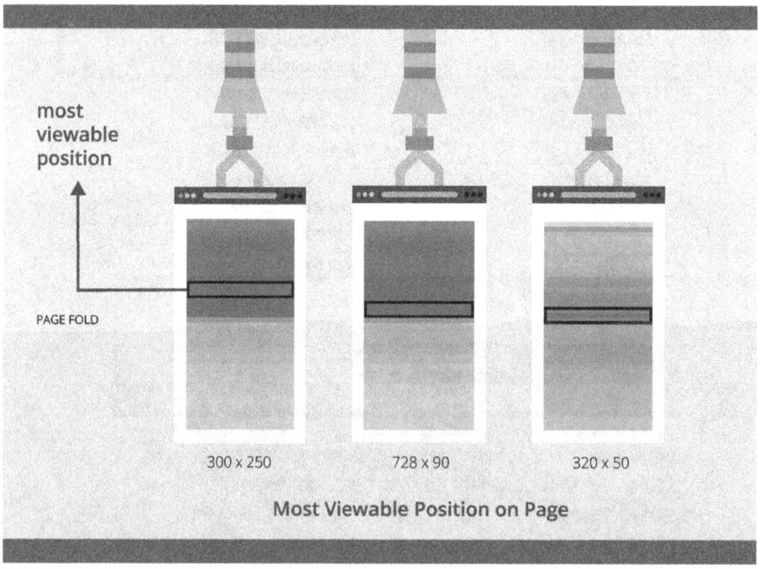

Most Viewable Position on Page

Source: Google viewability study, *https://adexchanger.com/data-exchanges/google-viewability-benchmark-more-than-half-of-all-ads-arent-seen. https://www.thinkwithgoogle.com/marketing-resources/data-measurement/5-factors-of-viewability/*.

Once you've determined the positioning of your ad, then you must consider all the features and functionality available for creative execution. For most campaigns, the challenge is cutting through the clutter when the ad has a chance to engage the user. There are many features that can be used to do this in the display world. For example, ad units that invite the user to engage can be very effective.

A car company, for example, allowed users to select and customize the colors on a car within the ad unit itself. This emphasized the customization opportunities of the real car and encouraged the viewer to interact with other features like safety structures and the like. Their customized car could even be shared with friends. A phone company launched a similarly engaging campaign by allowing people to submit their number or a friend's number to receive a humorous "robo-call" from a celebrity. Many stores do this around "Black Friday," where shoppers can sign up for a wake-up call from an actor or musician or other personality — cleverly incorporated in a form capture through an expandable ad unit. A good example is the ad forms and pictures used by Snickers below.

Sequence of Snickers Ads with Mr. T.

Even relatively less exciting products can be enhanced with carefully thought out expansions and interactions to achieve engagement. HSBC, for example, advertised a mortgage product by inviting users to slide a bar to determine mortgage levels in different cities around the world. This not only emphasized their messaging as "the world's local bank" but also focused on what people really are looking for related to a mortgage — a new home.

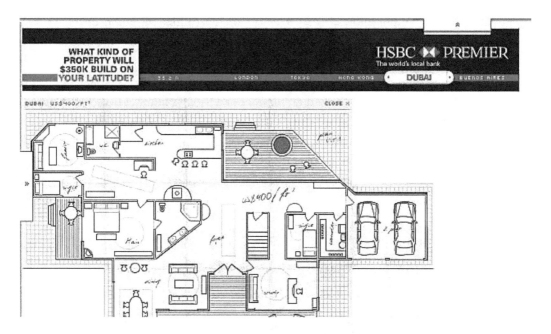

Other clever integrations take advantage of the fact that we have access to information beyond the ad itself through the web. An ad for a Jeep integrated a map to the nearest national park to use it; an ad for a movie integrated with the user's calendar by allowing them to add in the day of the premiere.

Other engagement methods include *page takeovers* and *synchronizations*. Page takeovers essentially eliminate competitive messaging by taking over all of the commercial space on a page for one advertiser; this can be particularly useful and effective in verticals like travel, for example. Synchronization can also be used effectively to tie the messaging between two or more ad units with motion or sound for maximum effect. A beer pouring from an ad unit at the top of the page into a glass on the side is a good example.

This can work with e-commerce as well. A recent IKEA ad unit actually took its catalog and condensed the entire thing into a single ad unit; customers could browse the expandable and interactive ad and click through to literally anything in the catalog.

IKEA "Smallest Store in the World" catalog. *http://www.smalleststoreintheworld.com/banner/en/index.html*.

Targeting is the Key to Success

Targeting in digital channels like display provides a deeper level of segmentation than possible with traditional media. Most brands have well researched demographic and psychographic targeting profiles and come up with optimal *persona*(s) and description(s) of a prototypical member of the target audience. Personas are created by examining *behaviors* (both online and offline), *attitudes* (about family and life, etc.), and *determining customer values*. This information is then used to create detailed understanding of segments that will benefit from highly targeted messaging and offers. Descriptions are designed to encourage empathy and enhance effectiveness in marketers trying to reach this customer.

Targeting in display can reach these segments at scale and open up new opportunities that simply aren't available in mass media. After all, we care about all people who are interested in buying our product — not just people who look like those who have already done so. An example might be video games. An assumption would be to target young men for this market, and that assumption might be the best option in a mass media world. But what about the "cool grandma" who wants to buy her grandson the newest console? Avid girl gamers? Small but potentially lucrative segments can be found online, whereas this might be all but impossible to address with traditional media.

Digital targeting can make use of context, behavior, and even identity to reach these goals. *Contextual targeting* is both about what content the user is consuming (an article on cameras, for example) as well as things like the time of day, their location, and even the operating system or device they are using. *Behavioral targeting* is also very effective. Targeting people on the basis of their actions (a purchase, a site visit, viewing a page or video, or filling out a form) can deliver enough information to offer much more effective messaging and reveal customers that might not match the standard profile. Digital can also target people more exactly based on their *identity. Cookies* on computers, a small piece of code to identify you as you, can allow marketers to offer perfectly personalized offers and promotions based on a user's browsing and buying history. For example, if you've bought a pair of pants, a retailer online can follow you with an offer for a matching shirt.

Compared to traditional media, these targeting methods provide unprecedented opportunity for everyone in the value chain. With a television commercial on broadcast media, an advertiser tries to find the audience with the highest concentration of likely customers, knowing that she will pay for the whole audience despite, for example, wanting to reach just men to sell them deodorant. The advertiser has one price for the inventory based on the size and quality of the audience. And the consumers in the audience may be forced to watch irrelevant commercial messages intended for a different target customer segment. (In this example, the women watching the male deodorant commercial.)

■ Figure 5.15 New Media versus Old Media Targeting

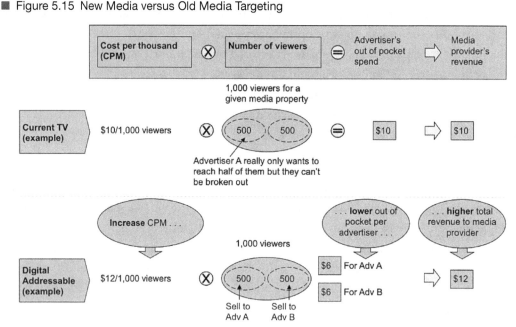

Source: Kagan, 2018.

As seen in Figure 5.15, the dynamics of targeting change in the digital world. The advertiser can purchase just the half of the audience she wants — the men — and cut her costs while targeting just the right segment. The publisher can charge a premium for the segment she wants — and resell the other segment to someone else, making more money. And finally, the consumer sees an ad that they are at least potentially interested in. It should be a win-win-win for everyone!

Retargeting and Remarketing

Perhaps one of the best ways to target someone based on behavior is to *retarget* them. Retargeting is what's happening when you find yourself followed around by ads from a website you've just visited. How do they know it's you? For most sites, it's the cookie that is dropped on your computer. This allows the site to recognize you as a unique visitor, as seen in the Hong Kong image below, which helps for login purposes, customization, retain your profile or history for convenience — and of course ad tracking and deployment for the marketer.

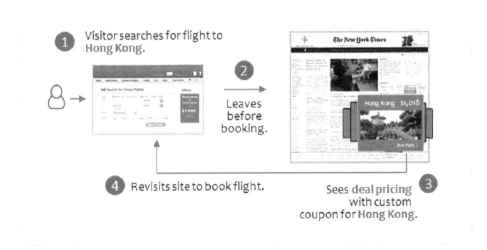

Once the site knows who you are, it can track what you do. That includes whatever you do on a website, including products you browse. If you are looking at a red baseball cap, you can be followed around the web using the cookie to target ads specific to the cap to bring you back. One great example of this is the shopping cart rescue. As seen in Figure 5.16, companies can now follow the potential customer who failed to complete their purchase around with that item, as a reminder, offering special discounts or calls to action like free shipping. This strategy has a very high success rate.

■ Figure 5.16 Different Types of Targeting

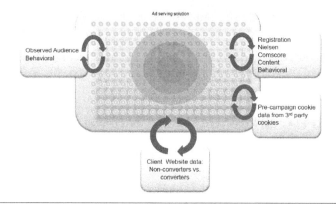

Source: Kagan 2018.

Targeting Challenges: The Devil's in the Data

Of course, this is in an ideal world. And that world depends on quality data. In many cases, our data is not as good as we'd like it to be. For example, someone who browses the sites of every major sports car manufacturer and spends time looking at specifications and prices could be a powerful executive looking for a new car (an "auto intender" in some data circles) — or just a teenage boy dreaming about being a race car driver. Behavior alone does not automatically demonstrate purchase intent.

Context can also be misleading. Most contextual targeting systems are based on keywords found on the page for their algorithmic assessment of where an ad should appear. However, common sense is not something computers generally display. As you can see in the sidebar, the ad team at a newspaper would know never to put an airline ad across from a story about a plane crash. Computers, however, have served up some of these actual gems. While these are actually fairly uncommon, this is a real challenge if the boss, a client or an offended potential customer sees it.

Tools and Resources

■ Extensive History of Online Advertising on HubSpot; *https://blog.hubspot.com/marketing/history-of-online-advertising*.

■ The IAB (Interactive Advertising Bureau) resource guide: *http://www.iab.com/wp-content/up-loads/2015/11/IAB_Display_Mobile_Creative_Guidelines_HTML5_2015.pdf*.

■ Ad galleries and search tools: *https://www.iab.com/guidelines/universal-ad-package/*; *https://www.richmediagallery.com*; *http://showcase.sizmek.com/*; *https://moat.com/*.

■ Double Click, Viewthrough conversion tracking resources: *https://support.google.com/adxbuyer/answer/166342?hl=en*

Despite best practice in development and targeting,
sometimes things just go wrong…

And, horrible ad placements happen in the real world too!

Endnotes

1. Joe McCambley, "Stop Selling Ads and Do Something Useful," *Harvard Business Review*, FEBRUARY 12, 2013; *https://hbr.org/2013/02/stop-selling-ads-and-do-something*.

2. "The History of Online Advertising," Adpushup Blog, *https://www.adpushup.com/blog/the-history-of-on-line-advertising/*.

3. Quora blog, Amar Hussain, "What are some of the most ingenious ways to increase traffic to a website?"; *https://www.quora.com/What-are-some-of-the-most-ingenious-ways-to-increase-traffic-to-a-website#!n=54.*

YouTube is an American video-sharing website and one of Google's subsidiaries. YouTube has over a billion users — almost one-third of all people on the Internet — and each day those users watch a billion hours of video, generating billions of views.

YouTube is headquartered in San Bruno, CA.

www.youtube.com

"Because YouTube is an interactive platform, people can respond immediately to your message and the way you deliver it. This may sound intimidating, but I really see this "no bullshit" culture as an opportunity for brands to cultivate greater self-awareness and transparency."

— Kevin Allocca, Head of Culture & Trends, YouTube

CHAPTER 6

Display Advertising: Advanced Topics and Trends

In Chapter 5 we discussed the "basics" of display ads, their versatility as a channel, and their essential role in any digital marketing strategy. Here we will cover the important advances in the way banner ads are both presented and targeted that have helped drive display advertising's amazing growth. With more and more inventory and advertising popping up (sometimes literally) everywhere on the Internet, better creative units have been developed to cut through the clutter. *Advanced topics* are necessary to understand where display is going, and the strategies and techniques needed to become an effective marketer in the broadest sense.

In this chapter, we will take a deeper dive into topics and trends such as how to deploy the most engaging forms of creative, the challenges of ad blockers and the rise of native advertising, programmatic display and real time bidding (RTB). In the last section, we will address the complexities of measurement and targeting strategies relative to these advances that enable the right audience to see the right ads, ensuring better performance and success for your marketing efforts!

Creative Trends in Display

The assortment of formats and creative options now available in display is truly amazing. Equally amazing is the exponential ability of digital to reach similar but more segmented audiences than traditional media, which continues to escalate brand advertisers transition of ad dollars from television and mass media to digital formats. As you will see in this chapter and the rest of the book, increasingly new brands are being built online first before expanding to more traditional distribution channels.

Creative: You Don't Have to Annoy to Succeed

As mentioned in the previous chapter, with the proliferation of ads on web pages, many consumers have come down with what's known as "banner blindness." They simply don't see ads in the commercial zone — the spaces on web pages that traditionally house the advertising messages. To combat this, there has been a rise in more interruptive ad placements (annoying ads), but also the evolution of more engaging forms of ad creative using rich media and video.

Another response to consumer blindness is the growing trend of so-called *native advertising*. These are commercial messages presented in a way that is often indistinguishable from editorial content. Their use has grown dramatically because of their engaging format and success in beating *ad blockers*.

These innovations in ad creative have led to challenges and pushback from users. As consumers experience heavier ad loads and more interruptive advertising, we have seen somewhat of a backlash, beginning with the adoption of ad blockers and other software tools that allow a user to manage or eliminate advertising from web pages completely.

While it's the worst offenders that drive people to use these tools, the good corporate citizen publishers who don't push the limits or annoy the user are also paying the price. We'll examine both the upside and the challenges that this type of consumer activism presents, as well as other trends in the fundamental infrastructure and deployment of display advertising.

Control is the Key

We know that audio, video, and interactivity are both more interruptive AND more effective. What's the key to balancing an advertisement's impact against the annoyance and irritation factors, avoiding the potential backlash from the consumer? In a word: *control.* Consumer research leads us to believe that ads are more accepted if they provide the user with some semblance of control. Opt-in ads or click-to-activate type ads with clear indications of how to stop them or shut them off are shown to be generally accepted and effective. However, ads that automatically blare sound and show video, expand to cover the text you are reading or pop up to block it, are generally loathed and as we've discussed, actually negatively impact a brand.

This is an important distinction, because without more moderate approaches, advertisers risk frustrating consumers so much that they actually increase the use of ad blockers — preventing all ads from being seen and seriously impacting the revenue models of many publishers. The risk of bad actors is always present, but the Interactive Advertising Bureau (IAB), the standards setter for most legitimate industry players, is trying to meet this head on. In recent years, the IAB — through its Tech Lab — launched the LEAN Ads Program as seen in Figure 6.1. The IAB hopes that these principles can guide advertisers towards a standard that achieves their goals without annoying consumers to the point of adopting blockers. LEAN stands for:

L: **Light**. Limited file size with strict data call guidelines.

E: **Encrypted**. Assure user security with https/SSL compliant ads.

A: Ad Choices Support. All ads should support DAA's consumer privacy programs.

N: Non-invasive/Non-disruptive. Ads that complement the user experience, without disrupting it. This includes covering content and sound enabled by default.

■ Figure 6.1 The Lean Ad Program

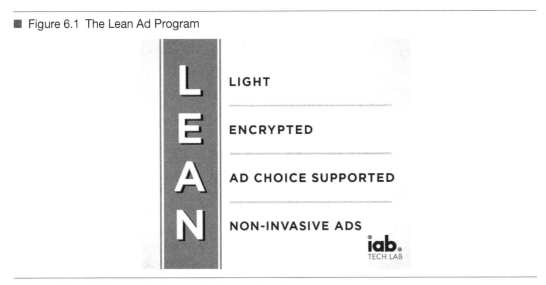

Rich Media and Video: Quality Drives Virality

Rich media and video have become perhaps the most effective forms of advertising. We are familiar with the classic 30-second spot on television: a commercial story encapsulated in a standard format. Some commercials are awful; some are so good we look forward to events like the Super Bowl to see the best. We even watch them online or on shows dedicated to the most compelling selection of these ads.

Online options can go well beyond simple 30-second spots. Whereas a 30 second commercial format is tolerable when weighed against 30 or 60 minutes of high quality commercial programming, online is different. It's acceptable to see a short cat video, so a YouTube ad spot might only be 10 -15 seconds long. Digital allows for much better targeting and personalization, with varied pricing options, all dependent on when, where and how the viewer accesses the ad.

While simple display ads sell with words and pictures, rich media ads offer an enhanced array of ways to involve an audience with an ad. You can access aggregated metrics on your audience's behavior, including number of expansions, multiple exits, video views, completions, and shares to get granular data on the success of your campaign (see the Blendtec campaign in the next section).

A good rich media ad contains images, animation or video involving some type of user interaction and engagement with the content; with attention to the concept of control discussed above. The initial load of a rich media ad is 40K or more. While text ads sell with words, and display ads sell with pictures, rich media ads offer more ways to involve an audience with an ad. The ad can expand, float, peel down, etc. For example, video can be designed in a variety of ways for greater audience involvement. The *Video Player-Ad Interface Definition* (VPAID), is a universal specification developed by the IAB for interaction between ad units and video players. This enables the rich interactive in-stream ad experience we seek. VPAID standards allow compliant video players to display rich interactive media ads, also known as an *executable ad unit*. VPAID linear creatives are video creatives that appear before, between, or after the publisher's video, and fill the entire video player. VPAID non-linear creatives overlay the video player without pausing the video, and do not fill the entire video player. When a user clicks a non-linear ad, the video can be paused, and the ad can expand.

Rich media enables agencies to create complex ads that can elicit strong user response. Using HTML5 technology, the ads can include multiple levels of content in one placement: videos, games, tweets from an ad, etc. If you have a simple objective to generate "likes" or clicks, or a more ambitious goal to create brand awareness, rich media, with a good targeting strategy, is a good format to go with.

It is the ability of video to break from the norm and become promotion at its best — showcasing the product and the brand — that has proven most effective. Given the high bar of investment for traditional media like television commercials or beautiful print campaigns, online video and interactive ads can level the playing field for all sizes of companies, as we see with these next two examples.

Showing the Product: Blendtec. One terrific example is the website WillItBlend.com. Blendtec makes commercial blenders for restaurants and the like — not exactly the sexiest or most exciting product to promote to the mass market. As a small business to business company, they wanted to expand their business, but simply couldn't spend millions on a national media campaign. Instead they reverted to one of the first principles of marketing — show the product in action, in a less expensive but accessible medium.

The CEO of the company — Tom Dickson, who looks remarkably like a classic high school science teacher, began filming videos of the product in action. Long before the Nutra Ninja Bullet, he showed the Blendtec blender making short work of pineapples, tomatoes, and other food items, but also things like 2×4s of lumber and marbles to demonstrate the durability of the product.

According to creator and producer Kels Goodman, "The honest truth is that Will It Blend? started with us fooling around. I mean, we had an objective, but YouTube was brand new and at the time we didn't really see the 'marketing' side of people posting silly videos on the Internet. George Wight, the marketing manager at the time, asked me to set up a shoot where Tom would blend a bunch of things (marbles, rake handle, can of Coke, Big Mac meal, etc). George got that inspiration from watching Tom test the power and durability of blenders by blending 2×4s down to sawdust. My job was to film Tom and make it interesting. If you watch the first 10 or so Will It Blend? episodes, you'll see Tom with almost no comedy, no lines, no gags or sound effects. Tom basically said, 'Here are some marbles; I think we'll blend these.' That's it."[1]

Blendtec "Don't Try This at Home" campaign.

Because the videos were unusual and funny enough, they began to be shared widely on the web. The marketing team at Blendtec, to their credit, picked up on this and began to work on the "Don't Try This at Home" section in earnest. Capitalizing on Internet memes, they leveraged things like launches of new video games, iPhones, sneakers, and other products in the news — even parodying other ads — all to generate viral traffic to the website. And it worked — soon brands approached them to join forces and get in on the viral traffic. Hundreds of millions of video views later, this low budget website continues to drive traffic, brand recognition and sales for the small blender company. [Check it out at *www.WillItBlend.com* — where iPhones, footballs, plungers... even a McDonald's Happy Meal get blended.]

Did it cost a lot? Using a simple set, the company's own product, and the CEO as the main actor certainly suggests not. It required a little social media savvy, a sense of humor, and some commitment to the series. At the time, Blendtec couldn't even sell blenders from its site — and it still refers you to stores for purchase. Yet the success lasts.

The "Create a Brand" Campaign from the Dollar Shave Club. Building a brand to compete with the consumer marketing giants in traditional media could cost millions of dollars in research, commercials, and mass media — with the risks of being drowned out by traditional marketing machines. Men's razors, the classic marketing case of razors versus blades, is a great example. Gillette and others spend millions on commercials expounding on their technology, spokesmen, and established brand to convince a small portion of the market that may be look-ing to switch that they should commit to their shaving brand.

Dollar Shave Club took a different approach. They sought to compete in this market by lever-aging online marketing and new business models to build a new way of reaching and keeping the consumer. By building their brand aimed at the younger adult male market — who spent their time online, consuming social media and viral content — they avoided a battle of wallets on traditional media while targeting the very customers that were most likely to switch.

Dollar Shave Club CEO Michael Dubin from his YouTube video, "A Better Shave Delivered."

The resultant video — again, low budget, humorous, and starring the CEO — was produced for the web. Longer than a 30 second spot, with an irreverence that nevertheless tackles the weak spots of the incumbents, the video has garnered more views than a Super Bowl ad online — for a fraction of the cost. It addresses the challenges of the market head on — quality, the high price and perception that it all goes to marketing, even the tedium of purchasing the blades themselves — in a humorous opener that people shared freely.

Soon brand expansion to "butt wipes" and other male products, with their own humorous videos, began to roll out. To be sure, the innovative subscription-based replenishment model was also key — as it avoided the challenge of constantly re-acquiring customers like the big brands do. But it was the low cost, high impact viral video that built and maintained the brand. The result: a $1 billion acquisition by traditional player Unilever, which is now rolling out the model globally.[2]

Challenges in Display

Although advances in technology, analytics and consumer awareness have offered many great examples and new opportunities for digital marketers to be more effective, progress does not come without its challenges. As marketers and advertising take over more and more of the user's experience in digital media, consumers are beginning to respond. From avoiding websites with heavy ad loads, to installing software to prevent interruptions and other problems, users have raised the stakes. Navigating between effectiveness and negative reaction from their target consumers is today's marketer's toughest assignment.

Ad Blockers: Consumer Response to "Bad Ad Behavior"

The use of tools to prevent advertisements from being displayed on websites, or *ad blockers*, is on the rise. Many people feel this is a natural response by consumers due to frustration at deceptive advertising, heavier and more interruptive ad loads, and general disregard for the user experience in favor of ad dollars. Industry organizations regard ad blockers as a threat to the very business model that provides the free content users are trying to enjoy. Certainly, both sides have valid points. The fact remains that ad blockers are here to stay, and only by responding appropriately can the online advertising model be preserved (see Figure 6.2).

■ Figure 6.2 The Cost of Ad Blocking in the U.S.

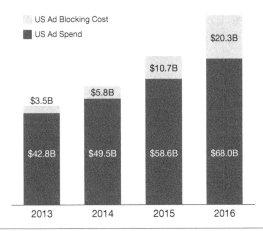

Source: Kagan 2018, from PageFair data, https://pagefair.com/blog/2017/adblockreport/.

Ad blockers, like one of the most popular "AdBlock Plus," are essentially pieces of software — usually plugins for the most popular browsers — that detect advertising by identifying the code on a web page and then simply prevent it from being shown. Without the advertisements showing, the publisher who is providing the content can't monetize a user's visit to the site. Ad blockers filter content in two main ways:

- Check against a (crowdsourced) blacklist of domain names of items loading on a web page, then stop them from loading.

- Check the page after it is finished loading and remove any items that fit prescribed rules; like images with standard ad dimensions or text within a box that says "sponsored."

Many publishers have made the user experience on their websites so onerous with various slideshows, pop ups, interstitials, lightboxes, and other euphemistically named ad units that slow down the experience for a few extra pennies, they drove users away. Forbes is an excellent example of brand that went too far in this direction (they found their way back), but many others are following its example for short term profits.

More troubling is the rise of social media driven sites that use provocative headlines or fake news to generate traffic. Given the post 2016 election backlash, Google and Facebook took aim at fake news sites with new consumer tools and algorithms to identify and remove these stories. Sites that do not address these issues have much less hope of capturing a repeat user as a destination, often attempting to squeeze every last dime out of each visit with an over-abundance of ads.

Figure 6.3 shows a simple model of how ad blockers work. Other than trying to improve their user experience while consuming content, users believe ad blockers are useful for concrete reasons. One is *performance* — ad blockers speed up the website by preventing the page from loading media and trackers that can seriously slow down the display of the core content a user is seeking. Blocking the trackers also enhances user *privacy,* as without the tracking pixels — which can number in the dozens on some pages — a user's behavior can be anonymous. The user can avoid the feeling of being "followed" around the web by re-targeters. Finally, the complex display ecosystem has led to many users having legitimate fears about *security,* given the many things that load can often include malicious software called *malware* that puts user's information at risk.

■ Figure 6.3 How Ad Blockers Work

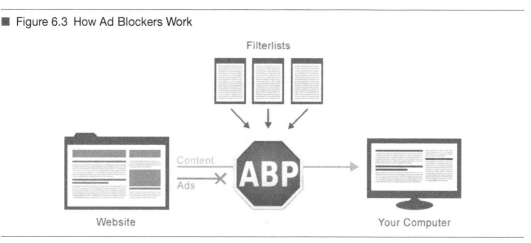

Source: Quora, *https://www.quora.com/How-does-Adblock-Plus-work-technically*.

Figure 6.4 indicates the use of Ad Blocking software is prevalent across many demographics, but particularly acute in some countries in Europe where privacy concerns are paramount. A continuing challenge for marketers is the fact that the ad industry has responded in multiple ways to the ad blockers. The simplest and most effective response seems to be notifying users (when an ad blocker is detected) that the ads supporting the content they want are being blocked; and asking them to "opt-in" and turn off blockers. This approach has many merits but ultimately forces sites to confront users with the advertising model, and hope they proactively accept it. The default is still to block ads and publishers to lose money. Other solutions include paying a fee to "verify" the ads with the ad blockers themselves; the industry, through organizations like the IAB, claims that this is effectively extortion — and doesn't make things any better for the user.

■ Figure 6.4 Ad Blocking Rates by Country

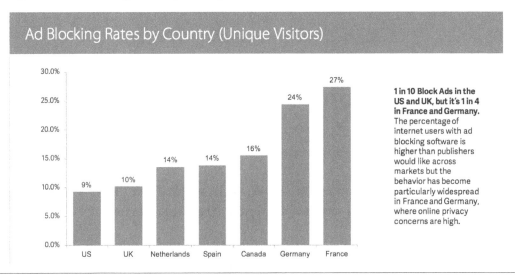

Source: ComScore 2015.

The brightest solution, seems to be the rise of so-called *native advertising*, which makes ads difficult to identify so that consumers and machines are fooled into thinking they are content and therefore prevent them from being blocked. However, good native ads may hold value for the consumer too. We'll discuss this more thoroughly in the next section.

The bottom line is that both sides are correct: the user experience has declined dramatically due to overzealous marketing and lack of respect for user privacy. The number of users' actively blocking ads has jumped from 6% in 2015 to 11% in just two years.[3] A breakdown of who these are is found in Figure 6.5. This trend places the business model of the web at risk, and unfortunately, legitimate publishers and users who are willing to accept a small amount of ads in return for content are paying the price.

■ Figure 6.5 Who Uses Ad Blocking Software?

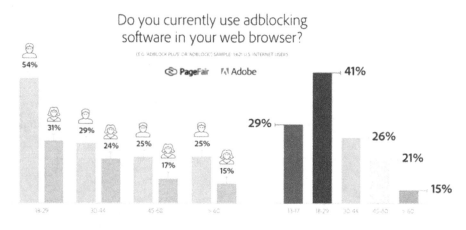

Source: PageFair, 2017 Global Ad Block Report.

Native Advertising

While many interpretations exist, the most agreed-upon definition of native advertising is "a form of paid media in which the ad experience follows the natural form and function of the user experience in which it is placed."[4] Essentially, an ad is considered to be native when it looks like it was meant to be there. The form of the ad will match the visual aesthetics of the page or rich media experience in which it is served. A native ad will behave and represent itself to function just like natural content.

Generally, there are four primary types of native ad integrations — *in-feed* native ads, *content recommendation widgets, promoted listings*, and *custom content units*. It will be important for marketers to understand each, how they fit with your brand and how to use them effectively. There is a great Marketing Land article that has many interesting examples of all four of these types of these native ads. Yahoo Gemini has some of the most interesting targeting options, which include search retargeting and mail domain retargeting. Links to both of these are found in our *Tools and Resources* section at the end of this chapter.

Programmatic and Real Time Bidding (RTB)

Publishers are monetizing more of their ad inventory through programmatic exchanges and real time bidding than ever before. Why? *Programmatic* offers an automated format of media buying that is more efficient and inexpensive, as well as reducing human error and inconsistency. *Real-time bidding* (RTB) is a type of programmatic, referring to a lightning quick auction that takes audience data into account to assess the value of an impression to a certain advertiser. While the most money and best placements are still being sold through sales teams at a premium — with guarantees and minimums of course — the sheer amount of unsold ad inventory available to be monetized automatically, has led to large amounts of display inventory winding up on *ad networks*, *exchanges*, and ultimately *RTB marketplaces*.

How does this work? Ad networks essentially take ownership of the inventory and the money they generate. Though sales is directly related to the price they get; they have an incentive to maximize value for the publisher, balanced with the need to provide long term value for advertisers. Exchanges differ in that they exist to create a marketplace with a clearing price for ad inventory providers (publishers and networks) and buyers (advertisers). Exchanges make money by facilitating transactions and focus on creating a secure and trusted marketplace for exchange.

Programmatic trading and RTB grew out of this infrastructure. Exchanges and marketplaces allow publishers to put inventory into the market and generate additional revenue, with the only requirement being that those impressions be reserved ahead of time. With a "real time" approach, impressions can be pushed out to the market as needed. If a publisher can't fill an impression with an ad at a premium price, that same impression can be offered in real time to an auction that will at least get a market-based price for the ad unit. As a perishable asset, like airline seats or hotel rooms, ad impressions need to be sold, or they are lost. While the revenue from leftover or "remnant" industry is often at a much lower price point, the dollar amounts add up quickly, as seen in Figure 6.6.

■ Figure 6.6 Display Ad Revenue Model

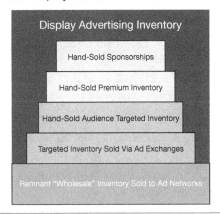 

The majority of revenue comes from the premium placements, but most of the volume comes from the remnant inventory.

Companies like AppNexus and a few others developed the infrastructure to handle this market. They liken it to creating a high-volume stock exchange in just a couple of years, and the comparison is apt. In real time, publishers provide inventory, and advertisers bid on it — and when a transaction clears, all of the traditional advertising operations functions of creative selection and deployment (the ad), data tracking and verification, etc., all take place as well.

Shown in Figure 6.7, the speed necessary for this to be unnoticed by the viewer necessitates computers being involved. The programmatic part of real time trading is simply the creation of the set of rules by advertisers the computers follow in regard to pricing and audience selections (among other things) for these marketplaces.

■ Figure 6.7 A Programmatic Ad Lifecycle

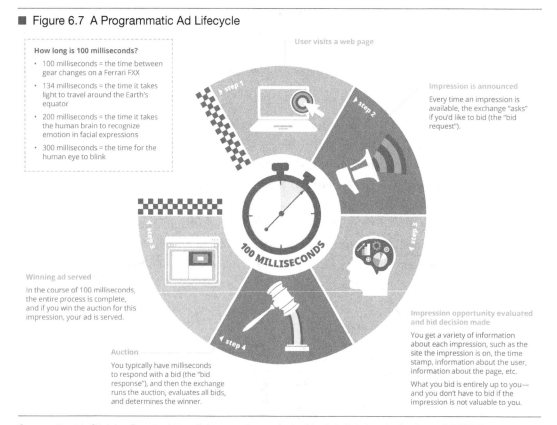

How long is 100 milliseconds?

- 100 milliseconds = the time between gear changes on a Ferrari FXX
- 134 milliseconds = the time it takes light to travel around the Earth's equator
- 200 milliseconds = the time it takes the human brain to recognize emotion in facial expressions
- 300 milliseconds = the time for the human eye to blink

User visits a web page

Impression is announced

Every time an impression is available, the exchange "asks" if you'd like to bid (the "bid request").

Winning ad served

In the course of 100 milliseconds, the entire process is complete, and if you win the auction for this impression, your ad is served.

Impression opportunity evaluated and bid decision made

You get a variety of information about each impression, such as the site the impression is on, the time stamp, information about the user, information about the page, etc.

What you bid is entirely up to you—and you don't have to bid if the impression is not valuable to you.

Auction

You typically have milliseconds to respond with a bid (the "bid response"), and then the exchange runs the auction, evaluates all bids, and determines the winner.

Source: DoubleClick by Google; *https://plus.google.com/+doubleclickdigitalmarketing/posts/UHMHAmYKZsE*.

A basic model for price setting can be seen in Figure 6.8. This automation allows advertisers to efficiently bid and purchase inventory they will never be able to review. Publishers, too, create rules to maximize their revenue from the inventory they have and avoid challenges to their premium advertising base.

Programmatic buying also allows buyers to include data (both their own and third-party data) to further refine targeting and optimization decisions. The buyer can use data from a third party, for example, to increase bids for a target demographic impression if the user has an "in market for purchase" profile. Data and transparency on the seller side can be limited, however, by paying a premium for greater specificity of exactly where the impression will be displayed. As the IAB notes, options range from knowing the Top Level Domain (example: publisher.com or news.publisher.com), Section Targeting (example: *publisher.com/sports*), or even the full

URL (example: *publisher.com/sports/NFL/Giants/article1235.html*). Alternately, the buyer may have little to no visibility on where the impression will show, a masked URL (example: *www. publishermarketplace.com*) or a completely blind purchase.

■ Figure 6.8 How Prices Are Set

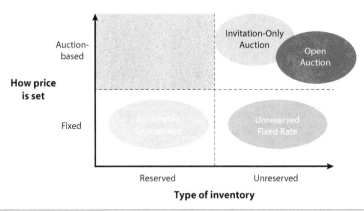

One thing is certain: the volume and revenues served through RTB are growing tremendously, as seen in Figures 6.9 and 6.10. As the RTB market often provides lower cost impressions, the sheer dollar volume may underestimate the impact to the industry. New methods such as header bidding are allowing for greater fine tune control of ad deployment and yield management technologies.

■ Figure 6.9 Digital Display Ad Spending 2015–2019

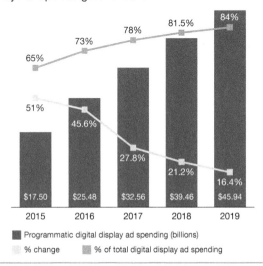

Source: Data from eMarketer, April 2017.

■ Figure 6.10 Digital Ad Revenue Buying

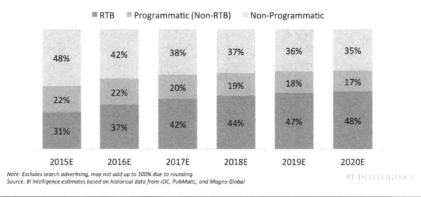

Share Of Digital Advertising Revenue *(US)*

■ RTB ■ Programmatic (Non-RTB) Non-Programmatic

	2015E	2016E	2017E	2018E	2019E	2020E
Non-Programmatic	48%	42%	38%	37%	36%	35%
Programmatic (Non-RTB)	22%	22%	20%	19%	18%	17%
RTB	31%	37%	42%	44%	47%	48%

Note: Excludes search advertising, may not add up to 100% due to rounding
Source: BI Intelligence estimates based on historical data from IDC, PubMatic, and Magna Global

BI INTELLIGENCE

Source: BI Intelligence, by *Business Insider*.

Trends in Ad Optimization: The Digital Difference

Unlike traditional advertising, digital media offers the undeniable benefit of being able to constantly improve the performance of ad campaigns. After an ad is deployed on television, little can be done except altering the media deployment plan: where to show and how much to spend. With digital, new creative and new targets can be tested as to the effectiveness of the ad. Various audiences are evaluated simultaneously, and performance improved. Advertisers can optimize the *media* (where the ad is shown), the *creative* (what is shown), the *frequency* (how often), and the *audience* segment (to whom) a message is shown, almost continuously.

Media. The types and placement choices for ads are one area where digital planners can have a huge impact simply by moving around media budgets to channels with the greatest return. Whereas TV has "upfronts" to buy as much ad space as possible to get volume discounts, many digital campaigns will deploy as little budget as necessary to acquire initial data on the media plan, then allocate the majority of the budget based on the results.

This "sanitized" media plan shown in Figure 6.11 has two kinds of metrics that can be used to optimize a media buy: click-through rate and conversion rate. It also illustrates a third point. If an advertiser did an initial buy against these 12 properties, they could look at the CTR — the blue bars — and quickly see that the difference in performance between high and low performers is 4×! Simply focusing the budget on top performers could double the performance of the campaign. But, is CTR the best metric to optimize on? If we're trying to drive people to a destination site, it's certainly a good one. But the jagged red line is another metric — conversion rate. If we're trying to get these visitors to, for example, fill out a form for more information, we'd better optimize on the desired action further down the marketing funnel. A quick glance tells us that the top three performers do six times as well as the bottom — some of those represent the lower CTR properties. Optimizing for CTR when we want leads, may not be as efficient. Taken together, however, it's possible this campaign could improve tenfold — turning a regular performer into a home run.

■ Figure 6.11 Example of a Digital Media Plan

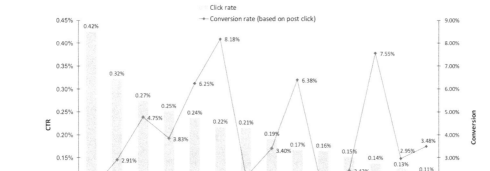

Source: Kagan 2018.

Creative. The design, content and type of ad is another area that can have huge impact. The high cost of creative in traditional media — like a TV commercial or magazine layouts — limits production and deployment to only the "best" ideas from the agency team. With digital, a campaign can deploy multiple versions of creative and determine which is most effective based on performance data. The difference between impact of the best and the worst creative can be an order of magnitude. With timely information on the performance of different variations of an ad, rapid increases in efficiency can be achieved (Figure 6.12). Everything can be tested, from the efficiency versus price of different sized ad units, variations in wording, images, offers, and the like.

Frequency. How often a potential customer sees an ad also makes a difference. The truth is that for a typical viewer of an ad, the impact is maximized in the first few impressions. Research shows that after I have seen an ad a few times, its impact is simply wasted on me compared to a new potential customer. Most advertisers want a user to take an action, like click on an ad, but cap the frequency that a single user will see an ad at a maximum of three times. If user *response* is your goal, it makes sense to either show a new creative message or target a new person at that point. If your goal is branding and messaging *awareness*, value can be derived up to about six impressions. This kind of "frequency capping," as illustrated in Figure 6.13, helps marketers limit the wasted ad spend of an online campaign.

■ Figure 6.12 Optimizing Ad Creative

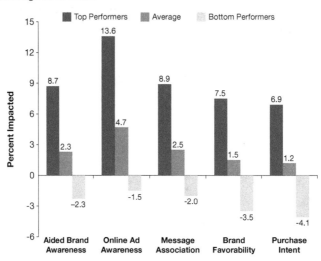

Source: Dynamic Logic Market Norms.

■ Figure 6.13 Frequency by Campaign Objective: Awareness vs Performance

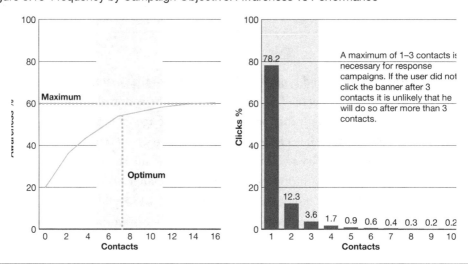

Source: Kagan 2018.

Audience. Finally, with timely data and appropriate adjustments, we can learn *who* is responding to ads and adjust our plan to include more of that audience segment to increase performance. If young men are responding to our ad for video games or shaving products, then we'll attract more of them with our media buy. Another great advantage, unlike traditional media, is that we can try and reach all successful segments — not just the obvious mass audience with the highest volume. While young men may be the main segment responding to our video game ad (high volume), but we may find other, perhaps unanticipated segments — like "cool grandmas" looking for that perfect holiday present — and target them too!

Opportunities: Targeting and Personalization

Ultimately, programmatic bidding and the associated technologies and techniques allow advertisers to define their media buys and creative campaigns by target audience on an impression by impression basis, rather than the media properties themselves that might have those audiences. Buying an audience rather than a property allows us to find our potential buyers in more cost-efficient places and reach them more effectively.

What's more, the innovations that began with standard banner sizes are moving rapidly into other forms of online ads like video. With proven effectiveness at driving results and buying efficiencies, these technologies and techniques will spread. Traditional media advertising will soon be available in this way as well, with addressable video and digital out of home already experimenting with ways to improve on the mass media model. As the buying process begins to shift from mass audiences to targeted segments, programmatic auctions, and real time processes, we'll see more and more of these techniques applied across the entire advertising budget — not just digital display.

Tools and Resources

- "How you should be leveraging native ads in 2017." Columnist Brad O'Brien of *Marketing Land* takes a close look at native advertising, what it means for your brand and how it can drive results at every stage of the marketing funnel. *http://www.marketingland.com/how-leveraging-native-ads-2017-199123*.

- Yahoo Gemini "Custom Audience Targeting" helps engage and expand your audience: *https://gemini.yahoo.com/advertiser/home*, *https://advertising.yahoo.com/solutions/native-advertising*.

- Top 10 Programmatic Ad Tools: *https://digitalready.co/blog/top-10-tools-in-programmatic-advertisement*.

Endnotes

1. *http://www.blendtec.com/blog/the-story-behind-will-it-blend/*.

2. *http://fortune.com/2016/07/19/unilever-buys-dollar-shave-club-for-1-billion/*.

3. "Who are the biggest ad blockers?" *Fortune*, September 21, 2015; *http://fortune.com/2015/09/21/apple-adblock-stats*. PageFair 2017 Ad Block report; *https://pagefair.com/blog/2017/adblockreport/*.

4. "How you should be leveraging native ads in 2017," *Marketing Land*, December 8, 2016; *http://marketingland.com/how-leveraging-native-ads-2017-199123*.

Hootsuite is the most widely used platform for managing social media, loved by over 16 million people around the globe. Big or small, Hootsuite helps organizations build trust and emotional connection to your brand, as well as protect your brand reputation. Hootsuite Enterprise empowers users to execute business strategies for the social media era and scale social media activities across multiple teams, departments, and regions.

Hootsuite is headquartered in Vancouver, CAN.

https://hootsuite.com

"You have total control over many elements of your organization's brand—things like your logo, tagline, tone of voice, and design guidelines. But no matter how carefully you curate the perfect brand identity, you can't fully control how people feel. By using social media to proactively strengthen and protect your organization's reputation, you can build the kind of brand loyalty that will separate you from your competitors."

CHAPTER 7
Social Media: Communities and Targeting Advertising

At the beginning of any discussion about social media, someone always asks, what is social media anyway? To the user, social media is the set of underlying websites, digital tools, and applications that facilitate the creation and sharing of user-generated content among groups of users united by a common interest. To others, it's the use of these technologies to turn communication into a dynamic, interactive dialogue versus a simple one to one publishing domain.

From a marketing perspective, these definitions are almost beside the point. What is the point is that for the first time social media technologies *and* the behaviors they enable have allowed the formation of *communities*, rich with information that allow marketers to target and engage these users to spread commercial messages and extend the reach of their brand. Social media captures the many behaviors that have existed for a long time in human interaction and makes them simple, leveragable, and trackable. Social media allows us to finally identify and interact with the enthusiasts and the detractors of our brands and products.

Source: Kagan 2018. A social media app for everyone!

We knew that individuals favorable to our brand existed, even depended on them for "word of mouth," but social media can actually pinpoint them individually and in groups. This capability has transformed marketing communications, from a monolog of brands shouting into mass media megaphones, into a dialogue of interaction on a much broader level, available to anyone, anywhere, with access to a smart phone, tablet, or a computer.

The Power of Communities

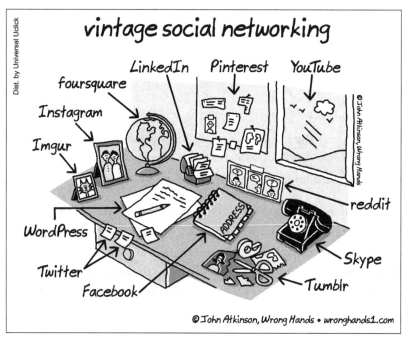

Courtesy of "Cartoons by John Atkinson," ©John Atkinson, Wrong Hands; *https://wronghands1.com/about*.

Mark Zuckerberg, CEO and founder of Facebook, defines social media as "the digital mapping of our real world connections."[1] From an Internet user's perspective, it represents something more fundamental and revolutionary. Mass media is defined by constraints and editors. Limited space on television, radio, and print channels means that professionals need to curate the things that make it to the consumer. In other words, a professional — an editor, media director, programmer, or DJ — decides what content reaches the user. The news stories on the front page are selected for their importance and we trust the editor to do their job.

Google, of course, approached the ranking of information differently — algorithmically. With the Internet allowing for an almost infinite number of information channels, computers (however sophisticated) began to make judgments on what a user could see — and what would be ranked highest in search results or news.

Social adds a third dimension, and new ways of filtering the firehose of information online using our networks of connections to determine what's important based on context. What articles are my colleagues reading? What events are my friends attending? What *user-generated content* (UGC) is being shared in my professional and personal networks? And by mapping our very interactions with each other and the content we create, social media and its technologies can make even better judgments about what we like and what we might be interested in next.

This generates more than just an interesting look at a favorite news feed on Facebook or pre-ferred social networks, but offers invaluable insight for marketers in the form of an *interest graph.*[2] Whereas social networks track the *social graph* of who or what a person is connected to, the interest graph tracks what they share and where they visit on the Internet, providing another layer of information on such things as what they might want to do or buy, where they might want to go, or who they might want to meet, follow, or vote for. This provides *perceived value* as it allows a marketer to begin to suggest things to people with similar interests and likes — for media consumption, product purchases, and more.

With users voluntarily sharing information about every aspect of their lives, and social net-works tracking what their activities say about their interests and relationships, finding and targeting the right user at the right time with the right commercial message become much easier. Users share a great deal of information beyond simple demographic data — things like relationship status, life changes, and other valuable information. Facebook touts a case study of a wedding photographer who targeted her ads just to women in her metropolitan area who changed their Facebook status to "engaged."

Three Elements of Social Media

Social Media has three distinct pieces: a portal to get information, user-generated content that fills the portal with media and information to consume, and the social graph, the filter through which content is placed. Each is important and necessary, but the social graph is the glue that holds social media together. Portals have existed online since early in the web's development. Yahoo, for example, provided a single place where you could get your news and stock quotes in a personal way. This information, however personalized, was still just mass media information being provided in a customized way.

User-generated content, the next element, is an important differentiator. This is simply media and information created by non-professionals such as text, photos and video, etc. While things like blogging and user reviews have been around for a while, early efforts often required some technical knowledge or were limited to a specific website. Before the widespread penetration of high speed Internet and digital cameras attached to phones, as well as enabling sites for photo and video storage like Flickr and YouTube, there was a significant hurdle in pushing out the most engaging and interesting content — pictures and video. Now, every user can be an author and publisher.

As we touched on earlier, the *social graph* is the layer of information about who is in a person's network and the nature and importance of their relationships. This provides the key to making it possible to provide personalized recommendations to you, and everyone else in your network, and keeping these elements, whether for individuals or commercial relationships, manageable.[3] On Facebook, for example, there are lots of baby pictures — but to me, the cutest ones are my friends' and family's offspring — and that's what I want to see. With the proper infrastructure in place for creation, sharing and distribution, as well as the evolution of simple and easy to use social media platforms and applications, the medium continues to grow and expand, creating exponential value for individuals as well as data and insight for commercial entities.

Social Media for Marketing

From a marketer's perspective, this is good information to know, but why do we care? Because people are spending more and more of their time in social media channels. So, if we want to reach them to tell them about new products and services, we need to be where they are. (How we do this in a way that isn't intrusive is a whole other story.) In Figure 7.1, we see that social media in its various forms is taking up more and more user time on an absolute basis, as a percentage of how we spend our time online, and even more of that time spent using mobile devices.

■ Figure 7.1 How People Spend Time on the Internet — Social is Huge

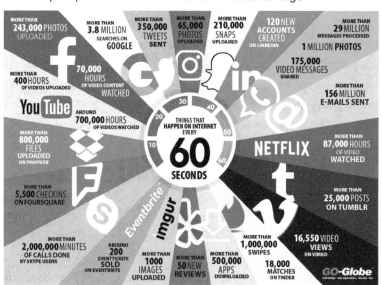

Source: Go Globe Blog, 2017; *https://www.go-globe.com/blog/things-that-happen-every-60-seconds/*.

■ Figure 7.2 Active Social Platforms, Globally by Users (including messaging platforms)

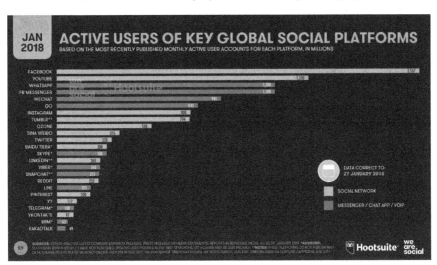

Source: 2018 Global Digital suite of reports from We Are Social and Hootsuite, Slide 59; *https://wearesocial.com/blog/2018/01/global-digital-report-2018.*

For marketers, this means, regardless of the specific choice of social media or channel, more and more potential customers are sharing information and joining communities of like-minded interests. This presents an unprecedented opportunity to find and reach potential customers. Social media in a sense has changed the traditional marketing funnel (Figure 7.3).

■ Figure 7.3 The Marketing Funnel

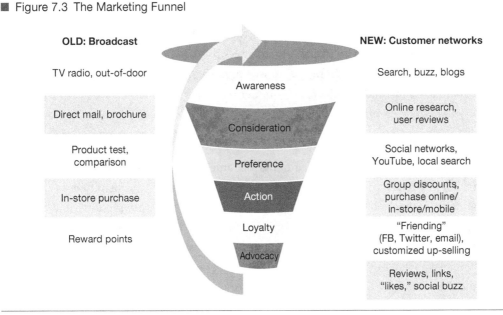

Source: © David Rogers, "The Digital Transformation Playbook," *www.DigitalTransformationPlaybook.com.*

Marketers used to use broadcast media to spread their message to the masses, hoping to reach some of the correct target customer prospects, then use sampling and coupons to "pull" a potential buyer into a trial and finally a purchase. Now the funnel is different. Customers may first hear about a product by searching or asking their network on social media; they might conduct online research and read user reviews, or interact with the social media presence of the brand itself. Motivation to make the initial purchase is likely to happen through a referral code or a friends and family discount. Social media can also take things one step further — negative experiences and positive experiences alike— by reaching a much bigger audience much more quickly.

With the self-selection of potential consumers into communities of interest, as well as the provision of large quantities of personal information and behavioral data, marketers have an opportunity to reach the right people with a precision they never could with mass media.

Major Social Networks

Social media's short history is notable for the constant emergence of new social networks to topple the old. The late 90s saw the emergence of arguably the earliest social network, *sixdegrees.com*, named after the academic research on social connectivity (and party game "Six Degrees of Kevin Bacon").[4] "Six Degrees" had some amazing features: you could connect with your contacts and share information, etc. To post a picture from a party you went to with your friends, for example, you simply took pictures with your disposable film camera that night. Next, you got the film developed. After receiving the pictures, you could review them to see if any were worth posting — good shots, not blurred, of the people you wanted. Next, you grabbed an envelope and some stamps, and placed the photo in the envelope, and mailed it to Six Degrees' address. After a few weeks, (enough time to deliver through the postal service and process) you'd see your picture... scanned and uploaded on *sixdegrees.com*. Obviously, without digital cameras (or even home scanning devices) there was no way to have the near real time impact and satisfaction of current social media. In fact, the founder of *sixdegrees.com* has said that he believes the inability to easily post pictures — some of the critical and engaging content for social networks — is the single biggest reason social networking didn't take off at the time.

As technology developed and digital cameras became the norm, mobile phones changed everything. Posting photos became ubiquitous; and newer, more successful networks emerged. First, Friendster arrived on the scene. With an easier ability to post pictures and a larger audience of web-savvy consumers, it grew rapidly. However, Friendster handled its astonishing growth poorly, allowing its user experience to deteriorate. It also prevented people from creating profiles of things other than themselves, like pets, bands, other projects, and groups. This opened the door for the growth of a rival network — Myspace.

Myspace, founded in August 2003 by employees of eUniverse, an Internet marketing company, allowed people to create profiles and post pictures of themselves. But Myspace understood its users, and did not restrict the content they posted, allowing the bands, pets, and anything else (even marketers and brands!) that one might want to profile. This led to enormous growth and its ultimate purchase by News Corp. for hundreds of millions of dollars. Sadly, it also contributed to its downfall. Soon people began to rack up thousands of friends — making the very concept of filtering the content through your network a challenge. Sifting through this avalanche of information became more and more of a challenge, and relevance and engagement dropped off a cliff as users fled to newer networks with less user saturation and information overload. This opened the door for networks like a small, elite college student-only social network that insisted that initial users had ".edu" email addresses to ensure its limited audience: Facebook.

Facebook was one of many social networks that emerged and began its growth by being a place where college kids could be shielded from the rapidly growing presence of marketers and parents on Myspace. Initially Facebook had a restricted membership — just open to certain colleges. It kept the clutter to a minimum and engagement high. Much as Google's simplicity replaced cluttered portals like Yahoo's in search, Facebook's clarity and usability allowed it to eclipse the larger but cluttered and corporate Myspace.

Today, the largest social network is . . . yes, Facebook. Facebook (and its subsidiaries Instagram and WhatsApp) dominate in both time spent by users and money spent by marketers in social media, with over a billion users and still growing. With this enormous user base, Facebook has been very successful at transforming the engagement and data collected from its users into

The story of social media is much richer than the summary just provided and can be found in other places. Three good books are "Stealing Myspace" by Julia Angwin, "The Facebook Effect" by David Kirkpatrick, and "The Art of Social Media" by Guy Kawasaki and Peg Fitzpatrick. You can also view a detailed timeline of the story of social media innovations and innovators at *https://en.wikipedia.org/wiki/Timeline of social media.*

the lion's share of social media revenue, with billions of dollars being generated through both desktop ads and successful forays into mobile, video, and lead generation. As we saw in Figure 7.2, other social networks like Twitter, LinkedIn, Pinterest, and Snapchat are also significant channels for users and marketers alike — with new ones arising every day. Having graphed its users' relationships and interactions, these popular social media channels offer anyone else interested in their users the ability to reach them with highly targeted messages.

In the next section, we will review the evolution of key social channels and their marketing value — as well as the marketing approaches used to meet consumers in these varied communities.

Marketing in Social Media

The opportunity of social and the time consumers spend there is showing up, naturally, in the growth of actual advertising spend across the various social media channels. As Figure 7.4 shows, most estimates indicate social media marketing spend is around $15 billion in the U.S. alone, with the lion's share going to Facebook/Instagram. (Globally, it's estimated at almost $35 billion, with North America accounting for almost half of the ad spend).[5]

■ Figure 7.4 U.S. Social Media Ad Revenue

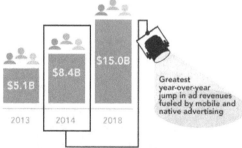

U.S. Social Media
Advertising Revenues

$5.1B — 2013
$8.4B — 2014
$15.0B — 2018

Greatest year-over-year jump in ad revenues fueled by mobile and native advertising

---

Source: Data from BIA Kelsey, Local Media Forecast, Social Edition 2013-2018.

Equally noteworthy is the shift in spending, with more and more of every digital ad dollar going towards social spend — approaching 20% — as advertisers increase their comfort and their budgets. The majority of that revenue is now derived from the mobile channel. We will address this specifically in Chapter 9.

Many brands report significant revenue from their investments in social media. A good example is KLM, the airline, that claims they are able to attribute over 25 mm Euros in sales to its efforts. KLM uses social media to support its 3 "pillars": service, brand and reputation, and commerce. They are willing to answer all questions in public, even if they have negative connotations. Their team works on thousands of queries per week often engaging in brand events designed to be picked up by social media — for example, delivering presents to passengers stuck in an airport due to a delayed flight during Christmas. KLM responds in more than a dozen languages and even publishes its response time on Twitter on its profile page![6]

Royal Dutch Airlines
@KLM

Official global account of KLM. We are here 24/7 for service in 13 languages. Share personal details only in private messages!

⚲ Amsterdam, the Netherlands
⦿ klm.com
📅 Joined July 2009

KLM places great emphasis on interacting with its customers through social media.

Even without the clarity of ROI that some brands like KLM realize, social media remains a huge area of growth for companies, in both time and resources spent on marketing efforts. As Figure 7.5 shows, more and more dollars are moving to both paid advertising as well as content in social channels.

■ Figure 7.5 Ad Spend in Social Networks

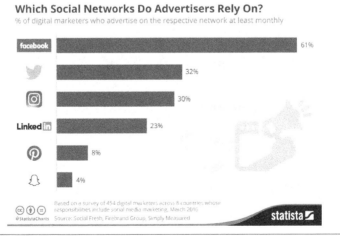

Which Social Networks Do Advertisers Rely On?
% of digital marketers who advertise on the respective network at least monthly

facebook	61%
Twitter	32%
Instagram	30%
LinkedIn	23%
Pinterest	8%
Snapchat	4%

Based on a survey of 454 digital marketers across 8 countries whose responsibilities include social media marketing, March 2016.
Source: Social Fresh, Firebrand Group, Simply Measured
@StatistaCharts

statista

Source: © StatistaCharts, 2016.

While much of this revenue is going to Facebook, we see that many other channels are important to marketers as well. Many will continue to grow in marketing value as they develop and deploy new ways for brands to connect with and monetize their user bases. Networks like Snapchat and Pinterest, for example, are just at the beginning of this process. All indicators suggest this trend will continue.

Facebook Dominates Advertising

The big daddy with billions of daily users is Facebook. The sheer size of the network (Figure 7.6) and the volume of the advertising opportunities has led to enormous growth in advertising on the network. Initial attempts at advertising stumbled a bit with privacy challenges, lack of engagement, and low interest as compared to other channels like search, but rapid improvement in these areas and Facebook's analytic tools have shown the true promise of social for marketing. (See Figures 7.7 and 7.8)

■ Figure 7.6 Facebook Community Network

Source: Facebook, July 2017.

Initially, advertising was limited to "right rail" display ads — the small text ads to the right of the desktop news feed with a limited message and simple graphic or picture. Facebook's initial foray into ads attempted to leverage its growing user base and the massive ad inventory available, but these types of ads often have click-through rates an order of magnitude lower than much maligned display ads in other environments.

In Facebook's auction-based, CPM and CPC based purchasing model, this massive ad inventory shows up as a relatively lower priced opportunity to advertise. These low prices have allowed for a lot of experimentation, sometimes providing a positive return on investment for brands through sheer volume and efficiency. With its enormous inventory and unique behavioral and targeting information found in *Facebook Audience Insights*, brands can learn more about their unique target audiences, custom audiences, as well as valuable re-targeting opportunities.

■ Figure 7.7 User Activity – Facebook

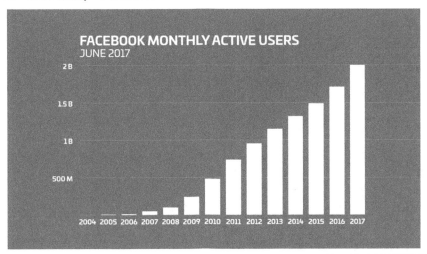

Source: Sprout Social.

■ Figure 7.8 User Activity – Instagram

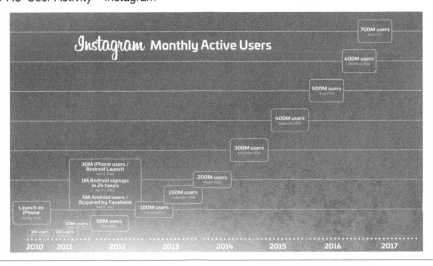

Source: TechCrunch.

The Facebook Advertising Challenge

A class exercise to demonstrate the targeting and power of Facebook's ad system. In class, a contest can be held to hit the target.

To explore the powerful and valuable capabilities of the Facebook advertising system, let's conduct a thought exercise. The reader can follow along using their personal ad account. Let's hypothesize that we want to test an idea for a new service for single people to meet. The service will be built around outdoor activities. To test ideas we have for marketing the new service and to see whether people are excited about the idea, we're going to target an audience on Facebook with some test ads. Our goal: to reach a group of 50,000 potential customers with our messaging.

Your exercise is to draft an advertisement targeted at this group and then select targeting parameters to reach this 50,000 person audience target. The ad itself isn't important (just a placeholder to get to the targeting exercise) and we're not going to run the ads so no payment methods, etc. should concern you. Simply focus on selecting a target audience that represents potential customers, and hitting the 50,000 person goal. You'll notice as you select different demographic and psychographic parameters, Facebook dynamically provides an estimate of audience size for you — this is the number you are trying to reach. You'll want to look at all the parameters but remember the target consumers are customers for a dating service.

[*Take this time to work with the Facebook system and come up with your target.*] Other suggestions — no one qualifies for the "finals" (review of their targeting) without being within about 10% of the goal (45k–55k). Note: this is an arbitrary exercise, not a well-designed business test, in order to make a point about Facebook targeting capabilities. Don't over-think it.

After some of the students (or you the reader) have hit the target, let's examine the parameters used to get there and some common mistakes. The goal was 50,000 people, ideally single adults capable of an active outdoor experience. One way to get there? Select an age range of 18-35, relationship status "single," and pick a single geography that might be a good test market (for example, Denver). Common mistakes include over-targeting, focusing on the number instead of finding potential customers, and forgetting that a dating service means that people have to be near each other! Selecting too many things can reduce the audience size — it's somewhat of a Venn diagram. Forgetting to select single people and those who like the outdoors ignores the need for them to like the product; ignoring the geographical reality of dating in the real world forgets this is a business test!

[*Ideally, you will be able to see these points in your own targeting successes or failures, or share them amongst the class.*]

Facebook's acquisition of Instagram and WhatsApp have solidified its hold on its user base and fueled growth of its entire ad ecosystem. Coupled with rapid innovation in ad products and unique data for targeting, it's no wonder that Facebook has seen explosive growth in ad revenues — Figure 7.9 — due in part to its emphasis on and a rapid rise in mobile users. Facebook has rapidly innovated, with larger and more intrusive newsfeed placements that capture higher prices with greater effectiveness. Also offered are new units like lead generation ads which use Facebook's knowledge and "insights" of its users to simplify the process of gathering information for an advertiser. *Remarketing*, too, is big on Facebook. It provides a way for brands to "re-connect" with visitors who failed to convert on a website by using the enormous reach and engagement of the social network.

Facebook has heavily invested in and relies upon the ease of sharing content within its network. By enabling users to easily post and tag humorous content or interesting brand messaging, some messages may have the chance at true viral spread. Video remains a huge focus area and they continue to experiment with both rich media content delivery and the advertising to support it. Of course, there's a lot of noise in the system too, so a well-crafted strategy is necessary to break through the clutter. Often, brands will "seed" potential viral content with Facebook advertising to the target segment in order to generate the initial momentum they need.

■ Figure 7.9 Growth in Desktop, Mobile, and Payments

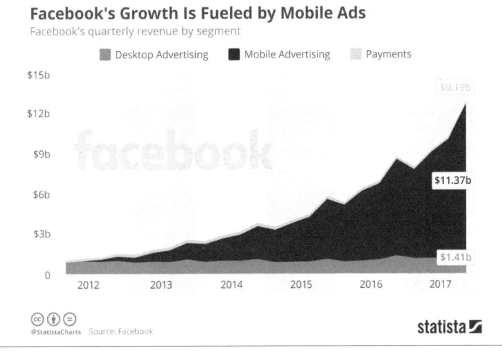

However, it's important to note that social's promise also comes with challenges. For example, Facebook's growth has not been without its problems for marketers. Initially, Facebook allowed marketers to build their communities on Facebook with the promise of reaching their fans and brand loyalists through an ongoing dialog. Brands spent millions of dollars to build their "likes" for their messaging and product pages as a permission-based asset to communicate with their fans and customers, much as building their permission-based email assets. Facebook, however, in what many marketers perceived as a bait and switch, adjusted the formula for showing marketers brand posts. This makes it almost impossible for even a fan to see messaging organically. Marketers now must pay to "boost" or sponsor posts in order to get their message out to their target audiences, despite their previous investment in "free" social media.

Perhaps more troubling was a spate of continuous revelations by Facebook in the 2013/2014 timeframe regarding major issues with its metrics and other data shared with marketers. Video views were overstated, engagement miscalculated, and other mistakes were made. Facebook was purported to have been aware of this for years — compounding mistrust by marketers and advertisers.[7] Without confidence in the data and analytics, marketers would not be able to continue to justify social media expenditures. Facebook's dominance, accompanied with its dedicated efforts to fix these issues, has avoided any mass exodus.

LinkedIn for Professionals

With roughly 500 million users, LinkedIn does not have the revenue and reach of Facebook, but its huge professional audience has proven it to be a valuable channel for marketing outreach. LinkedIn advertising is less well developed than some of these other channels, but the "Simply Measured" program for professional context, and "LinkedIn Matched Audiences" provide excellent opportunities to target and retarget people and measure ad effectiveness by their professional interests, industries, and positions.[8] LinkedIn also owns SlideShare, which is a great platform for sharing content such as white papers, presentations, tools, and resources to help develop and nurture leads. LinkedIn is essential in broad based corporate marketing as many potential stakeholders, customers, and recruits will check a company out on LinkedIn as part of their research.

Twitter for Real Time Influence

While not as network-based as other social channels, Twitter is an extremely powerful distribution network for real time content as seen in Figure 7.10. As Twitter allows one to follow another person without the relationship being mutual (Lady Gaga, Katy Perry, and Justin Bieber have between 39m and 42m followers respectively but they do not reciprocate with each one!), the social aspect appears primarily in the ease of sharing and distributing user-generated content.

For many media and technology influencers who focus on real time sharing, the Twitter feed is *the go to place* for quick release of current information.

Twitter ads allow for exposure of brand messaging, including video, and lead generation with excellent targeting data. Content marketers can spread "word of mouth" messaging with greater quality, clarity, and context, without the labor intensive community and engagement management of other channels.

■ Figure 7.10 User Demographics – Twitter

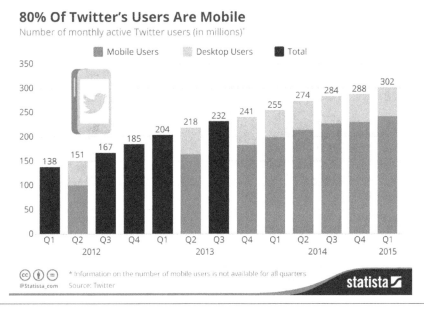

Source: *https://www.statista.com/chart/1520/number-of-monthly-active-twitter-users/*.

Pinterest for Purchase Intent

Self-described as the "World's Catalog of Ideas," the photo sharing community Pinterest has many unique characteristics. For one thing, it was the first major social network whose rapid growth was not driven by young, tech-savvy, bi-coastal early adopters in the U.S., but rather by middle-aged women from the Midwest — scrapbooking moms. Pinterest's organization serves as a virtual scrapbook. Its retention of source links for the photos shared also added an important layer of accountability and validity to the network.

Pinterest's real differentiator, however, is that those who share on Pinterest are sharing pictures of things — often aspirational items — that they might want to purchase. Most photo sharing on other social networks revolves around pictures of people and social activities (remember the baby pictures?). Pinterest's virtual scrapbooks represent items organized by theme: wedding planning, cooking, collections, housewares, clothing, and the like. Figure 7.11 provides a clear picture of their demographics. For e-commerce brands the math is simple; studies show that traffic from Pinterest converts into sales at a rate almost *5 times* that of Facebook. This suggests that the purchasing power and *intent* of Pinterest users are much higher than other traditionally low and challenging social media channels, where their users are focused more on communication between members.

■ Figure 7.11 User Demographics – Pinterest

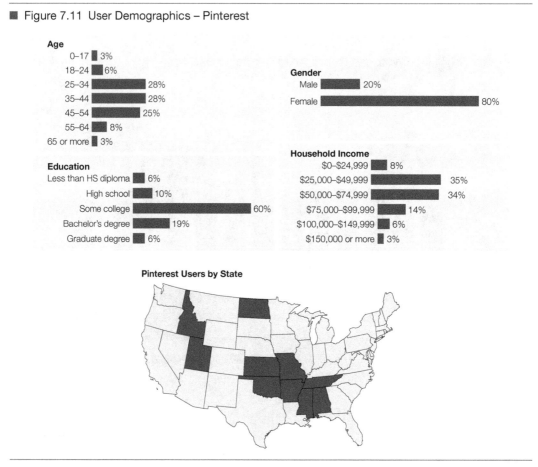

Source: Comscore 2017, *https://www.ignitesocialmedia.com/social-networks/pinterest-demographic-data/*.

Snapchat for Millennials — On the Watch List

No longer seen as a sketchy area of social media, Snapchat (now Snap) has come of age as a preferred messaging tool of millennials and early adopters. With its disappearing messages, vertically focused video, filters, and other quirks, Snapchat has a large and desirable audience; it is the focus of much experimentation by youth oriented and consumer-focused brands. Recently, Snapchat has launched a new feature that allows you to add Giphy animated stickers to your snaps. Additionally, Snap will introduce a new feature called Tabs, which will help users organize and see the stories they want. Currently, Snapchat is not a major channel for advertising for the typical business, but due to the hype around its IPO (NASDAQ) and its growth and engagement among millennials and even younger generations, it's definitely on the radar for brands appealing to those groups.

Which Network is the Right Network?

Hint: It depends on your audience...

With the myriad of choices and properties, as well as the promise of invaluable information and analytics, advertising on social media seems like a sure thing. However, the reality is a bit more complex. Advertisers face many unique challenges on social networks if they are to effectively get their messages out. The advertising units themselves range from simple and easy to set up — perfect for even small businesses — to complex, expensive, and custom units only available to large brands. It can also be difficult to find and engage with a desirable audience in an organic way — for example on Snapchat — especially for brands that aren't specifically youth oriented.

Social Media: Advertising Considerations

Advertisements in social media environments are by definition interruptive in the ongoing communication and conversation of the medium; indeed, the more interruptive the ad unit, the better the performance. The low click-throughs and engagement rates often seen in basic display ads are offset here by the large amounts of inventory and low market prices, which make the units very cost-effective. However, most advertisers find that to truly have impact they must "pay up" for more interruptive ads — sponsored posts, placements, native ads, and other new formats. We covered many of these in Chapter 6. This has caused some pushback from advertisers and brands who have invested early in building up a large organic following of customers in these channels to reach with their marketing messaging. Now, to connect with the communities they have built, they must pay for the ads to ensure their content is seen.

Facebook and Instagram (and to a smaller extent Twitter and LinkedIn) currently have the biggest adoption by advertisers today. Facebook captures the significant majority of all social ad revenue through it sheer size and analytic tools. The ubiquitous "right rail" simple banner ad, small, simple and easy to create, can also be very cost-effective. With a simple text message and millions of available stock photos for use, even a small business can rapidly set up an advertising campaign. Targeting to a geography or demographic is easy and can be used to create a local activation campaign and drive people to a store or restaurant. The simplicity is somewhat offset by the low response rate, but with pay per click and other performance-based pricing, businesses find this an acceptable tradeoff.

More engaging units are either more interruptive, more "native"/deceptive, or take advantage of the knowledge the network has of the user and their behavior to make things easier for the advertiser. Sponsored posts — otherwise normal text, photo, and multimedia posts from Facebook pages that are "boosted" — have noticeably higher engagement and click-through rates. This "pay to play" model can ensure the posts are seen by both fans and targeted audiences right in their news feed or within the desired UGC from friends and family. This makes them disruptive, harder to avoid, and somewhat more difficult for users to separate from legitimate content.

Other units simply play to their strengths. Lead generation units on Facebook, for example, allow businesses to capture information and follow up with users who are interested in their product or service. Since Facebook already has a great deal of the information that would be used for the forms to be filled out, it pre-fills these for the user, making conversion rates jump since much less effort is required on the part of the user. This also makes mobile conversion much easier than if people had to fill out forms on their small phone screens.

Advertisers can also use re-marketing strategies to reach people who have already visited their sites for continued messaging on Facebook. To begin with, they can simply upload email lists to cross-check and target custom audiences of customers or prospects. This ability to link existing customers or prospects thanks to social network profile information is effective and powerful. Twitter and LinkedIn have similar lead gen and targeting advantages.

Social Media: Privacy Considerations

While it's possible for advertisers to use information about you to have great impact, there are practical, ethical, and legal questions that surround this. For some categories, legal restrictions and regulatory requirements make it difficult to be creative and effective in social media formats. Health care, financial products, and products aimed at kids all fall in this category. With disclosure rules, limits on what can be said in copy, and reporting and other requirements, many companies walk a fine line to implement creative yet compliant advertising strategies for these types of audiences. For the rest of us, there are additional concerns. Recent testing found that racial, ethnic, and political targeting was easy and not blocked by the platform, enabling much of the troubling politically based sponsored posting of "fake news" and sensationalist posts. Facebook has begun to crack down on this, but the problem remains.

> *During its initial investigation, the social media platform allowed ProPublica reporters who bought ads to block anyone with an "affinity" for African American, Asian American or Hispanic people. That possibly put Facebook in violation of the Fair Housing Act, which make housing discrimination for certain protected groups illegal. In response, Facebook announced an antidiscrimination initiative that included an automated system to spot problematic ads.*[9]

Data collection practices and their impact on privacy is another key area of concern on the part of users and advertisers. This includes tracking people's activities and capturing personal data in the context of these interactions. This is the data in some form used to enable the targeting and retargeting of ad campaigns we discussed earlier. People might argue that there is implicit consent when users share personal data in social media. But there is also an implicit trust that social media companies will act ethically and adhere to their own "terms" and privacy policies. "Leaking" data, identifying information about those who are using them without their knowledge, is another concern. This involves capturing and sharing personal metadata (profile information, user histories, or location based) acquired from "access tokens" or cookies, found in the likes, tweets, shares, and other buttons users click on.

How do we protect our privacy? Enforcement agencies like the FTC used to enforce only those privacy policies articulated by each social media company. Today the FTC works to exercise much greater vigilance, from gaining 20-year consent orders from online providers to protect consumer data, to new rules on transparency related to endorsement and disclosure in advertising and misrepresentation of individuals in online profiles and communities. But, at the end of the day the best things we can do is to remain informed and cautious about who we share with.

Social Media: Where to Engage

The myriad of choices in social can seem bewildering to a business or advertiser looking to reach consumers. But for a strategic thinker, the choices need only to be filtered through a very simple lens: where are my customers? For most marketers, this means a "Facebook plus..." strategy. With its massive global user base, Facebook can be used with proper messaging and targeting to reach almost any audience for any marketing goal. Some businesses with more business to business products, or complex, longer lead time sales funnels have some concerns about reaching people who may be on a personally focused social network, but the reality is that any given CEO is there looking at pictures of his grandkids; the sales and marketing team is sharing their travel pictures with their friends; and the accounting director is engaging in a political discussion. In short, the targets are there and reachable.

One ever-changing filter is generational — the age of the target consumer is an important determinant of where a campaign should be deployed. Millennials and Gen Z use Snapchat quite heavily and youth-focused brands have experimented a lot with paid filters and the like. For other generations it's virtually a non-issue. Younger Facebook users tend to access the network on mobile devices and through Instagram; older users tend to be still browsing the desktop newsfeed. Female housewives from the Midwest, the scrapbooking moms, might be reached on Pinterest. Thus, smart marketers keep a close eye on trends reflected in demographics, as shown in Figure 7.12.

■ Figure 7.12 Trends in Age Demographics

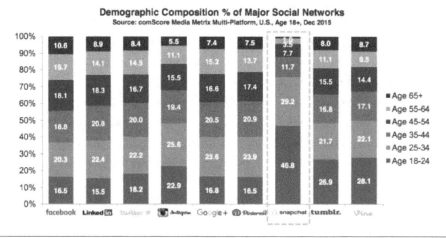

Source: comScore.

Globally, it's important to realize that much like search, if the language and alphabet are different there are likely other prominent social networks. Asian countries like China and Japan often skew towards local messaging-based networks like QQ or Wechat; WhatsApp and other text-based messengers thrive in low bandwidth, low budget environments around the world, as shown in Figures 7.13 and 7.14. Global campaigns need to check engagement and usage of different networks in their target countries for this reason.

■ Figure 7.13 World Map of Social Networks

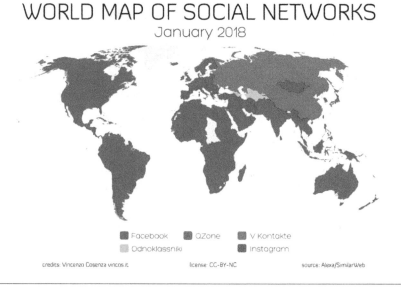

Source: http://vincos.it/world-map-of-social-networks/.

■ Figure 7.14 World Map of Social Networks — Ranked Second

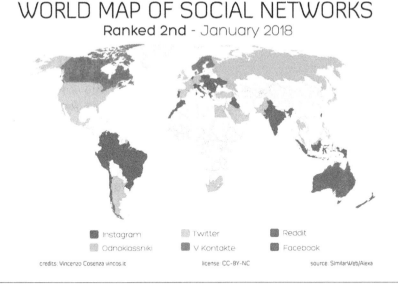

WORLD MAP OF SOCIAL NETWORKS
Ranked 2nd - January 2018

■ Instagram   ■ Twitter   ■ Reddit
■ Odnokiassniki   ■ V Kontakte   ■ Facebook

credits: Vincenzo Cosenza vincos.it   license: CC-BY-NC   source: SimilarWeb/Alexa

Source: http://vincos.it/world-map-of-social-networks/.

For business marketing, LinkedIn is almost a no brainer. The targeting ability of titles and companies makes reaching the right decision makers relatively clear. It's also possible to target messaging to professional groups whose members indicate the right profile. With more limited options and functionality than Facebook and other channels, as well as less inventory, LinkedIn is part of, but rarely the backbone of strategies. (However, LinkedIn is more useful for a content driven expert engagement strategy or community group management — to be explored more next chapter.)

Twitter can be used for promoted Tweets or trends and too has excellent targeting capability. People can follow brands and communities on Twitter without being "friends" from a social media perspective, thus it's possible to target on this basis. A business selling a software tool that works with Salesforce, for example, can target those following the larger company with lead generation ads. It's also great for rapid response to customer support or other challenges, or riding a wave of interest in a brand relevant topic.

Pins and "promoted" (paid) pins on Pinterest for fashion and household goods are excellent for targeting segments primarily populated by women. L'Oréal more than tripled their referral traffic from Pinterest. Instagram's image-based ads, and the like can all be part of a well-executed social ad strategy; the key is to use the creative and targeting tools appropriately. The first consideration is to use the "voice" and content type appropriate to the medium; photos are obviously a must for an image-based network like an Instagram or Pinterest. Advertisers must also be very aware of the social content distribution aspects of each network — a bad ad or tone-deaf approach can be not just a mistake, but magnified. Using a humble and open approach is almost always necessary with social ads, and preparation for potential negative reception should include real time monitoring at a minimum.

Ultimately, the challenge for an advertiser is not utilizing tools and reach of the bigger networks, but often understanding that the appropriate networks might be smaller. For example, there is a community in the tens of thousands for those who avidly collect and trade athletic footwear — *sneakerheads*. While not likely to be a great place for a software campaign, this is a natural fit for an Adidas or Nike! Smaller and niche communities rich with potential customers abound in social media — indeed, sometimes they are most abundant in areas that were previously difficult to reach. Specific industry sub-groups on LinkedIn, enthusiast communities of collectors, or even sufferers of a variety of health afflictions all find likeminded individuals online in social environments.

With new networks springing up all the time, and old networks changing and fading, developing a general strategy is perhaps the most appropriate. HubSpot, the well-known inbound digital marketing and lead gen firm suggests eight questions that should be asked when evaluating whether or not to incorporate a potential channel into a social media strategy:

Evaluating New Social Networks: 8 Questions to Ask[10]

1. Who are the current users?
2. Who's likely to go there over time?
3. Are these people potential customers, or influencers of customers?
4. What kind of content do they like to share?
5. How does content get shared?
6. Can you create this type of content?
7. How much time and resources will it take to participate?
8. Do you foresee a positive ROI?

Whether considering an advertising strategy or a content and community-based strategy, these questions are an excellent place to start. Knowing where your customers are, how to reach them, and ultimately whether it's worth it depends on asking these questions — and reviewing them and the multitude of data sources supplied in this chapter regularly to see whether the reasons still apply.

Tools and Resources

- Video for class intro: Eric Qualman #Socialnomics2014 *http://youtu.be/zxpa4dNVd3c*.

- Hootsuite is a simple but powerful tool for the average social media marketer: *https://hootsuite.com* .

- New tools and ideas to manage social media advertising: *https://optinmonster.com/23-tools-that-will-take-your-social-media-marketing-to-the-next-level/*.

Endnotes

1. Zuckerberg Quote: *https://www.theatlantic.com/technology/archive/2017/...mark-zuckerberg*.

2. Interest Graphs: *https://en.wikipedia.org/wiki/Interest_graph*.

3. "The Rise of Social Graphs for Business," Sangeet Paul Choudary, *HBR*, February 02, 2015: *https://hbr.org/2015/02/the-rise-of-social-graphs-for-businesses*.

4. Six Degrees of Kevin Bacon — Wikipedia: *https://en.wikipedia.org/wiki/Six_Degrees_of_Kevin_Bacon*.

5. "Social Network Ad Spending Worldwide 2013-3017," eMarketer: *http://www.emarketer.com/Chart/Social-Network-Ad-Spending-Worldwide-by-Region-2013-2017/168356*.

6. eConsultancy blog source: *https://econsultancy.com/blog/65752-klm-we-make-25m-per-year-from-social-media*.

7. "Facebook Overestimated Key Video Metric for Two Years," *WSJ.com*: *https://www.wsj.com/articles/facebook-overestimated-key-video-metric-for-two-years-1474586951*.

8. "LinkedIn Matched Audiences: A Remarketing Guide for LinkedIn," *Social Media Examiner*: *http://www.socialmediaexaminer.com/linkedin-matched-audiences-remarketing-guide-for-linkedin/*.

9. "Facebook Still Lets People Target Ads by Race and Ethnicity," *MIT Technology Review*, November 22, 2017: *https://www.technologyreview.com/the-download/609543/facebook-still-lets-people-target-ads-by-race-and-ethnicity/*.

10. Hubspot: *https://blog.hubspot.com/blog/tabid/6307/bid/33213/8-questions-to-evaluate-if-that-new-social-network-is-worth-your-company-s-time.aspx*.

Since 2006, HubSpot has been on a mission to make the world more inbound. HubSpot is an inbound marketing and sales platform that helps companies attract visitors, track and convert leads, and close customers. Today, over 37,000 total customers in more than 90 countries use HubSpot's software, services, and support to transform the way they attract, engage, and delight customers by being more relevant, more helpful, more personalized and less interruptive than traditional marketing and sales tactics.

HubSpot was founded at MIT in 2006, and is headquartered in Cambridge, MA.

www.hubspot.com

"Your success with inbound marketing and sales is much more dependent on the width of your brain than the width of your wallet."

— Brian Halligan, Co-Founder & CEO

CHAPTER 8

Social Media: Content Marketing, Influence, and Amplification

In Chapter 7 we explored some of the basic ways social media communities and applications differ, and how the rich information they provide on users creates excellent opportunities for marketers to find, reach, and engage new customers. Now, we'll look at ways digital marketers can go beyond reliance on advertising and the old models of CTR and paid outreach, using *content marketing* and *community outreach* strategies to generate results.

Content marketing is often described as a strategic marketing approach focused on creating and distributing valuable and relevant content to attract and retain a targeted audience — ultimately to drive profitable customer action and interaction. Content strategies within social media categories are key to successful inbound marketing and customer relationship management programs. They offer marketers powerful new tools and techniques to build and sustain customer interactivity and loyalty. They allow potential customers to find and interact with the brand, as well as keep existing customers engaged, active, and happy. Finally, content marketing and community outreach strategies help marketers integrate public relations or publicity efforts in their marketing mix, engaging with or *amplifying* the voices of influential figures to drive positive messaging for the brand — or address problems and concerns before they become a major incident.

Consumers Trust Each Other

At the core of social media marketing is a simple fact proven over and over again by research: *consumers trust one another far more than they trust advertisers,* see Figure 8.1. In survey after survey consumers indicate that they trust recommendations from friends over all other sources of information about products and services — at rates approaching 80% to 90%. Even the opinions of strangers — other real consumers they don't know — are trusted over advertising by roughly 70% of respondents. Online banner ads reach a measly 42% trust level, with traditional media faring slightly better, peaking in the 60th percentile. In short, whether deserved or not, marketing messages are not as trusted as the voice of the consumer and their peers.[1]

■ Figure 8.1 Trust in Advertising

	Trust Percent who completely or somewhat trust format	Action Percent who always or sometimes take action on format
Recommendations from people I know	83	83
Branded websites	70	70
Editorial content, such as newspaper articles	66	63
Consumer opinions posted online	66	69
Ads on TV	63	69
Brand sponsorships	61	62
Ads in newspapers	60	63
Ads in magazines	58	62
Billboards and other outdoor advertising	56	58
Emails I signed up for	56	63
TV program product placements	55	59
Ads before movies	54	54
Ads on radio	54	54
Online video ads	48	53
Ads served in search engine results	47	58
Ads on social networks	46	56
Ads on mobile devices	43	50
Online banner ads	42	50
Text ads on mobile phones	36	46

Source: Data from *MarketingCharts.com* research study.

What if there was a way for marketers to tap into the trusted comments, reviews, and opinions of a typical consumer? There is — by following, finding, and aligning with content created by regular people, the users of the social networks. *User-generated content* (UGC), one aspect of the broader field of content marketing, can be leveraged across social media to help brands communicate a more trusted and effective message. User-generated content spans a wide range of types. Here are just a few examples:

- Consumers can create content by simply clicking a "thumbs up" to like something — an endorsement.

- Reviews or comments on a product or service directly in a post.

- Sharing an emoji or sticker in text messages or posts that mention a product.

- Images and videos with embedded captions and comments about products.

- User-generated "unboxing" of new products (creating video clips that capture them opening and reacting to their favorite purchases).

- "How-to's" featuring consumers talking about products are a very popular category.

An example might be a teen blogger showing other teens how to use makeup. She might address problems unique to teenagers, and showcase products she finds useful, as she shares her own experiences. If you're a company that makes a teen-friendly product that is featured here, this can be a very powerful voice to share with your other social communities. Unlike your own marketing efforts, this originates from a more trusted, consumer voice, and is more likely to be shared and engaged with than a traditional marketing message.

Content Marketing: Amplifying UGC

Content marketing utilizing user-generated content is a key benefit of why some brands manage or sponsor online customer communities. Encouraging consumer discussion and commentary in the community, from reviews and support, to showcasing successful case studies, companies can not only encourage and generate valuable content with which to populate their online presence, but select the best for further social promotion across all their social channels. This is called *amplifying* UGC. This also creates volume in trusted content for consumers to view and engage with without the company bearing the expense and effort of generating their own content assets.

Another tactic can be found on Facebook/Instagram, Twitter, Pinterest, and LinkedIn. Here one can pay to promote posts or images to both existing followers and a wider audience to ensure that it's seen. A positive and well written comment from a customer on a Facebook page can be highlighted to customers who are more likely to trust another customer's voice, amplifying the effectiveness of the paid outreach.

An example of content promoted by the brand for amplified reach.

In the traditional media world, only brands could create content and get it out to their audience. The cost of creation was high and there were limited channels in which to distribute the content. Television commercials, special sections in magazines and newspapers, and other mass media had a high cost of production and distribution and demanded a level of production quality to be a worthwhile investment. With a limited and controlled environment, media and brands could be the authoritative message.

The new media world allows virtually anyone to produce content. Everyone has a phone in their pocket with the capability to create and distribute incredibly high-quality video and images, with built-in editing software. With these simple, easy to use tools, individuals are producing and sharing more content with each other than ever before. Within social networks, peer to peer communication to one's community and groups becomes easier than mass media ever was to reach targeted audiences.

Platforms like YouTube and other media based communities share text like blog posts, images, video and live streams. They host and disseminate this user-generated content using built-in tools to share and embed wherever one might want.

Social and user-generated content, then, are two sides of the same coin. While social media provides the filter for consuming information, UGC provides the interesting niche content that powers the networks, fills them with rich content, and makes users come back for more. Creating and consuming content from their friends is the gas in the social media engine.

A fun example of a good UGC campaign comes from our friends at HubSpot, where they showcase numerous instances of good UGC. This one on Instagram features the online furniture store Wayfair. It launched a campaign to let customers showcase the results of their online shopping sprees. Using the hashtag #WayfairAtHome, users post their home setups featuring Wayfair products. Wayfair reposts this UGC and provides a link so users can shop for the items featured in a real customer's home — an ingenious strategy for combining customer testimonials and design inspiration all-in-one. The HubSpot showcase also features examples from companies like IBM, Netflix, Hootsuite, and others.[2]

As you see, content marketing allows marketers to tap into this engine, making their brands go further by blending use of both UGC with their own original content and messaging. UGC is unique in that it creates a two-way conversation in marketing. Where in the past a marketer could stand with a megaphone and send their message out whether the consumer wanted to respond or not, now the consumer can speak back — and that message can be spread farther than ever through social media.

Sound easy? Like other areas of social media, content marketing presents distinct challenges for the marketer. For this reason, a well-designed and managed content strategy is essential. Content marketing can take advantage of the positive content created by consumers to spread the brand's message and values with a more authentic and trusted voice. However, it's also important to monitor and manage comments from existing customers and others to ensure a continued positive outlook for the brand. It's critical to have a proactive strategy in place to manage negative comments and respond quickly to the new two-way dialogue consumers are having with your brand. This is not optional. Brands cannot "opt out" of this dialogue. It's happening on websites, blogs and in forums whether the company

> *"Technology is shifting the power away from the editors, the publishers, the establishment & the media elite. Now it's the people that are in control."*
>
> — Rupert Murdoch

and marketers want it to or not. Whether you are a small business or large corporation with many brands, it is the necessary and practical approach to actively manage the conversation around your brand, as you will read in this next section.

Customer Relationship Management: Supporting the Community

Perhaps no area of social media marketing has the potential to spiral out of control worse than an unsatisfied customer actively sharing their discontent. Customers post, tweet, and review their way into the Internet's dialogue about your brand. If those comments are negative, they can cause significant damage. However, this is also an opportunity to display the brand's care and values. Marketers should be prepared to prevent the negative from spreading widely as well as turning it around into a positive experience, as shown in this example in Figure 8.2.

■ Figure 8.2 Turning the Negative into a Positive

Source: Originally shown in *BusinessWeek*, Oct. 18, 2007.

One of the first brands to learn the power of the crowd was Dell. More than a decade ago, Dell had a quality problem with its computers. One customer who bought one was a professor — and blogger — named Jeff Jarvis. After many fruitless attempts to get help for a problem-ridden computer he had purchased, Jarvis created "Dell Hell" — an online forum where he shared his unsatisfactory experiences with Dell and their support team. He also allowed others to do the same. It turned out many other people had similar frustrations and took to the Internet to complain. Through their participation, linking and sharing, *Dell Hell* became quite a popular site — and moved up enough in the search engine rankings that it became one of the top sites in many search results for Dell computers.

When Dell discovered this — anecdotally through Michael Dell himself seeing the site after Googling his name — the company had to begin a massive action to respond. Dell built a team, began to address the problem, and started a more proactive approach to interact and engage with their customers. Rather than leave them to their own frustrations through telephone support lines, Dell created websites of its own where customers could seek help and even support each other. Today, Dell hosts moderated community support forums on its own websites in multiple languages. This isn't just good for Dell's image and relationship with its customers — the online support has transitioned the volume of calls from expensive phone support to more effective and cheaper online and social channels, saving the firm real dollars.

Even media companies, trying to create traffic and the resultant ad revenue with provocative pieces, news or issues that ignite passions, need to have a plan for social media engagement. Every media company talks about creating a forum for discussion around a story, but not all discussion will be civil or courteous, fact-based and productive. A great example of effective moderation is the *Washington Post*, as seen in Figure 8.3.

■ Figure 8.3 Example of Effective Moderation

Source: Twitter feed, retweeted, and shared widely.

It shows that while moderation likely can't and won't change the mind of a negative Internet commenter, properly handled the brand can indeed continue engaging conversation in a way that continues to win attention and even praise. In this instance, a supporter of a politician reacted to a negative story about his candidate with inflammatory remarks and nasty language. The paper handled the interaction so well that it drew a response from the larger community, deflecting the negative and increasing the attention it received in a positive way.

Having a proactive social media plan is much better than the potential alternatives that many brands face. Time and again, brands respond to negative commentary on blogs, review sites, or on social media by trying to take down or remove the message — through legal action in some cases. This frequently has the opposite effect — leading to unintended consequences of the action. Given the speed of information exchange online, the very act of trying to suppress or muffle negative comments often risks drawing the unwanted attention of more people to the very comments you were trying to suppress and inadvertently bringing additional negative publicity for the brand.

A better approach? Acknowledge the customer's negative experience, and attempt to solve it. AT&T, for example, began to respond to customer complaints about bad cellular service in an effective way. They apologized first, and then provided information to the customer on how they were investing in improved service in their area — with a link to further information. This not only showed empathy and awareness of the problem to the customer, but had the added impact of appearing right alongside the negative comments in the social feeds of that person's network — showing other potential customers that the company at least cared and was doing something. This reduced the spread of negativity and prevented other customers from "piling on" with negative comments of their own.

Social as Online Public Relations

In the world of marketing, media is often broken into three pieces: *owned, paid*, and *earned*. In the digital space, *owned media* includes things like a company's websites, apps, and even pieces of social networks like a Facebook page, a YouTube channel, etc.

The key here is that the company *controls* the media and original content in these locations. *Paid media* — such as advertising, sponsorships, and the related content — is when the company controls the message but must pay to push it through other media — where content and audiences are controlled by others. *Earned digital media* includes stories, testimonials, and articles created on websites (much like the traditional way stories were placed in the press by PR professionals), but also encompasses social media postings (like the Wayfair and makeup examples) and items people share on their own — essentially *PR and publicity* to the mass audiences.

Since everyone online "is a publisher," and can share what they want with a built-in audience in social media, *viral marketing* depends on marketing professionals creating valuable content that people want to share too, and make it easy for them to do so. Figure 8.4 compares and contrasts these three media types in more detail.

■ Figure 8.4 Online Media Types for Content Marketing

Media Type	Definition	The Role	Benefits	Challenges
Owned media – Website – Mobile site – Blog – Twitter	Channel and brand controls	Build for longer-term relationships with existing potential customers and media	• Control • Cost efficiency • Longevity • Versatility • Niche audiences	• No guarantees • Company communication not trusted • Takes time to scale
Paid media – Display ads – Paid search – Sponsorships	Brand pays to leverage a channel	Shift from foundation to a catalyst that feeds owned and creates earned media	• In demand • Immediacy • Scale • Control	• Clutter • Declining response rates • Poor credibility
Earned media – WOM – Buzz – "Viral"	When customers become the channel	Listen and respond, earned media is often the results of well executed and well-coordinated owned and paid media	• Most credible • Key role in most sales • Transparent • Lives on	• No control • Can be negative • Scale • Hard to measure

Source: Data from Forrester Research; *https://go.forrester.com/blogs/09-12-16-defining_earned_owned_and_paid_media/*.

Clearly, there are many benefits to using all types of content strategies to earn social media exposure. First and foremost, it can be extremely cost effective for a brand or company to directly distribute its own content to its built in digital audiences (email lists, social communities, etc.) to achieve measurable impact — rather than paying for expensive advertising. Secondly, with search results incorporating links and other social signals into a company's search rankings, a good content strategy can have a significant impact on SEO and discoverability online. Finally, with more and more consumers seeking answers and product solutions on social media, the audience is not only there, but actively looking for content to consume and share. To refine your approach or approaches, it's important to understand the role, benefits, and challenges of each content strategy, and decide the correct mix of content types (paid, owned, and earned) for your brand or product.

Another positive impact of a good content strategy is in the event of a crisis. Company created content provides a buffer of sorts when and if something negative happens and it is released in the news and shared online. By having a lot of very visible and findable positive content associated with the brand, it's much less destructive to a company's reputation than if all that can be found are the negatives that are trending in the news.

Reputation management is the essence of what we have been discussing. It is important from a purely self-interested perspective as potential clients, partners, employees, and customers are all looking online to find information in order to form an opinion about your company, its products and services. As seen in Figure 8.5, online PR offers a company many options to manage their messaging and dialog, all of which are supported through effective social media and content marketing strategies.

■ Figure 8.5 Online Public Relations Strategy Options

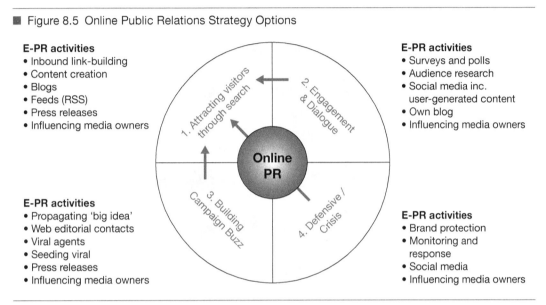

E-PR activities
• Inbound link-building
• Content creation
• Blogs
• Feeds (RSS)
• Press releases
• Influencing media owners

E-PR activities
• Surveys and polls
• Audience research
• Social media inc.
  user-generated content
• Own blog
• Influencing media owners

E-PR activities
• Propagating 'big idea'
• Web editorial contacts
• Viral agents
• Seeding viral
• Press releases
• Influencing media owners

E-PR activities
• Brand protection
• Monitoring and
  response
• Social media
• Influencing media owners

1. Attracting visitors through search
2. Engagement & Dialogue
3. Building Campaign Buzz
4. Defensive / Crisis

Online PR

Source: *https://www.slideshare.net/monikaskarzauskaite/7-lecture-online-reputation-management-ethics-webpr*, slide 26.

The subtleties of techniques for content marketing are an essential part of this overall process. By creating valuable and discoverable content, marketers have a chance to speak to customers both ahead of and after the conversion point. Instead of saying "buy now!" — like most advertising — the marketer can build and maintain a more meaningful relationship through content that entertains, informs, or provides a solution. Perhaps most importantly, this can be much more cost effective and efficient. Whereas outbound marketing like a television commercial or banner ad is ephemeral and simply disappears after it's shown, content marketing can be "evergreen" and continue to attract interest and traffic well into the future.

Content Marketing: Attracting and Retaining Customers

Unlike our discussion on leveraging or amplifying UGC, the broader concept of content marketing almost always involves content created by professionals aligned to a strategy developed to appeal to and attract potential customers and leads. This content tends to be created in the *voice of the expert* or partner, not the marketer or salesman. The goal being to build a trusted relationship without making customers feel they are being "sold to." It's a brand building, lead nurturing approach compared to the variants of performance based advertising we discussed in Chapter 7.

For a consumer-focused product with a more impulse-based purchase pattern, like a snack, this might be humorous or otherwise entertaining information to keep the product top of mind (see Oreo examples below in Figure 8.6). For a business to business or more complex sale, it might be the creation of detailed and thoughtful content like stylish buyers' guides, white papers, market analysis, slideshows, testimonials, and the like, designed to educate the potential customer and position the brand as a trusted expert.

■ Figure 8.6 Examples of Agile Content Marketing from Oreo

Oreo's Ad Team Responding to News and Events through Creative Content.[3]

A social content marketing strategy, then, has to be aligned with the goal of the overall content campaign, meaning that the type of content being created must match both the customer's needs as well as the capabilities and branding of the company. HubSpot, for example, uses ebooks, blog posts, graphics (we've shared some with you), and other online content to promote its inbound marketing practice — "eating its own dog food," so to speak. By creating the type of content that answers a potential customer's questions about inbound marketing, HubSpot positions themselves as both a *trusted expert* on the topic as well as a company in the consideration set for people who are looking to purchase tools and consulting expertise to help them — which is their goal.

A Word on Inbound Marketing

nbound marketing, mentioned earlier, is a defined approach focused on attracting customers through creative content and interactions that are relevant and helpful — not interruptive. With inbound marketing, it's about enticing potential customers who find you through channels like blogs, search engines, and social media — unlike outbound marketing, which fights for their attention. By creating content designed to address the problems and needs of your ideal customers, inbound marketing attracts qualified prospects and builds trust and credibility for your business.

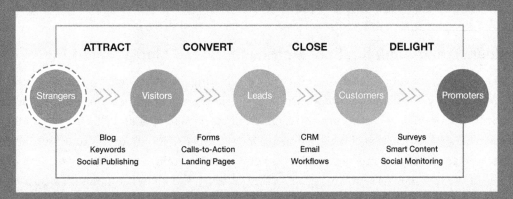

In essence, the term captures all of the things a marketer can do holistically that aren't direct selling to maintain and build a trusted relationship with a potential customer. From capturing interest with content marketing that impacts SEO and viral social sharing, to trading lead information for valuable content, to nurturing leads and building community with new and existing customers on an ongoing basis, inbound marketing is perhaps best identified in its opposition to traditional, outbound marketing — advertising. With the advent of digital tools, marketers aren't forced to use broadcast- based advertising as megaphones to get their message out — it can be done on a more subtle, sustained, segmented, and expert basis by entertaining or informing potential customers to create and build a relationship.

Source: *https://www.hubspot.com/inbound-marketing*.

Before choosing the goal of "the content," it is first necessary to understand the purchase process. If the product or service is high priced, high consideration, or infrequently purchased with a long sales cycle, this suggests an "educate and inform" content strategy for generating qualified leads. An example of this might be a series of case studies on savings of existing customers; a cost benefit analysis calculator; a positive profile from an industry analyst; or a buyer's guide. A more impulse-based purchase might require content that is solely about entertaining the consumer to keep brand awareness high until a purchase opportunity comes up — ensuring the brand remains top of mind.

Whatever the goal, the company should set clear metrics for success to ensure that the content strategy can be judged and measured for effectiveness. If the goal is qualified lead generation, then the metric might be completed qualification forms. For some brands it might be free trials, sales, or subscriptions. For a brand awareness goal, it could be permission-based asset growth (building email lists or increasing followers and friends in social media) or other engagement and awareness measures. Secondary metrics for success might be related to traffic generated from search and social media, improvement of SEO ranking, and the like.

Influence and Amplification: Metrics for Social Media Marketing

Another important set of metrics — crucial for evaluating the effectiveness of a social media content strategy — will include some measure of influence and amplification. These will allow marketing to properly measure, prioritize, and evaluate engagement and effectiveness in their social media plan. When reaching an audience in social media, it's important to tap into *social influencers* to amplify the message. In the traditional media world, a brand would tap into professionals like columnists or reviewers or celebrities to try and influence a potential customer. Otherwise, just encouraging current customers to share and generate good word of mouth was the best we could do. In both cases, it was often impossible to measure the impact.

In the world of social media, a new group of influencers — in between mass media giants and peer-to-peer word of mouth — has been born. This group, called *prosumers*, are amateur creators with a broad audience, and can often be the best target for a brand. Bloggers, YouTube channels, even just social influencers with a substantial following on Instagram or Snapchat, can be the most effective leverage for a content strategy.

Influence in social media is not just about audience size — it's also about the trust and expertise the influencer has with relation to your brand. Again, amplification, the ability of an influencer to get an audience to act even if simply to share a message, is what we are seeking. Identifying influencers to target then becomes a combination of both their audience size (followers, friends, subscribers), their impact with that audience, and their affinity with your brand or expertise in your area. If they tweet, do they get re-tweeted? Do their posts get shared and commented on? Examples of influencers can be seen in Figure 8.7.

This kind of social engagement is the *leverage point* for viral content. Without the ability to spread past the initial outreach, the audience size remains the same as with traditional media and advertising. Viral marketing with content depends on influencers sharing with the right people to amplify the message and increase the reach of the content shared.

■ Figure 8.7 Influencers and Their Reach

Network	Audience Size (largest age group)	Engagement	Prototypical Influencer	Representative Advertisers
Instagram	**200M** users 18 – 29 yrs.	**75M** daily users	Chris Ozer, 32 Brooklyn, NY 559k followers	JOHNNIE WALKER, Cole Haan
YouTube	**1B** monthly unique visitors 18 – 29 yrs.	**100 hours of video** uploaded every minute	Zoe Sugg, 24 U.K. 5.1m followers	MAYBELLINE NEW YORK, TOPSHOP
Pinterest	**70M** monthly unique visitors 25 – 34 yrs.	**88 minutes** average session	Joy Cho, 34 Los Angeles, CA 13.6m followers	TARGET, SEPHORA
Snapchat	**30M** users sending 18 yrs.	**700M** snaps per day	Meghan Hughes, 16 Los Angeles, CA	TACO BELL, Clean & Clear
Vine	**40M** users 20 yrs.	**5 Vines** tweeted per second	Nash Grier, 16 Charlotte, NC 8.4m followers	THE HOME DEPOT, BMW
Tumblr	**48M** monthly unique visitors 18 - 29 yrs.	**154 minutes** average session	Tanesha Awasthi, 34 San Francisco, CA 900k followers	H&M

Source: Business Digital Media Institute, Influencer Marketing Overview, *Slideshare*, August 2014.

Content Strategies and Examples: Notes from the Field

So, we know that creating and deploying content is the core of any marketing strategy designed to engage users of social media. As previously mentioned, the first step is to start with the goal: brand building, lead generation, sales, engagement, or the like. Mapping this goal to a trackable metric is the next step of the process and critical to measurement. A best practice at this stage is to identify current and future channels that customers are using for possible content distribution and narrow the focus to the best choices for your strategy. An important consideration at this point is what kind of content is shared on these networks — and can the brand realistically create or develop it easily. High quality video and real time media deployment require much more in terms of resources and expertise than a weekly blog post or an occasional Facebook post.

Before we get into the next steps of a well-formed content strategy, you might want to take a look at Figure 8.8 — a creative overview of all the varied elements that impact a content marketing plan.

■ Figure 8.8 The Key Elements in Content Marketing

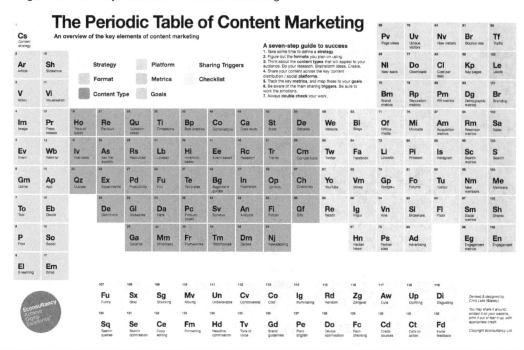

Source: Chris Lake from Econsultancy; *https://econsultancy.com/blog/64539-introducing-the-periodic-table-of-content-marketing.*

One way to approach content development and distribution is to determine which of three methods of generating content best fit your goal and audience: *Collection, Curation, or Creation*, as seen in the matrix in Figure 8.9. An additional consideration when determining the type of content is to evaluate your internal resources, budget and capabilities. Using this basic framework, you can now implement an ongoing strategy. Let's look specifically at the factors that differentiate these three content types.

■ Figure 8.9 Example of Simple Content Strategy Matrix

Channel	Type of Content	Frequency	Distribution
Twitter	Created, Curated, and Collected	Daily or more	Twitter, Facebook, Blog
Blog Post	Created	Weekly or more	Blog, Facebook, LinkedIn
Created Content (white papers, PPTs)	Created	Quarterly or more	Site, Slideshare

Source: Kagan, 2018.

A *collection strategy* is the simplest. With a Google alert of key topics or by simply tracking key sources of news and information, a company can aggregate and repurpose a relevant stream of information. This is often applied to create a weekly newsletter, a blog post, or a regular feed on Facebook or Twitter. Aggregating and sharing headlines or topics from that week is useful to keep followers informed. "Local business news" or "notable this week in the industry" type of information can add value, particularly when filtered to only what's relevant to your audience.

Curation takes this up a level. Here we are not just collecting everything, but judging what's most important with a critical and expert eye. In a curation strategy, adding value by explaining and adding context by commenting on timely news and information can present an informed and expert voice to the community at large. This can apply to both user-generated content and industry news. Strategies like "meme-surfing" and "news-jacking" — picking up topics or news trending online and tying those to relevant industry or brand topics — can have a great impact. ("Ten reasons the new president will be great for business" will get attention — although with some risk.)

A *creation strategy* is the most difficult, but ensures that the content is unique and adds a higher level of value by being new, relevant, and fresh. It's also the most likely type of social content to be shared, generating attention as it has the best chance of rising above the noise of social sharing about the same topics. Brands can often be intimidated by the necessity of committing to high quality content.

But, many brands may already have the foundation and assets in place for creating unique content valuable to their audience (as we saw earlier in the Oreo examples). Customer interviews and case studies, for example, may already be among the necessary tools the sales team has generated. Often these can be easily repurposed for use in a social media content strategy. Interviews with successful customers, maybe originally featured in the company blog or newsletter, can be recast for social channels, generating new content, loyalty, and goodwill. Industry events where the company has a booth or an executive speaking can be captured, edited and shared on social media. Awards and the like are great ways to spread good news. Even simply surveying existing customers about interesting industry topics — and then sharing back the results — can generate valuable, engaging, and welcome content.

Interactivity and response planning are a final critical element of any social content strategy to ensure success. The major difference to remember between social media and traditional media is that *customers can and will respond* — with praise, with questions, with comments, and even with insults. You can see some of these "triggers" in Figure 8.10. Only by designing for, and being prepared for, these kinds of interactions with a response plan at the ready, can brands avoid the challenges and risks associated with a transparent content strategy.

■ Figure 8.10 Checklist to Evaluate Content Creation for Virality Potential

	VIRAL TRIGGERS	Example
MIND	**FUNNY...ROFL!** Humour is notoriously subjective: will your audience be tickled by a witty quip or a banana slip? Parody or farce? Either way, a top-notch 'pay-off' is a must-have.	Toyota "Swagger Wagon"
	HOT...SEXY! This one's a slippery pole, ranging from booty-shaking through to celebrity upskirts and full blown sex tapes. Approach with caution: this is hot stuff. Misjudge your target audience and you'll get your fingers burnt.	Agent Provocateur "Kylie"
	SHOCKING...OMG! As a species we find disturbing content strangely compelling. There's a certain thrill in being 'frightened' by the unexpected and the ghastly. Hence the popularity of car-crash TV and hard-hitting road safety ads.	Carlsberg "Carlsberg and Mentos"
BODY	**UNBELIEVABLE...AWSM!** Has to be seen to be believed. Brilliantly done stop-motion sequences, people performing on the edge of what's humanly possible, creative teams pushing the boundaries of human & technological achievement.	Gillette "Federer Trick Shot"
	CONTROVERSIAL...GENIUS!/F**** S****** Love it or hate it? Some videos divide opinion and split the online community into opposing and vociferous factions. Not for the faint of heart. You'll need to be prepared to stand your ground.	Bud "9/11"
	GLEEKY...COOL! This is brain-food for aficionados. Could be the unboxing of a limited edition game for Xbox fans, a Jen Aniston meta-viral for meme fiends, or Sue Sylvester voguing for Glee fans.	Blendtec's Will it Blend? "iPad"
	ILLUMINATING...FIRST! Will open your mind and rock your head. Unveilings, sneak peeks, breaking news. Eye-opening facts, trends or technology. Useful as well as entertaining. Guaranteed to make your synapses tingle or your money back.	TFL "Awareness Test"
	ZEITGEIST Confounded, surprised? Bewildered? Random clips often involve a verbal, visual, or conceptual non-sequitur that is as funny as it is bewildering. Why is that gorilla playing the drums? I Like Turtles? You bet we do!	Cadbury's "Gorilla"
	RANDOM...WTF? Does this video ride the crest of a current meme or develop a current news story? Does it capture the public mood or celebrate a public holiday? Timing is everything. Yesterday is nothing.	Volkswagen "The Force"
SOUL	**CUTE...AWWW!** Sneezing pandas, laughing babies, fainting kitties, these are the videos that melt our hearts.	Evian "Roller Babies"
	UPLIFTING...YAY! I love this! Want to escape the tedium of everyday life? Bring a smile to the faces of fed-up friends? For a shot of Feel Good factor 40, look no further. Flash mobs, group dances, good causes tend to coalesce around this trigger.	Alphabet Photography "Hallelujah Chorus"
	MOVING...WOW. Made me cry. These videos are intense, with the power to evoke strong emotions: hope, pride, faith, nostalgia, love, anticipation. The best ones give us goose bumps, uplift our souls, and renew our faith in humanity.	Pantene "Extraordinary"

Source: Data from Econsultancy blog on video sharing triggers; *https://econsultancy.com/blog/7851-the-12-video-sharing-triggers-that-you-really-need-to-know-about*.

An excellent example of not only responding to negative social chatter — but turning it around and getting a positive brand message — can be found in Figure 8.11 from Smart Car. A few years ago, someone on Twitter made a humorous comment about a Smart Car he saw being pooped on by a wayward bird. The Smart Car team responded in kind — with a humorous, well-researched and well-designed infographic that refuted the negative implications while keeping the tongue-in-cheek tone!

■ Figure 8.11 Humorous Response to an Off-the-Cuff Tweet

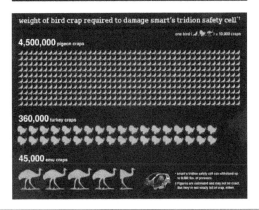

Source: "How Much Bird Poop Does it Take to Total a SmartCar?" Published by Mashable.

The biggest complaint from many marketers, is that their organization is "too conservative" — that there's no way they could design and execute a responsive social strategy that would get approval from the legal team and still be timely and effective. Others might say their organization is too controversial to risk engagement in social media at all.

To that, I simply present the following example of an engagement response guideline prepared by none other than the U.S. Air Force. If the military can find a way to engage online with their disgruntled "customers," so can your organization — no matter how conservative!

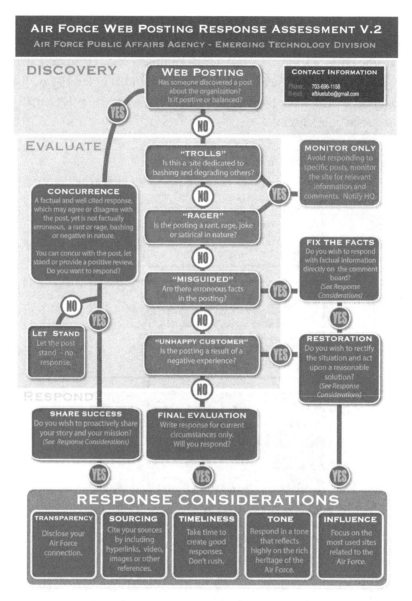

As far as the Air Force is concerned, social media is a good thing. "The enemy is engaged in the information battlespace, and our Airmen must engage there as well."

But Does Social Drive Sales?

The short answer is yes. Although it can often be tough to track and attribute, and the time frames are often longer than with a simple ad campaign, a good social media strategy can tie directly to sales conversion. But, just as many of the world's most valuable brands sell billions of dollars of product without being able to track directly to a television commercial, it's clear that while direct one-to-one sales attribution is difficult, social is clearly having an impact — both positive[4] and negative[5] — when used properly in the context of a broader digital strategy.

> ### Unilever Finds Social-Media Buzz Really Does Drive Sales
> Coke, Where Unilever's Top Researcher Once Worked, Found Otherwise

> ### Buzzkill: Coca-Cola Finds No Sales Lift from Online Chatter
> Marketer Finds Digital Display Nearly as Effective as TV

Two sides of the social media conversation, from *AdAge* articles (September 2015 and March 2013).

At the beginning of this discussion we noted that the most important thing is to "map your goal to a trackable metric." For social, this often means tracking a number of key metrics against the stated goals of the social content strategy, and continuously improve against them to eventually show their impact on sales. For example, many researchers see social as the #1 driver of traffic to a website (roughly 31%). Is there a plan in place to convert those visitors? A second key point is to establish a baseline for the brand as well as a "relative range" of target success. Knowing where a brand stands on key metrics when a content marketing effort commences provides an appropriate reference point to be able to demonstrate how well the effort is doing. *Knowing what a reasonable target is allows the setting of reasonable goals for success.*

For example, establishing a goal of 100,000 followers in key social channels sounds like an easily trackable target. If a brand is at 100,000 Facebook followers at the end of the year, they might want to declare their efforts a rousing success. However, a baseline is critical in determining this. If they started with 1,000 followers, this could be an incredibly effective strategy. If they started with 90,000, the effort will likely be discounted, attributing the extra 10,000 to natural growth with the social effort deemed completely ineffective.

However, if all brands in the space have between 50,000-75,000 followers, our brand's strategy is nothing short of a major victory. Similarly, if our competition has one million fans and followers, we have set our sights too low and our strategy should target a much more aggressive number to be effective when competing for attention in social channels.

Setting a baseline can be fairly simple. Most brands have a known *competitive set* — or comp set, which is a selection of key competitors to benchmark against. A good first step is simply scoping out the friends and followers' count of both the brand and its competitors in key social networks where customers are active. The brand's initial counts serve as the baseline, while the competitive set can determine the relevant range to try for when setting brand goals in social.

More advanced metrics, such as content engagement and brand sentiment (whether customers feel positive or negative about a brand) can also be tracked using a social media monitoring tool. Many high quality tools exist for those with the resources to employ them. However, free tools like social mention (see screenshot in Figure 8.12) are easy to use, configurable, and can help you make the case for action when starting out.

■ Figure 8.12 Social Mention Dashboard

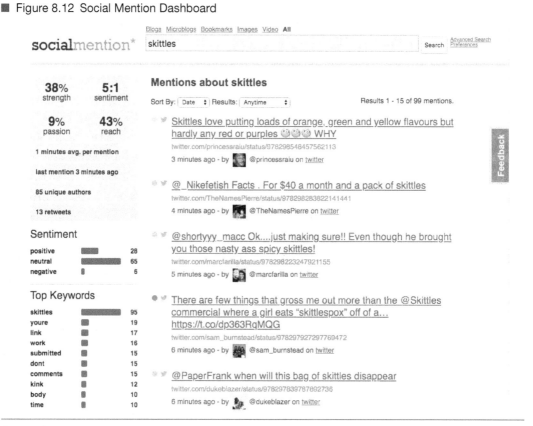

Source: *Socialmention.com*.

Final Thoughts

In today's exponentially more social and content driven world, a social content strategy is crucial to building a brand, generating sales, and retaining customers. It also plays a critical role in online reputation management in the event of a crisis. Marketers need to identify the key networks current and future customers use to communicate, identify the types of content they share and how the company can contribute. Then, craft a strategy that is right for their brand to generate and distribute the content. A key element of any strategy must be tracking and accountability, so matching brand goals with trackable metrics, setting a baseline and relevant target range for impact, and monitoring these over time are key tools in ensuring success from a business perspective.

Tools and Resources

- ▦ Video about branding and reputation management: *https://www.youtube.com/watch?v=nXG7zYWKH-GU*.

- ▦ "BrandYourself DIY Reputation Management Tools," looking better on Google! *https://brandyourself.com/info/about/howItWorks*.

- ▦ Social Mention real time social media search tool: *http://www.socialmention.com/*.

- ▦ Google Trends, explore and search media by phrase or topic: *https://trends.google.com/trends/explore*.

- ▦ FollowerWonk, tools to explore and grow your social graph including Twitter analytics tools: *https://moz.com/followerwonk/*.

Endnotes

1. "Global Trust in Advertising" Report, Nielsen, September 2015: *https://www.nielsen.com/content/dam/nielsenglobal/apac/docs/reports/2015/nielsen-global-trust-in-advertising-report-september-2015.pdf*.

2. "The 10 Best User-Generated Content Campaigns on Instagram," HubSpot: *https://blog.hubspot.com/marketing/best-user-generated-content-campaigns*.

3. "The Secret Behind Oreo's Social Media Marketing," Shopify Blog, April 2013: *https://www.shopify.com/blog/7589919-the-secret-behind-oreos-social-media-marketing*.

4. *AdAge, http://adage.com/article/digital/unilever-social-media-buzz-drive-sales/300426/*.

5. *AdAge, http://adage.com/article/cmo-strategy/coca-cola-sees-sales-impact-online-buzz-digital-display-effective-tv/240409/*.

"Apps have revolutionized the way we approach business — because apps have transformed consumers' lives."

— Bertrand Schmitt, CEO, Chairman, & Co-Founder

App Annie delivers the most trusted app data and insights for businesses to succeed in the global app economy. If you're serious about promoting your mobile app, the products App Annie offers are so useful and the data they provide so complete you can't really go without, as evidenced by their 800,000 store stats subscribers, 100,000 app analytics and intelligence subscribers, and 1 million plus apps they cover (growing every day). App Annie's most famous product is their consumer index which tracks downloads of the top apps in stores with all the data behind each one. They also offer detailed market intelligence (as a platform) with what's ranking and why, what keywords apps and their competitors use, engagement metrics and many other statistics or insights.

App Annie is an app market data and insights company headquartered in San Francisco, California.

App Annie

www.appannie.com

CHAPTER 9

Mobile and Its Impact

For years the promise of mobile was just that: a promise. The consensus was that mobile Internet would be big, but that it would happen at some point in the future. In the U.S., carrier-controlled platforms ruled. To get "on deck" — making your app available to the users on a carrier's phone — you had to undergo a long, complex, and costly arrangement with the mobile phone company. Naturally, this hindered innovation, causing the U.S. to lag behind more forward-thinking markets like Europe with its WAP phones and Japan.

The history of mobile in Japan is somewhat of the tale of an "Island of Geniuses" — a single, dominating company controlled and advanced exciting new innovations in mobile technology, but regulatory issues and unique business factors hindered their success outside of the country. In Europe, the early European-developed GSM standard reigned supreme, allowing for growth and innovation within a unified market. GSM became the first system to introduce the SMS (short message service) texting technology that later became the global standard. On their way to global domination? No. Europe too regulated itself into a similar situation as Japan with roaming restrictions, regulations, and proprietary technology standards that curtailed growth beyond the region.

Back in the U.S., AT&T was broken up into seven regional companies. Mobile was assigned to them as a business because the Bell Labs folks (back in 1979) forecast that the market size for mobile "could" reach 1 million subscribers by 2000. Each of the Bell companies chose its own technology and built out its own incompatible networks. Roaming was a difficult process, wireless frequencies were different, etc. Even today we can see the legacy of this.

All this changed with the introduction of the iPhone in 2007. The phone was an exquisitely designed piece of equipment for using the Internet, creating a more pleasant user experience with both hardware and software innovations. It offered a critical marketing innovation as well: the *unlimited* iPhone data pricing plan from AT&T as a condition of them getting the exclusive distribution rights from Apple.

Much like the pricing transformation that created an explosion of interest and utilization of Internet for AOL in the 90s (from a per minute to unlimited browsing that resulted in busy signals as plenty of people explored the emerging world wide web), the removal of the meter on the iPhone's data and browsing capacity was a catalyst towards mobile web usage. Even before apps and serious mobile broadband, this shift from voice only to messaging, search, and content sharing changed the world in ways we are still experiencing.

The Evolution of Mobile

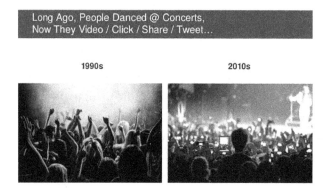

Source: KPCB Mary Meeker's annual presentation 2017.[1]

As you can see from our short history lesson, the changes over just a few decades have been drastic. Ironically mobile telephony is only one of many functions we are able to access through what has evolved into a personal mobile computing platform in everyone's pocket. Email, banking, entertainment, travel booking, and more are with us all the time and at a moment's notice. Since 2015, the majority of all Internet activity occurs through mobile devices of one kind or another. Indeed, everything in this advertisement from a couple of decades ago for Radio Shack is now part of your phone — including a dynamic version of the ad itself!

Radio Shack newspaper ad circa 1990s.

The dream of mobile has been around for longer than people realize! As long as there have been communications technologies, people have been exploring ways to take them on the go. (Figure 9.1)

■ Figure 9.1 Wireless Telephone Patent 1908

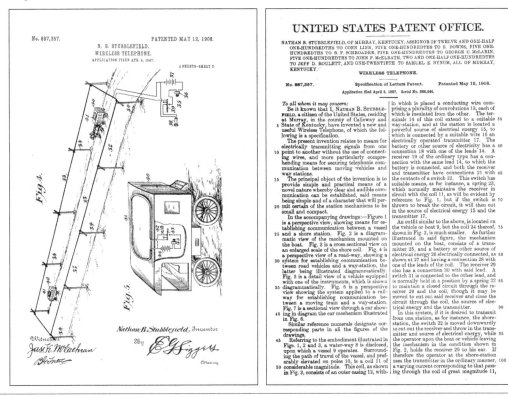

The world's first mobile phone patent (1908). Found by a researcher in the Pathe vaults, this clip shows that more than a century ago, mobile phone technology as well as music on the move was not only being thought of but being trialed; *https://www.google.com/patents/US887357.*

Despite early experimentation, mobile phone technology didn't truly take off until the 70's and 80's. Even the most informed business leaders didn't truly see the explosive potential of the new medium. Today, there are more cellphone users than people on the planet — some have more than one! Mobile technology impacts both business strategy and operations in ways previously unimagined. Bell Labs' forecast of limited usage by the year 2000 was, of course, off by orders of magnitude (see Figure 9.2).

As mobile access to information and services from the Internet continues to grow we will see user behaviors continue to evolve. Marketers will need to adapt.

■ Figure 9.2 Worldwide Mobile Subscriptions 2010-2020

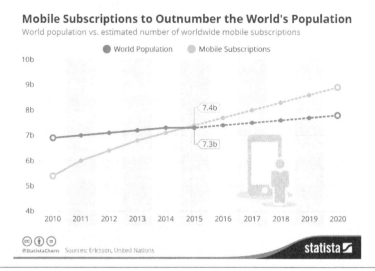

Mobile Subscriptions to Outnumber the World's Population
World population vs. estimated number of worldwide mobile subscriptions

Source: © StatistaCharts, based on Ericsson's mobility report, UN data.

Mobile as a Marketing Channel

Today, billions of people are dependent on their mobile phone — in fact, it's the primary computing device for most of the world, and the way the majority of people now access the Internet. What does this mean for marketers? For the first time ever, this gives marketers the opportunity to be with consumers at every relevant moment in their day to day life. We now know where they are located, who they're connected to, and how and when to provide help with searches, purchases, or other services people require on a regular basis.

A major difference from desktop computers is that mobile phones are much more *personal*. Not just the choice of phone — the teenage girl with a "Hello Kitty" branded phone case making a fashion statement or a businessperson with a more conservative case — but, their ubiquity, portability, and configurable utility enables wireless devices to become an invisible extension of each of us, and in some cases even a status symbol or personal statement.

As potential customers spend more and more time in the mobile channel, marketing spend now over-indexes in declining traditional media channels like newspapers and magazines. Translated: money is moving from old media channels to mobile as marketers refine ways to reach consumers where they are now, not where they used to be. Mobile broke the barrier and flooded the digital ad space with 51% market share by the end of 2016.[2] Research indicates this trend will grow each year as marketers catch up to new consumer behaviors. But in order to be effective, mobile marketing tactics must be designed to align with and support consumer behavior, from search to the very beginning of their purchase journey.

One obvious example of this shift is the growth in mobile advertising. As you can see in Figure 9.3, this jump in ad spending has mirrored that of the Internet as a whole — focused on search and display ads, with video and rich media added to attract customers. While these two channels are fairly well understood from desktop usage, we'll look closely at the important differences with mobile.

Not only does growth in search and display spend outpace that of other media, but they lead spending in all other mobile ad formats. By 2019 search and display spend is projected to reach over $33 billion and $28 billion respectively.[3]

What is the nature of this spending? Most of it is going to two current behemoths: Google and Facebook. Both are innovating and adapting their existing business to the new mobile channel as fast as they can. Facebook's revenue growth, for example, has been entirely driven by mobile ads.

■ Figure 9.3 Snapshot of Mobile Share and Ad Spending versus Other Media

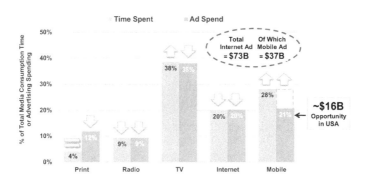

Source: *2017 Internet Trends Report*, KPCB, May 31, 2017.

However (as we saw in Chapter 7), many other players are beginning to seek a piece of the pie in mobile spend, creating a future that is fluid. One major area of growth is *applications*.

An explosion of computer programs available on the mobile platforms, called *apps*, have become one of the biggest places that consumers spend their time. Good apps are not simply the mobile version of a website, but a uniquely designed dedicated platform. Since many of these apps are ad-supported, this has caused a great deal of growth and innovation in the ad ecosystem, as marketers spend their budgets in different places inside apps.

As marketers, we have many decisions to make as the world shifts to the mobile channel. Where to advertise? How to adapt to the differences between desktop and mobile? Should we use mobile sites, apps, or both; and for what purposes? Guiding these decisions requires new data to understand consumer behavior on mobile and to create better and more effective messaging.

Mobile Platforms: iOS and Android in Control

The rise of smartphones and the explosion of web traffic coming from them has overturned the previously established hierarchy of web browsers and operating systems. As web traffic transitions to mobile, computers and their browsers are yielding to the phones. This shift in usage has led to the shift in control of the browsing experience from the carriers to the operating system. The wireless giants that acted as gatekeepers to the mobile consumer are losing their grip to the technology giants that supply them with the services they crave.

Before smartphones, the mobile phone service providers — carriers like Verizon and AT&T — dictated what information and Internet sites their consumers could easily access on their cellular phones. They maintained a "walled garden" of selected providers, who paid for the privilege but needed to conform to the carrier's specific programming languages and other technical specifications in order to get on deck. Predictably, the result was that only big companies could pony up the money, navigate the process, and invest the time and resources to his new medium, so choices were limited, impeding consumer adoption.

If you didn't want to use the carrier-provided partner for, say, sports news, your choice was likely too difficult to access using only the default web browsing features available, resulting in a terrible user experience. Internet utilization also required that consumers pay by the minute — severely limiting growth and discovery given that the experience was bad *and* the meter was running.

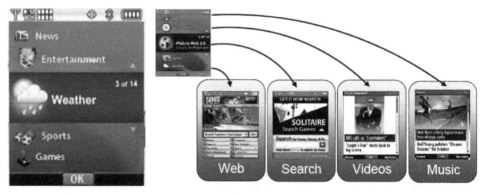

Archive version of an early Verizon phone to the "Verizon Wireless Dashboard," easy-to-use application which acts as the primary platform for discovering, purchasing, and personalizing multimedia content and services on the device. *https://www.amazon.com/LG-VX8360-Silver-Verizon-Wireless/dp/B001PKV39Q.*

Arguably, the iPhone — which launched the smartphone revolution — changed all that. Released with great fanfare through AT&T in 2007, the iPhone wasn't just a superior device for experiencing the Internet and its multimedia websites, but it also came with a pricing plan that encouraged browsing and experimentation — the *unlimited* data plan.

With a user friendly, larger sized touchscreen capable of providing a pleasant experience, and no per minute charges to discourage use, mobile access of the web exploded. Anyone with a website could reach mobile consumers without dealing with the carriers' defaults. And, with the advent of apps, Apple and Google and their app stores became the new mobile gatekeepers.

■ Figure 9.4 Utilization by Operating System

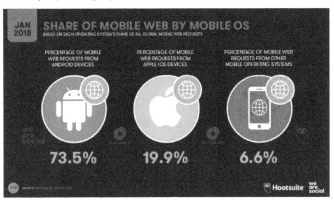

Source: 2018 Global Digital suite of reports from We Are Social and Hootsuite, Slide 113; *https://wearesocial. com/blog/2018/01/global-digital-report-2018*.

For website owners and content providers of all shapes and sizes, this was a new world — and a new and fast growing base of potential mobile customers, as we see in Figure 9.4. No longer would the carriers control access and favor a single, large, slow-moving partner. Pioneers like Google and Apple had a vested interest in encouraging usage of the mobile web. With the emergence of app stores and marketplaces, and the growing revenue these companies received from facilitating the sale of apps, app purchases blossomed into a billion dollar businesses. The mobile carriers now operate more like *Internet Service Providers (ISPs)* — sellers of access to the broader world.

Mobile Design and the User Experience

Another important difference between the advent of mobile first and what marketers have been doing in desktop environments for years — are the required subtle (or not so subtle) technical changes. Marketers must now take into account how mobile search is handled from both a SEO and advertising perspective; the technical implications for display ads and video; and how to take advantage of new ways of reaching consumers in mobile heavy social channels. Beyond the technical issues, but certainly not to be discounted, are the many design considerations that go into optimizing for mobile or for websites in general.

Mobile browsers tend to be the defaults that come with the phone, as compared to desktop where browsers are independent from the operating system and easily changed by the end user. On Apple devices, Safari's mobile browser dominates; Google's mobile version of Chrome has similar standing on the Android platform. This manifests itself in specific ways. Many websites used to use a web technology called Flash for complex animations and interactive media. Apple doesn't support Flash in its browser, supporting instead HTML5 with easy loading and lower bandwidth requirements. As mobile grew and Apple's browser share grew with it, designing websites using Flash made it impossible for a large number of mobile web browsers to display a website properly — so the technology stagnated and died. Similar impacts can be felt in other areas as technology evolved and standards changed.

One such area is the design of a company's website with the mobile user experience in mind. There are many factors to consider. One key area is *user interface design (UI)*. Desktop designs have always been optimized for *landscape* (broader horizontal) screens, fast desktop connections to the Internet, and precise mouse controls. They are rich with multimedia like video and images and have detailed menus and forms that pre-suppose a keyboard interface. Mobile websites are very different. They are generally consumed on smaller screen sizes, with a *portrait* (vertical) orientation. Mobile devices generally don't experience the same speedy connectivity of an always on, high speed wired desktop connection, so technical considerations for bandwidth and page speed become very important. Even the interface is different. The touch screen on a mobile device is a wonderful invention, but is only as precise as a person's fingers. Thus design must modify for the "fat finger" problem — taking in to account that some menus and controls designed for desktop are simply too difficult to access on a small, touch focused screen.

There are two major ways of handling websites to make them more mobile friendly. The first, and most common, is using *responsive web design*, which allows a business to build one website that can be used across different devices and screen sizes. A responsive site uses flexible HTML templates, scripts, and cascading style sheets (CSS) to adjust images and layouts according to the screen size and interface of the device viewing it.

An alternative approach is to create a separate website for different devices. This involves both a dedicated mobile and desktop site, each with different focus and functionality, requiring more development and maintenance. Sometimes called *adaptive design,* this can make for a better experience but result in maintaining multiple sites depending on how many devices are supported. To be truly adaptive, some designers recommend all six most common screen widths (see Figure 9.5).

■ Figure 9.5 Alternative Platform Interfaces

Created by Freepik; *https://www.freepik.com/free-vector/responsive-web-design-on-devices_724794.htm*.

More and more we are seeing sites that are simply going *mobile first*: that is, designing first for the most complicated use case — for mobile — and then adapting the design for desktop and tablet users.

Regardless of the method used, there are basic best practices for mobile viewing. First, with a smaller screen and planning for bandwidth constraints, it's often best to simplify the page design with smaller and fewer images and video, bigger text, and a general attentiveness to making controls larger to accommodate touchscreens. The "fat finger" problem is real — if I can't use the controls on the page, or click a button or link, I can't make a purchase or fill out a form! Other design considerations like swiping and gestures, or a "click to call" feature, take advantage of mobile device functionality and support ease of use.

Equally important for marketers is *intent*. Users on a mobile device are generally using a personal device with only one user. They are pinpointed in time and space (geolocated), and often have different intentions, involving immediate goals or local commercial needs. Because of this, a site might prioritize nearby store locations or directions for a mobile user, or target them with hyper-local ads and specials to entice them into a physical location. In other words, the very content displayed may be different. More on this later in the chapter.

Digital Marketing: Strategy & Tactics

Channel Differences between Mobile and Desktop

Google's recognition of the major shift in the source of searches — more than 50% are now coming from mobile devices — led to 2016's significant changes in how SEO and search advertising work. With so many searches coming from mobile devices, new formats and new information are available. This has caused marketers to adapt both search engine results pages and the ads that appear around them.

Search engine optimization (SEO) changes were primarily due to Google's new emphasis on location. With mobile searches, particularly those of commercial intent, Google is now weighting *proximity* — the nearness of a local business to the search — as an important factor. Someone searching for "pizza," isn't looking for the authoritative site on pizzas — they're still looking for lunch! Indeed, it's no surprise SEO has been impacted as Google noted the meteoric rise in the number of searches for things coupled with the words "near me." It's also worth noting that Google now penalizes the search rankings of sites that are NOT mobile friendly.

Search advertisements have also been modified as seen in Figure 9.6. Google made the switch to a unified format of 4 ads before and 4 ads after the search results on both desktop and mobile, recognizing that the old model of having two different styles made it tougher to create campaigns. Google compensated for the lower number of ads per results page by providing expanded text ads — a format with twice as much headline space and body text for more detailed creative messaging, as well as other subtler design changes.

■ Figure 9.6 Google's Best Practices for "Mobile Friendly" Development

Google's guidance on why and how to make websites mobile friendly. Google and the Google logo are registered trademarks of Google Inc., used with permission.

Google now calls the mobile element of the purchase process the *Zero Moment of Truth*.[4] As seen in Figure 9.7, this recognizes that in the traditional influence cycle of marketing, the first moment of truth was seeing the product in the store and the second was using the product. Now, before these occur, the consumer is often online or on a mobile device gathering more information or familiarizing themselves with a potential purchase.

180

■ Figure 9.7 Google's Zero Moment of Truth Model

The traditional 3-step mental model

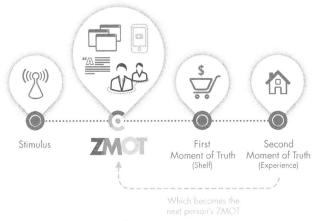

The new mental model

Source: "Think with Google." "ZMOT. Winning the Zero Moment of Truth" by Jim Lecinski/Google, June 2011. *https://www.thinkwithgoogle.com/marketing-resources/micro-moments/2011-winning-zmot-ebook/*. Google and the Google logo are registered trademarks of Google Inc., used with permission.

It's essential for search marketers to make sure they understand and adapt both the behavioral and technical changes in the new mobile friendly world. Sites need to be mobile friendly to rank highly for SEO, and businesses need to make sure their local information is accurate in Google's data. Marketers can use the free *Google Mobile Site Testing Tool* (*https://testmysite. thinkwithgoogle.com/*) to ensure they are fully optimized to rank well. Google's "My Business" (*https://www.google.com/business/*), also free, can ensure that the search engine has the proper information when local searchers are seeking products and services.

Mobile ads also have one extra feature that's particularly beneficial for mobile searches: mobile click-to-call. Rather than simply asking searchers to click through to a website, advertisers can provide a telephone number and pay by the call when it originates from the search ad. With so many new communication methods accessible from our mobile devices, people might overlook that the smartphone can make the basic phone call. For marketers, it's been proven that the calls are actually additive when presented to mobile users — an additional 10-15% on the actions on the ad. In other words, some people prefer to call, and these calls don't cannibalize the clicks.

Display ads have also required adaptation to the medium. With a smaller screen, display ads have less room to communicate their message. For this reason, *expandable ads* are much more common in the mobile environment. Also common are full screen *interstitials* (ads that appear in between screens or activities) or *takeovers* — where the ad takes over the entire screen and obscures the content during display. Even video ads are affected. Many commercials need to produce extra film footage or edit a "vertical version" so advertising content can display better in the portrait/vertical orientation.

Mobile Ad Options for Social Media Advertising

Facebook and other social channels have experienced most of their advertising growth from the successful monetization of their own mobile traffic (Figure 9.8). As their user base increasingly moved to mobile access, new ad units were introduced that enabled this traffic to begin generating revenue. Many ads, like sponsored posts on Facebook and sponsored tweets on Twitter, have the advantage of appearing in the natural flow of the newsfeed, thus are much less interruptive to the social experience and more accepted by users.

■ Figure 9.8 Growth of Mobile Advertising and Payments

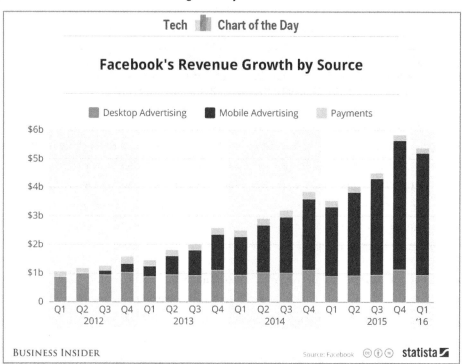

Source: Facebook, Statista; *https://www.statista.com/chart/2496/facebook-revenue-by-segment/*.

An added benefit of social networks is the large amount of personal information tied to your identity — your personal profile and user activity history that marketers are able to exploit. This has allowed many sites to offer new ad units that have done quite well, particularly for local businesses and more complex sales. One type is a *lead generation ad*. This capitalizes on the users' *personal information* — like your email, address, or phone number as well as many other important things (metadata) that a social network has tied to your real identity. On a mobile screen, a potential lead for a business is much less likely to ask a consumer to fill out a detailed form to get more information. By using the information they already have on you, Facebook for example can provide a one-click "send more information" type of ad unit so that businesses can reach relevant leads, and leads can easily respond.

This personal information is critical to the success of social advertising on mobile, from targeting the ads, to allowing for simple identification and information sharing. Another key piece of information is *location* (and time). When you are logged into Facebook or another network on your mobile device, the site not only knows who you are, but where you are and when you logged in. This allows real world businesses to promote themselves based on geographical parameters and drive "foot traffic" to nearby, likely to be interested customers. *Retail activation* is being used more and more to target nearby customers — within a couple of miles — and only when the store is open.

One final ad type that has driven a lot of revenue growth on all mobile channels is *app install ads*. The enormous growth of the app ecosystem has forced apps to acquire customers like anyone else. Since app publishers' customers must download to use their services, many app marketing campaigns focus on mobile devices and pay the App channel on per install (app download) models. When a customer views an ad for an app on their phone, it's often a one-click process for them to download that new game or application since they are already in the mobile environment. And since the advertiser will know the users operating system and other key information, the Android user will get a link to the Android version of the app and so on.

The Mobile Application Ecosystem

For a business that didn't even exist ten years ago, mobile apps are doing quite well. Mobile applications, software designed to run on a phone or tablet, can be used for web browsing, utility functions like banking, travel, getting information like weather updates, or accessing entertainment like music or movies. More than a billion downloads a month on both the iPhone and Google app stores make this a multi-billion dollar business.

The Apple app store launched in July 2008 with just 550 apps. Only 30 were free. Fast forward to today, and you'll find millions of apps in both the Apple and Android app stores. As seen in Figure 9.9, cumulative downloads are in the billions — Apple alone recognized over 150 billion downloads a year. Apple said developers earned $20 billion in 2016, up 40 percent from the prior year. Given that Apple keeps 30 percent of sales, App Store annual revenue is more than $28 billion. That sum is in line with expectations.[5]

■ Figure 9.9 Apple App Store: Number of Downloads as of June 2017

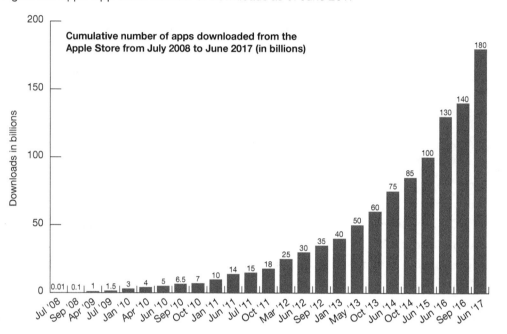

Source: Apple. Worldwide survey conducted by Apple, July 2008 to June 2017, *apple.com*.

For a marketer, the question is often whether to invest not only in a mobile friendly website strategy but perhaps also in a mobile app for a brand or service. Certainly apps can create a more personal and more functional experience for the user when designed properly. As seen in Figure 9.10, users spend more of their time in apps than on the mobile web.

> *"In the I-want-to-know, I-want-to-go, I-want-to-do, and I-want-to-buy moments of life, people are increasingly turning to their phones with the intent to act—and they expect brands to deliver. When it comes to shopping, users want immediate, relevant, and frictionless mobile experiences.*
>
> *Given that 30% of all online shopping purchases now happen on mobile phones, the stakes have never been higher for retailers. To meet the needs and expectations of today's omni-channel consumers, retailers must transform their mobile experiences."*
>
> — Think with Google.[6]

■ Figure 9.10 Time Spent in Mobile Apps

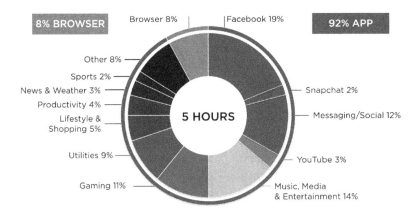

US Time Spent By App Category

Source: Flurry Analytics, comScore, Facebook, NetMarketShare.

To design a successful app, a marketer must follow some basic principles and design parameters. But, at its essence, an app needs to make the user's life easier and accomplish something useful or entertaining. While the technical aspects of mobile app design is beyond the scope of this text, from a business perspective *removing friction* is the key concept. Users want to accomplish their goals quickly and efficiently.

■ Figure 9.11 Mobile Design — Website versus App

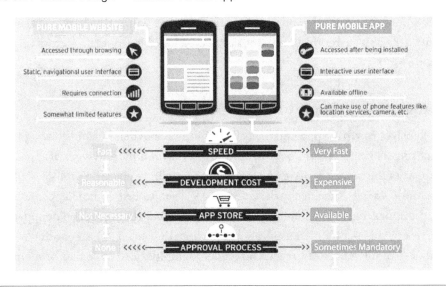

Source: Quora Blog, mobile app or mobile website and why.

As seen in Figure 9.11, from a business perspective, the best outcome for a company or brand would be to have both a mobile friendly website and a mobile app. Mobile websites are quicker to deploy, cheaper to maintain, and able to do most of the things an app can do with proper design. For occasional use or infrequent purchases, customers may not be willing to invest in and use a brand's app. On the other hand, if an action will be done more habitually — like banking, checking the weather, following a favorite sports team, or catching up on the news — a well-designed, secure, and customizable/personalized app that can make use of the native features of the smart phone (like camera, location, contacts, etc.) will be well received.

As we discussed in the early chapters of this book, these decisions are essentially strategic, relying on answers to the basic business questions surrounding a company's ultimate goals and results, and how they will measure success. A mobile website might be sufficient if intended for a broad and shallow audience, a business driven by ad revenue, or to ensure easy access, timely updates, and compatibility of user experience across devices. A mobile app might be best for a company with invested customers, or a smaller set of known devices streamlining access to functions they use regularly.

From a pure cost perspective, a website is a cheaper and more durable way to reach a broad audience. A mobile app requires expensive, specialized development, as well as ongoing maintenance. It must be constantly updated to reflect new devices and technology (think how many app updates you receive). Apps often have to pass a gatekeeper's review (for example, the Apple Store) in order to be downloadable at all. On the flip side, apps can be used offline, access native functions and controls, provide new streams of revenue, and provide richer and more engaging experiences for users.

Long term, it does seem that the mobile optimized website will win as bandwidth and access only expands. The app currently dominates in the U.S.[7] but that's not true across the world, as seen in Figure 9.12.

In App Advertising: Opportunity Knocks?

With the explosive growth of apps, and many firms monetizing their business through ads in the app, it is not surprising that there's been a rapid increase in volume and types of app advertising on mobile. One of the newest is driven by the need to distribute apps themselves — mobile app *install ads*. These are ads specifically designed to get users to install more apps. As we saw in Figure 9.9, the app business is booming, with billions of dollars being spent. For app install, the connection is obvious — potential users are right where they need to be. For other advertisers, it's often about branding to hard to reach target demographics like millenials or moms.

■ Figure 9.12 Apps versus Web by Region

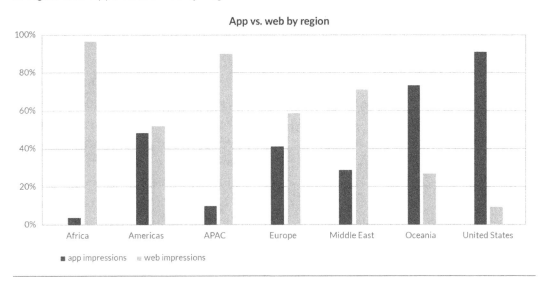

Source: *https://morganlinton.com/native-apps-vs-mobile-web-debate-rages-on/*. Original by Opera MediaWorks, *http://operamediaworks.com/innovation-and-insights/state-of-mobile-advertising-2015-q2.*

Mobile app advertising is growing even faster than mobile advertising as a whole, and represents almost three fourths of the spend on mobile. App install ads, promoting downloads directly, is almost 10% of the total.[8]

App advertising is generally subject to the same design challenges noted for display and social ads discussed in earlier chapters. However, the unique environment does provide a new level of potential for targeting, reaching, and retaining users where they are most interested in a topic or use case.

Mobile Has the Momentum

Mobile is in its moment. By almost every measure growth is huge — as is the engine behind overall digital growth. According to App Annie, the leading global provider of app market data, App downloads grew by 15% from 2015-16, while overall time spent in apps grew 25%, 30% for shopping apps. Usage of video, social, commerce, and messaging, as well as mobile gaming, continues to ramp.[9]

In their *Market Data* blog App Annie projects an even rosier picture, with researchers announcing that 2018 started with the strongest quarter the app economy has ever seen, shattering records set in Q4 2017 for both consumer spend and downloads. Global iOS and Google Play combined downloads grew more than 10% year-over-year to 27.5 billion — the highest of any quarter. Global iOS and Google Play combined consumer spend grew 22% year-over-year to $18.4 billion.[10]

"The trend has been mobile was

winning. It's now won."

— Eric Schmidt, Google

Although growth is slowing for mobile adoption (given that most of the world has already acquired phones), the same cannot be said for revenue opportunities in mobile. Although U.S. advertisers are still heavily overindexed in traditional media as compared to mobile, it is estimated that there is over $22 billion in projected growth as the ad dollars follow the customers to where they are clearly spending their time.

It's worth a revisit of the data in Figure 9.13 from earlier in the chapter now that you understand the true magnitude of the mobile opportunity for marketers!

Figure 9.13 Time Spent in Media versus Ad Spend (Percent)

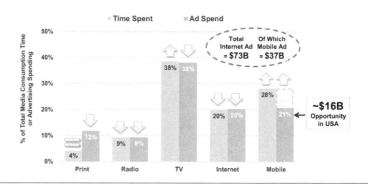

Source: *2017 Internet Trends Report*, KPCB, May 31, 2017.

Tools and Resources

■ Marketers can use the free *Google Mobile Site Testing Tool http://www.youtube.com/watch?v=ILiLaRX-HUr0* and *https://testmysite.thinkwithgoogle.com/* to ensure they are fully optimized to rank well.

■ The site *Google My Business* makes it easy to create and update listings—so you can stand out, and bring customers in. *https://www.google.com/business/*.

■ A resource for more information regarding responsive versus adaptive design of websites: *https://www.uxpin.com/studio/blog/responsive-vs-adaptive-design-whats-best-choice-designers/*.

Endnotes

1. KPCB Internet Trends 2013, *https://www.slideshare.net/kleinerperkins/kpcb-internet-trends-2013/9-Long_Ago_People_Danced_ConcertsNow*.

2. eMarketer, "U.S. Mobile Ad Spending by Format 2014-2019."

3. KPCB, *2017 Internet Trends Report*, May 31, 2017, *kpcb.com/InternetTrends*.

4. "Think with Google," "ZMOT: Zero Moment of Truth," *https://www.thinkwithgoogle.com/marketing-resources/micro-moments/2011-winning-zmot-ebook/*.

5. App Store annual revenue: *http://www.zdnet.com/article/apples-app-store-2016-revenue-tops-28-billion-mark-developers-net-20-billion/*.

6. "The Web is Dying; Apps are Killing It," *WSJ* 2014; *http://online.wsj.com/articles/the-web-is-dying-apps-are-killing-it-1416169934*.

7. "Apps Solidify Leadership Six Years into the Mobile Revolution," Flurry: *http://www.flurry.com/bid/109749/Apps-Solidify-Leadership-Six-Years-into-the-Mobile-Revolution#.VHNaDfnF-Sq*.

8. eMarketer, "U.S. Ad Spending, In App vs. Mobile Web," 2014–2016 and "U.S. Mobile App Install Ad Spending" 2013–2015.

9. "App Annie 2016 Retrospective; Mobile's Continued Momentum": *https://www.appannie.com/en/insights/market-data/app-annie-2016-retrospective/*.

10. App Annie *Market Data* blog, April 9, 2018: https://www.appannie.com/en/insights/market-data/q1-2018-apps-record-downloads-spend/.

Just over a decade ago, Shopify started an online store to sell snowboard equipment directly to those who loved the sport as much as they do. Today, merchants use the Shopify platform to manage every aspect of their business — from products to orders to customers, selling online, in retail stores, and on the go. Merchants use the software to design, set up, and manage their stores across multiple sales channels, including web, mobile, social media, marketplaces, brick-and-mortar locations, and pop-up shops. The platform also provides merchants with a powerful back-office and a single view of their business. Shopify currently powers over 600,000 businesses in approximately 175 countries.

Shopify is headquartered in Ottawa, ONT, Canada.

www.shopify.com

"Entrepreneurship is the foundation of the global economy and it's not easily done alone. That's why our mission has always been to make commerce better for everyone to encourage anyone, anywhere to become an entrepreneur."

— Tobias Lütke, Co-Founder & CEO, Shopify

CHAPTER 10

E-Commerce and Shopping: Product Listing Ads

One of the most common online business models is e-commerce: selling goods and services through digital storefronts. The growth and acceptance of buying physical things online for later delivery has created a world of new challenges and opportunities for marketers both online and offline as they compete with traditional retailers. For marketers, e-commerce presents unique and interesting choices, whether in promoting an *online storefront* — or trying to compete with one.

Online storefronts are websites that offer goods and/or services for sale; and where customers or digital "window shoppers" can visit at any time, from anywhere. Storefronts present an opportunity to capture data at every level of the marketing funnel, from making a consumer aware of the existence of a brand or product, through consideration and purchase, and even to loyalty and relationship management. As online retailers are endemic to the medium, analytics and tracking can be used to manage and optimize the purchase process. For many companies, the entire marketing and sales process is based on these digital channels.

To this point, we have broadly reviewed the digital channels available to online marketers and the varied advertising and engagement models utilized within these channels. In this chapter, we will focus on some specific advertising units that are unique to sellers of products online — *product listing ads* and their related formats. These e-commerce ads are unique for several reasons, making them worth discussing as part of a larger marketing program. We'll also review site analytics (using Google Analytics as an example), and show some of the basic methods of tracking and testing that savvy marketers can use to improve sales conversions and marketing efficiency overall.

As in most of the digital world, e-commerce is always evolving. We will take some time towards the end of the chapter to briefly review new forms of buying models that e-commerce makes more valuable, specifically subscription commerce and its forms. And of course, no discussion of e-commerce would be complete without some analysis of Amazon — and the opportunities for marketers within that e-commerce ecosystem.

The Growth of E-commerce

From modest beginnings, e-commerce has seen tremendous growth — from less than 10% of all retail sales in 2016 to becoming the dominant channel in some categories. Retail e-commerce sales worldwide will increase at four times the rate of retail sales this year, jumping 23.2% to $2.290 trillion. E-commerce sales growth will stay in the double digits throughout the forecast period seen in Figure 10.1.[1] The importance of this is that the portion of the purchase process that takes place in digital channels, regardless of category, is big enough across most B2C and B2B segments that its impact will be felt on all sales — not just the online commerce. People will still test drive a car before buying, but using consumer friendly online shopping sites first, they can find the best price and desired features as they work through the different stages of the purchase funnel. According to Nielsen research, the top consumer e-commerce activities are collecting product information, checking/comparing prices and searching for deals, promotions, and coupons, directly impacting the *omnichannel* strategy of retailers and other companies.[2]

 Figure 10.1 E-commerce Sales Worldwide

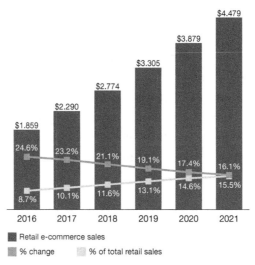

Retail e-commerce sales
% change % of total retail sales

Source: Data from eMarketer, 2017, *https://www.emarketer.com/Report/Worldwide-Retail-Ecommerce-Sales-eMarketers-Estimates-20162021/2002090*.

In many ways, e-commerce is the digital evolution of the traditional mail order, catalog-shopping business that began back in the late 1800s, from the earliest days of Sears Roebuck and Co. providing items and selection through delivery options that simply weren't available to many customers. A bit later when direct sellers became more sophisticated, the business was driven more by statistical analysis and testing than traditional retail. Catalogs were sent with different front covers to different groups, and response and conversion rates were painstakingly tracked and optimized against purchase data. This has transitioned nicely to online selling, where the level of analytics has taken this to new heights. Today's digital retailers use dynamic pages and continuous testing and optimization to track consumers across the purchase funnel ... and beyond.

With an *online storefront*, it's possible to track buyer behavior from the first awareness ad, through consideration, to the last touch before purchase — even extending this to loyalty and lifetime value. Using the right tools, retailers can both optimize the marketing and the store experience to maximize revenue. Consumer sophistication has also increased, distinguishing between simple marketing messages, to sites that actually help their shopping efforts such as advanced order placement, or mobile price-matching features. Online storefronts that have the right assets and insights fuel the context-aware engagement — customized experiences and products that consumers desire.

Amazon Is E-commerce

The poster child of this new economy is Amazon.com. What started as a bookstore has truly become the "Everything Store" (read *The Everything Store: Jeff Bezos and The Age of Amazon* book for further info). Whereas Google owns the interest graph — what people are looking for, and Facebook owns the social graph — what they like and share with their network, Amazon owns the *purchase graph* — the most detailed view and understanding of what and how people buy online.

Amazon's start as a bookseller has been a story of relentless expansion of product lines and optimization of the channel to the point of domination in many categories. From books to fashion, cars to groceries, Amazon sells almost everything — competing as much on limitless selection of products personalized for each consumer as price. In fact, Amazon is now generating revenue from its own private label products at a rapid clip, having learned what its customers want and what they are willing to pay for it.

For example, in the battery category, the "AmazonBasics" brand now accounts for around one-third of online battery sales and is seeing 93 percent year-over-year growth. And again, the majority (94%) of total online battery sales — a $113 million market — are taking place on Amazon.com.

AmazonBasics Batteries.

Amazon private label Mama Bear
brand for baby products.

"Amazon is leveraging its dominance to sell their own private-label brands which compete with traditional suppliers," said Jed Alpert, Senior Vice President of Marketing at 1010data, in a statement about the firm's new report.

"Reasons for Amazon's success across different markets vary. In batteries, they have a price competitive product in a largely commoditized market with little brand loyalty. In speakers, they've developed truly innovative products that are redefining the market. The bottom line for brands is they can no longer view Amazon as solely a channel and need to acknowledge them as a competitor," he added.[3]

Amazon's years of experience and vast reach amongst consumers are the result of learning and growing, leading them to build the infrastructure that underpins the world's largest store. For many other would be "e-tailers," that learning curve would be and has been their undoing. Amazon's excellence at both e-commerce systems and logistics means it can get things from the website to a customer's door better than any other retailer out there. This is, after all, the company that patented one-click purchasing and other innovations. One of these winning e-commerce strategies is crowd-sourced content that makes a site "sticky." Amazon attracts millions of consumers by encouraging them to share their opinions on items from books to tools to electronics. Having these crowd sourced reviews "pop up" next to a user's personal shopping preferences was a huge early differentiator and becomes exponentially more valuable to loyal customers.

Amazon was the first to serve these online reviews directly with product listings. This invaluable content comes from its customers, who are encouraged to share their opinions. Add this to Amazon's data on its customers, from purchasing information to the buying patterns across its millions of customers, gives it the credibility to suggest new products to its base, and create competitive moats that few have been able to overcome.

Toys"R"Us, for example, had an absolutely disastrous holiday season in the late 90s — it simply couldn't keep up with its website sales and the logistics. The company then partnered with Amazon to handle its online toy business. But after many disputes about exclusivity that ended in court, Toys"R"Us sued to get out of the deal and control its own online destiny again. The court noted that Amazon had invested very heavily to fulfill toy orders, especially during the holiday season, with 14 around the clock fulfillment centers at the time.[4]

Toys"R"Us turned to Amazon to handle its Internet sales after it was unable to keep up with orders on its own website. In August 2000, the companies signed a 10-year contract that created a co-branded virtual store where, for $50 million a year plus additional fees and commissions, Amazon would sell toys and baby goods for Toys"R"Us under a separate tab on its site. The contract gave Toys"R"Us the right to designate exclusive items that were not to be sold by Amazon but could be sold by third parties on the site up to a ceiling of 3.5 percent of Toys"R"Us revenues on those goods.

The deal broke down over Amazon's expanding relationships with other toy sellers, aided by a technological advance that enabled it to sell new and used goods side by side.[5]

E-commerce and SaaS

E-commerce is now established enough to allow any company looking to sell online to easily adopt established SaaS (Software as a Service) infrastructure to support their efforts. Companies like BigCommerce, for example, sell the storefront software and services that allow new entrants to avoid having to build from scratch and learn from trial and error. Instead they can begin by deploying an optimized platform, hosted by BigCommerce and others, for success. Smaller retailers can utilize SaaS platform providers like Shopify, which offer sophisticated template storefronts and services at an affordable price.

Shopify's customers number over 500,000 already and include smaller retailers as well as brands like Nestlé and Red Bull. Shopify provides everything merchants need to set up and run an e-commerce business. Its customers don't even have to create a Shopify-specific website; they can add a "buy" button to their blog, existing website, or even Facebook messenger to get started. Shopify provides the customer-facing platform as well as the back-office tools for inventory management, shipping, payments, and analytics. It simplifies a merchant's multi-channel business into a single view for the entrepreneur that they can manage from their phone.[6]

Shopify's "Sell on Amazon" integration is available and designed to seamlessly connect Shopify store owners to the millions of customers searching for products to buy on Amazon. Merchants can now manage all their product catalogs for their e-commerce website all in one place. Storefronts for Tattly, a tattoo store, and Uproot, a wine store, on the Shopify Platform are seen here.

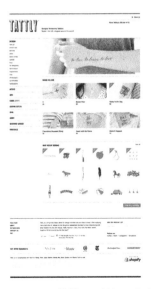

Tattly and Uproot storefronts supported by Shopify.

E-commerce Evolution: Subscription Models and Beyond

Constant innovation in the marketing and business models of e-commerce continues despite Amazon's success. *Subscription commerce* is one example where new and established brands are beginning to rethink the way retail has traditionally been done. This takes place in several forms. However all subscription models benefit from a simple change to their economics that drives an enormous uptick in customer value. Rather than acquiring a customer for a single sale and having to cross-sell or upsell them for additional value, subscription companies begin by establishing beachheads for long-term fulfillment. This drastically increases the LTV of an acquired customer — and makes the "allowable spend" of customer acquisition all the greater against this higher value. In other words, the higher value of a committed repeat customer through subscription models justifies greater spend in acquiring a customer in the first place.

There are several variants of this approach, all with success stories. In the *replenishment* model, a commodity product like Proactive or Dollar Shave Club grooming and skin care products, is sent to the customer at regular intervals (monthly, weekly). They must not only deliver a good product, but also an experience that makes the end user feel good about being part of a larger branded community of satisfied users. Often these types of companies offer the community free education, advice, and free trials of new products.

The *discovery* model is even more promising. It offers a subscription to a curated experience that delivers new, hard-to-find, or customized items periodically to the customer's doorstep based on a personalized profile. Here site visitors are demanding one-of-a-kind experiences that cater to their stated needs and interests with the convenience of a regular shipment of new products for them. Examples include Bombfell.com for men and Fabletics.com for young women for athletic outfits, and Try the World, a service for trying new gourmet foodstuffs from around the globe.

Online Advertising and E-commerce

Online retailers are able to take advantage of additional types of advertisement beyond the channels already discussed in previous chapters. While each of the channels, search, display, social, etc. can be used to promote products, the online retailer can use product focused advertisements driven by the very systems used for sales to target the online shopper as they seek to make a purchase. At the very bottom of the purchase funnel is the *product listing ad,* a highly efficient ad channel for e-commerce specialists. This ad unit is available to online retailers; driven by product SKUs, it is designed specifically for comparison and shopping online.

E-commerce: the Product Listing Ad (PLA)

Product listing ads (PLAs) are a relatively new ad unit from Google and Google search channel that have mushroomed into a multi-billion-dollar line of business (Figure 10.2). Born as a data feed, the product listing ad is unlike a typical ad. No creative is written or display ads created; no keywords are targeted. Instead, the retailers' own feeds of product images, descriptions, and prices are used to dynamically create a carousel of relevant products aligned to searches deemed to have high commercial intent. Ads appear on Google Shopping, Google Search, and some Google partner websites like YouTube and Google image search.

■ Figure 10.2 Results Page with PLAs for "Funky Socks"

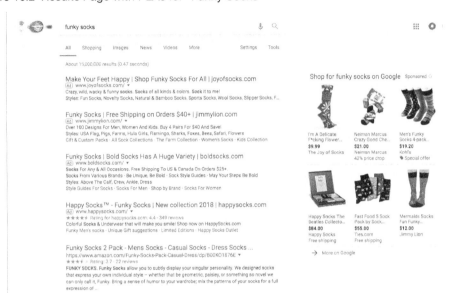

Source: Screenshot, Google results page. Google and the Google logo are registered trademarks of Google Inc., used with permission.

Product listing ads started out by connecting e-commerce retailers' inventory to Google through the *Google Merchant Center*. This is essentially a single sign on to the control panel, linked to a retailer's existing Ad Words account, designed for uploading the retailer's data feed of its products to Google to ensure they are discoverable through search channels. This is how e-commerce targeting occurs — Google decides when a relevant, product-oriented search is occurring — not through simple keyword targeting like regular search.

PLA's are cost per click and auction based just like regular search ads, so you only pay when someone clicks. Since the ad unit shows your product image, your product description, your price and your store name, the clicks are highly qualified leads. The potential customer already knows who's selling, what it costs, and even a little about the product. Interestingly, in this environment, brand value can shine through — a little known retailer selling a branded product for less can do well by leveraging that brand's strength.

Amazon also has a product listing ad format called *Sponsored Products*. While not as high volume as Google, Amazon has the advantage of being where people are searching from when they are ready to purchase. Much like Google Shopping, they are at the bottom of the funnel. Amazon's ads are targeted by keywords and are available in most categories.

They are also priced on a CPC basis, so a merchant only pays when a potential customer clicks through to a detail page. Stores must have an active Amazon sellers account in order to run ads, but for most merchants this is a no-brainer (see Figure 10.3).

■ Figure 10.3 Amazon Product Results Page

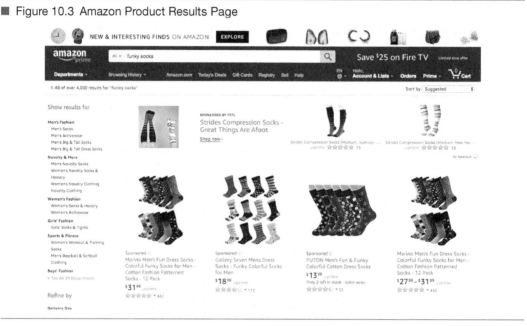

Source: Amazon results page.

Social networks have begun to feature more product listing-like ads in their own formats. Facebook and Instagram, for example, have the *product carousel* (Figure 10.4). The product carousel is an ad unit that features multiple, rotating, or swipeable images of products that link directly back to a website or storefront for sale. The pictures can be of different products, highlight features of a single product or for services that walk a potential customer through the benefits of the service. Instagram ads often feature swipeable imagery. Both Facebook and Instagram now have buttons with e-commerce calls to action like "Shop Now" as well.

Pinterest, the photo-based social network, is notable for its "Promoted Pins," as seen in Figure 10.5. These are "pinned" photos that are actually paid placements to products featured in the pictures. (Pinterest users are also noted to convert at a higher rate — presumably as they are already thinking of and reviewing products in their "pinboards." See social chapters for further information on their strategy.[7])

■ Figure 10.4 Facebook and Instagram Product Carousels

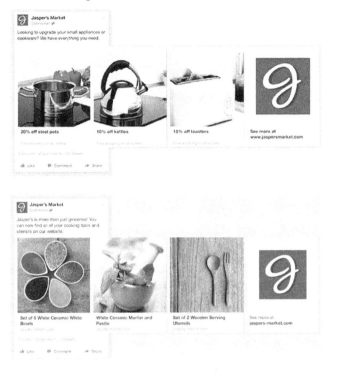

Source: Facebook and Instagram — examples of Product Carousel multiple product images.

■ Figure 10.5 Pinterest Promoted Pins

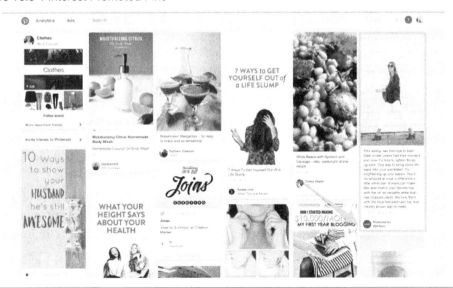

Source: Pinterest Promoted Pins; *https://cdn.searchenginejournal.com/wp-content/uploads/2016/02/Pinterest-Promoted-Pins_Old-Navy-Promoted-Pin-760x444.png.*

Tools for E-commerce: Google Analytics and the Merchant Center

One of the best things about e-commerce is the ability to track marketing from the advertisement to the purchase. As we discussed in earlier chapters, correlating the digital ad or marketing action to an actual sale or conversion is often the "fuzzy" or most difficult part of digital marketing. When the sale takes place offline, it's often tough to attribute it to the correct marketing effort. The endemic nature of e-commerce can alleviate this challenge.

Tracking and attributing digital marketing campaigns properly — and being able to prove value to the boss! — is realistic in e-commerce. But, it's essential to have the right analytics strategy in place. Many online stores will start with *Google Analytics*, a powerful, free website analytics package from Google. Not only is the price right (there is a more powerful version available for a premium price) but it easily integrates with other Google products, like AdWords, Google Shopping or the Merchant Center, offering a broad ecosystem of technical support and guidance.

Google Analytics is based on a package developed by Urchin Software, which was acquired by Google in 2005.[8] Google Analytics is easy to implement. It simply places a small snippet of JavaScript code called a page tag on each page of a website. This allows Google to track users on the site on behalf of the site owner. Tracking uses cookies to identify unique users and provides detailed information on how visitors to a site are behaving. Google even provides tools to test different pages to optimize for best performance.

Whereas AdWords and other ad tracking consoles provide detailed information on how advertising campaigns are performing (optimizing to drive traffic, for example), Analytics provides information on what happens once a visitor reaches a website that is optimized for purchasing. By reviewing the potential customers' journey through a website, a retailer can identify page views, average time on any part of the site and the points where visitors drop off. The site owner can then work to make the process smoother, stickier, and more personalized. Integrating with AdWords allows a *full funnel view* of the marketing flow — from advertising to purchase and beyond.

E-commerce and the Moment of Truth

The "Moment of Truth" in e-commerce is the customer's first experience with the brand in real life — and the packaging creates a first impression even before the box is opened and the product handled. This is a key opportunity, then, for retailers to make an impression with their brand.

Pure play online retailers for the most part understand the value of this moment and plan accordingly. Just as a luxury retailer invests in a nicer shopping bag to hold your high value purchase, online brands understand that the shipping and packaging experience projects the brand image to the end consumer in lieu of the in-store experience. There are a couple of key ways to achieve this.

First, a *distinctive box* itself can stand out from the pile of brown cardboard in the typical mail-room or delivery truck. Having distinctive colors and branding on the box has a visual impact. Even Walmart and Amazon do a little extra to create branded boxes with their distinctive logos. Spending a little more for a colorful and distinctive package can also create a perception of quality beyond the norm for a customer used to handling a more typical package. And, a branding bonus? This packaging is often seen by others in its journey — potentially an opportunity to inform and impress new customers.

Walmart, Amazon, and e-commerce companies packaging examples.

Second, the *inside material* — and the paperwork — can present another opportunity to impress the customer and reinforce the brand's value. High quality boxes may even be used for storage (as my kids have done with monthly subscription boxes) instead of being discarded! Adding a personal note, a thank you, and even distinctive packaging like tissue paper around clothing, further distinguishes this purchase from the plastic bag or drop shipping crowds.

Warby Parker provides a high quality case for its eyeglasses, which come in a heavy grade high quality box. Indeed, with some highly anticipated products, the "unboxing video" is part of the excitement. Early adopters and fans (for example, Apple customer loyalists) will rush out to buy a product and video themselves opening up the box and describing the experience. These videos are narrated so that every element — the visual and tactile elements but also any surprising touches — grab the attention of the maker, and its broader audience.

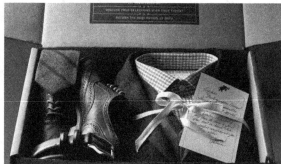

Examples of high quality interior packaging and personalization.

Including gifts, samples of other products, or carrying cases and related items (both complimentary and complementary) can make the customer feel like they are special by providing just a little bit of extra unexpected value. There's also the added benefit of testing new product lines and extensions. This "surprise and delight" strategy can extend the customer's lifetime relationship with the company — a significant value proposition for an e-commerce retailer.

Dollar Shave Club "surprise and delight" materials.

Unboxing is the unpacking of new products, especially high tech consumer products, where the process is captured on video and uploaded to the web.[10]

According to Shopify, customers are more likely to buy again from retailers that invest in custom or unique packaging, and more likely to share the experience with others. Areas where retailers can be creative are:

- **Packaging:** the box, tissue, filler, and even the tape can be customized and color coordinated to support the brand.

- **Personal paperwork:** receipts, thank you notes, promotional inserts, and coupons should all be created to be brand supportive rather than treated as an afterthought.

- **Surprises and samples:** welcome gifts, samples of additional products, and even seasonal or other types of stickers and branded promotional items can make the purchase feel a little more special and more valuable.

This description from Shopify reflects the very things that a typical customer might notice. Clearly, this kind of product excitement and user enthusiasm, creating content that is shared and leveraged online, is one of the positive impacts marketers seek with the investment in product design and packaging.

> *"Packaging in e-commerce came out of necessity for protecting the most important thing — the product that the customer ordered. However, as e-commerce evolves and as consumer habits shift, delivering a complete brand experience extends beyond the product itself and transcends into the whole experience."*
>
> — Shopify[9]

Full Circle: Guide Stores and the Return of the Storefront

One of the ironies of the most sophisticated online retailers is the emergence of physical storefronts as part of their strategy. Amazon is now opening bookstores in many cities and has tested lockers and other fulfillment center options for deliveries. Bonobos and Warby Parker have "guideshops" for their menswear and eyeglass lines respectively, allowing customers to have a tangible experience that includes touching the product and checking sizing and styles — but unable to walk away with it as it's still delivered to their home. Even Harry's, an online razor brand, has gone so far as to buy a barber shop in New York's SoHo neighborhood — despite its mundane use as a home product!

In these examples, the store itself has become part of the marketing experience — both as a reaffirmation of brand strength and identity, as well as a way for many brands to extend beyond the early adopters and meet the large majority of potential new customers in the real world where they customarily purchase their products. Most of these stores are in high profile retail areas, with a lot of foot traffic. Importantly, they are organized along very different principles than traditional stores. For example, Amazon is shelving some books next to each other physically based on its understanding of similar products bought from online customers. Even "guideshops" have a different look and feel; the store has a smaller footprint than a traditional retailer since little stock is held in inventory and all sales are fulfilled through a central distribution point.

One thing is certain: the ongoing travails of traditional retailers reflect the shift the Internet and e-commerce is causing in the physical goods space, much as it has for media. The future of the physical location may lay in part in its value for marketing — capturing new customers at the point of sale. When coupled with the value of a physical presence for deliveries, returns and other customer service necessities, online retailers are finding that for a large portion of the population, real world storefronts continue to provide the critical element — meeting them where they already shop — to convert them to a new brand that may have originated online.

Tools and Resources

- *The Everything Store: Jeff Bezos and The Age of Amazon* book. Available (yes!) on Amazon: *https://www.amazon.com/Everything-Store-Jeff-Bezos-Amazon-ebook/dp/B00BWQW73E#46938.*
- Google Merchant Center: *https://www.google.com/retail/solutions/merchant-center/#?modal_active=-none.*
- Website analytics, Google Analytics etc.: *https://www.google.com/analytics/#?modal_active=none.*
- Post sale — loyalty and cross-sell/upsell — what is the resource?

Endnotes

1. Retail E-commerce Sales Worldwide 2016–2021, eMarketer report, July 2017: *https://www.emarketer.com/Report/Worldwide-Retail-Ecommerce-Sales-eMarketers-Estimates-20162021/2002090.*
2. 2016 Nielsen Global Connected Commerce Report: *http://www.nielsen.com/us/en/insights/news/2016/what-are-connected-shoppers-doing-and-not-doing-online.html.*
3. Amazon battery sales, Techcrunch, "Amazon's private label brands are taking over market share": *https://techcrunch.com/2016/11/03/amazons-private-label-brands-are-killing-it-says-new-report.*
4. "Toys"R"Us Wins Suit Against Amazon": *http://www.nbcnews.com/id/11641703/ns/business-us_business/t/toys-r-us-wins-suit-against-amazoncom/#.WZ3hXHeGNTY.*
5. "Breach of Online Marketing Deal With Toys"R"Us Will Cost Amazon $52M": *http://www.americanlawyer.com/id=1202431721403/Breach-of-OnlineMarketing-Deal-With-Toys-R-Us-Will-Cost-Amazon-51M.*

6. *https://www.fool.com/investing/2017/03/22/youve-likely-used-shopify-and-didnt-even-know-it.aspx.*

7. Pinterest Promoted Pins: *https://cdn.searchenginejournal.com/wp-content/uploads/2016/02/Pinterest-Promoted-Pins_Old-Navy-Promoted-Pin-760x444.png.*

8. "Urchin Software Corp.: The unlikely origin story of Google Analytics, 1996–2005-ish": *https://urchin.biz/urchin-software-corp-89a1f5292999.*

9. *https://www.shopify.com/blog/16991592-how-to-create-a-memorable-and-shareable-unboxing-experience-for-your-brand.*

10. *https://en.wikipedia.org/wiki/Unboxing.*

Dollar Shave Club's creation of a dominant men's lifestyle brand began with their intuitive understanding of direct to consumer marketing; content, conversation and community to attract and grow subscribers. By exploiting the rapid adoption of mobile and analyzing vast amounts of customer data to refine their service and products, they not only grew – but have far exceeded retention metrics of most subscription businesses.

Sure they offer high value, highly-differentiated products (with high product margins), but their retention success is also attributable to the transparency and flexibility of their service plans. They made it easy for customers to "stay in the club" allowing them to control the frequency and selection of products — fueling their financial success, but also laying the groundwork for unlimited growth.

Dollar Shave Club is headquartered in Venice, CA. (Dollar Shave club was acquired by Unilever in 2016).

www.dollarshaveclub.com

"A lot of entrepreneurs find subscriptions attractive because in theory you have a consistent cash flow. But that's not always sustainable if you're selling something that people want and don't need."

— Co-Founder Michael Dubin

CHAPTER 11
Evolving Business Models

The Internet's powerful impact on businesses isn't just a transfer of existing businesses to a new distribution channel, commerce model or marketing strategy. Internet businesses are now freed from the constraints of the brick and mortar foundations that, as we have discussed, have defined traditional retail and commerce for centuries. It allows companies to make "smarter" products, enable smarter decisions about business operations, and impact how, where and when consumers interact with their products and services. Perhaps most exciting, digital based business models have brought real innovation to traditional industries; providing organizations the ability to address new markets, new delivery and distribution models, new pricing systems, and adopt new media channels to engage and serve their customers.[1]

Many of us depend on services like Uber or Waze for transportation, social media for news, reviews, and recommendations, and online services for information, banking, shopping, booking and reservations, or completing many other real world transactions. All of these rely on the search and social network infrastructure built as the Internet has grown, as well as the explosive adoption of smartphones by the general population. Even payments — through platforms like Venmo and others — have dramatically changed, all enabled by this infrastructure. In this chapter, we will explore some of the impacts of these innovations on traditional business models.

We'll also look at some of the technologies that may continue and accelerate these business model changes. As the "Internet of things" — the connection of newly smart devices like home appliances to the grid — becomes more of a reality, we'll see business models follow the new functionality and leverage the data generated in new and exciting ways.

It's not a stretch to foresee new services developed that integrate with smart appliances in the same way Waze leverages smartphones in cars, creating completely new value propositions. And, as these newly smart devices become more common, each will become more and more customized and personal to the consumer. Just as the Internet and smartphones have become the new foundation upon which businesses build custom and personal solutions for targeted customers, the potential appears even greater as computing devices are embedded in more and more of the everyday objects we use.

But, first we'll review a new way to look at demand for products and services called the "Long Tail" that has us thinking completely differently about the traditional business models for selling to customers.

Revenge of the Niches: Selling Fewer "Hits" and Many More Misses

In a provocative article in *Wired* magazine entitled "The Long Tail" — later expanded into the bestselling book — author Chris Anderson suggests that relieving the constraints of physical stores and services has actually changed the nature of what we can sell and who we can sell it to.[2]

The theory of the *Long Tail* is that technology has enabled our culture and economy to increasingly shift away from a focus on a relatively small number of "hits" (mainstream products and markets) at the head of the demand curve, and toward a huge number of niches in the tail — which in aggregate add up to a greater volume than the hits.

So what does this mean? Conventionally for a store in the real world to be profitable, it needed a physical site or retail location where they can draw enough customers and demand from the surrounding area to stay in business. This applies to broad based retailers, specialty shops, business to business sales, and even movie theaters. If enough customers can't get to the physical location to support the sales needed for the business to be profitable it will die. In New York City we might have a block with four or five wine, electronics, or flower stores on it. But, the reality is that smaller population cities, less dense rural areas, or even many college towns can't support specialty retail. The selection in the local superstore, Walmart, or downtown generalist store is what you have to choose from, meaning a more limited variety of a limited range of products.

As the largest retailer in the world, Walmart's 2.3 million associates meet the needs of more than 260 million customers every week (*https://corporate.walmart.com/our-story*).

Bricks and Clicks

Most traditional stores are also constrained by the hours they are open — the 24-hour store being the exception, often with only broadly appealing fast moving items — and convenience. Not only is a traditional store likely closed at 3 am, but the transportation and other infrastructure might not be available to get there. Online stores can sell you anything day or night, and you can shop in your proverbial underclothes.

Of course, physical stores have to absorb the costs of overhead, in other words they pay rent and costs associated with inventory. This means their limited shelf space needs to be filled by goods that sell frequently enough to pay their way. The result being that only the most popular products are worth stocking. A book store in a high-rent limited space location like an airport might carry only a few hundred bestselling titles. A book seller in a typical shopping mall might have thousands or tens of thousands of titles — with a bigger selection of mysteries, for example. A large suburban Barnes & Noble might carry over 100,000 titles in stock. Offering a complete selection of books, or even depth in a niche like mysteries, would involve an enormous amount of expensive real estate — an impossible proposition.

Anderson observed that Amazon was not just selling an enormous number of books in competition with brick and mortar book retailers like Barnes & Noble, it was selling books that weren't popular enough to be stocked at all. Amazon was selling just a few copies of many less popular titles — niche titles — but collectively, they added up to more in volume than the most popular books sold by the brick and mortar retailer! In other words, the hits were overrun by the sheer volume of lots and lots of less popular titles — the misses. And these titles, either stored in low cost areas near vast distribution centers, or simply delivered digitally, often have higher profit margins — since Amazon was the only place to get them.

Media Moves to Digital

We see this same phenomena in the way people consume music, movies, and entertainment. A suburban movieplex might have 15 screens with 5 showing the same crowd-pleasing big budget blockbuster — but not a single screen dedicated to an independent film, documentary or the like. Another hit driven business faced with a distribution constraint — limited screens — needs the titles that will put the most "butts in seats." So despite latent demand from documentary lovers and independent film buffs, there's simply not enough of them in one place to regularly fill theaters in all but the biggest cities.

Netflix, on the other hand, can offer every obscure movie genre, old television show and more because its customers can stream to their own screens on demand. An evolution in delivery created a new business model in an established industry, with the marginal cost essentially the same.

With these constraints of traditional retail sales removed, online stores can aggregate demand from around the globe — even with previously "niche" products that would be unable to support a physical storefront. An online store dedicated to hot sauce for example, can "go deep" in its inventory of the condiment, offering every kind of hot sauce for the spice-loving gourmet. Opening a retail location to do the same might not have enough hot sauce fanatics to draw on, but online, millions of dollars can be made from stores that can aggregate deep but diffuse demand. Whether custom clothing for people with unusual sizes or tastes, specialized plumbing parts, or items for niche hobbies and interests, you name it, it can be sold profitably online.

Online Infrastructure and Tools Enable the New Sales Models

One could argue that this is simply a new version of the catalog economy popularized by Sears more than a century ago. However, modern enabling tools supporting the digital storefront make this bigger and better than traditionally possible. Now with online distribution and retail, consumers can leave the world of *scarcity and constraint* and "enter a world of abundance" and the differences are profound.[3] The keys to the success of the *Long Tail of Internet* commerce for customers is the vastly greater ability to discover, access, and purchase niche and custom products. For businesses, it's the same: discoverability and access means lower costs of customer acquisition and larger markets to serve — and the direct connection to customers through email and social channels, as well as changing business models, can make each customer worth more over their lifetime as well.

Online sellers can aggregate demand for a product or products designed for a small group by amassing the selection into one place, making it easy to sell and to buy. As online communities form and gather by interest, this provides a natural environment for marketing. *Access* to the demand aggregated from everywhere not only becomes possible, but desirable.

For a buyer, niche products are now easily *discoverable*. Search engines like Google can pull the needle out of the proverbial haystack — from hot sauce to hot dogs to hot pants, whatever you want will be returned in a simple-to-peruse page of results. Indeed, Google's own advertising program and tools vacuum up dollars from niche product advertisers looking to reach this very demand.

Perhaps most importantly from a business perspective, specialized products with less availability in traditional retail but better meet the needs of a particular customer are now more *profitable* to sell online. Margins are better when there's no competition from the Walmart down the street. Unique products like those found on Etsy or eBay can't be comparison-shopped. And, with lots of low volume sales coupled with demand aggregation, niche stores can thrive.

■ Figure 11.1 The Long Tail Demand Curve

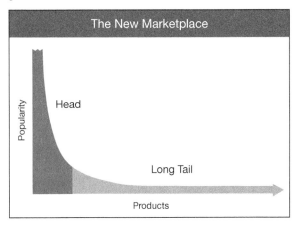

Source: "The Long Tail demand shifts the demand curve"; *http://www.longtail.com/about.html*.

As seen in Figure 11.1, the theory of long tail commerce suggests that there is latent demand in the head of the demand curve that would be actually better served by more unique or appropriate products and services that were previously unavailable. Now, with easy access and discoverability, we are seeing a shift down the demand curve — resulting in a flattening of the hit driven popularity of traditional products.

It's important to note that none of this could thrive without the advances in infrastructure of payments, platforms and logistics present in developed countries. Without secure and trusted payment systems, transactions couldn't take place online. Without efficient shipping and logistics systems, e-commerce couldn't compete with retail distribution and time to market. Streaming services that enable online media, games, software and services all depend on a dependable, high bandwidth Internet infrastructure to ensure viewability (for example movies) and consumption and access.

The Evolution of Next Generation Business Models

The changes to traditional commerce models spawned by the Internet aren't the only business evolution. Entirely new business models are now possible. Some of the most disruptive are based on the ability to disintermediate middlemen and go directly to stores and customers alike. Figure 11.2 depicts the old model of retail (which is very similar in almost every B2C and B2B product category with some variation). Large physical retail chains controlled the end user or customer experience, reducing the power of manufacturers of products and forcing them to do whatever they could to get represented by major distributors or stocked on the shelves of the nation's stores. Sophisticated marketers like Proctor & Gamble knew a lot about the purchasers of its products — but its biggest customer was actually Walmart. The pilgrimage to Bentonville, Arkansas, and the hard-driving price concessions the retailer drove are legendary. Similarly, every toy manufacturer on the planet had to work with Toys"R"Us (now defunct), auto parts manufacturers were beholden to GM, and so on. Getting shelf space (access to the consumer) involved low margins, commitments to marketing, and sometimes outright payments (slotting fees) to get prime positions and maximize sell through. A typical brand might get 20 cents on the dollar to supply the giants and made it up on volume — if they could.

■ Figure 11.2 Impact of Disintermediation and Source

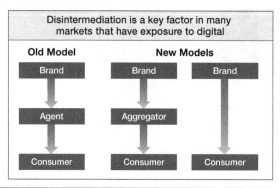

Source: Jeremy Kagan, 2018.

In the new world of online commerce, it's entirely possible for new models without the middleman to exist. Indeed, many new brands and "startups" launch online first, where they can connect with and maintain relationships with customers directly, as well as build new value exchanges and pricing models that reflect this new way of doing business.

We also see a wide range of transformative business models that mirror those of the real world; but attack entrenched and long-standing sales, distribution and service models in new ways. We will walk through a few of the most widely utilized, and their impact in greater detail:

- **Direct sales**, where a retail company offers a good or service directly to a consumer. This model is most commonly associated with online retailers like Amazon or eBay.

- **Disintermediated sales** is when a company facilitates the sales of products or services by taking the place of offline middlemen, like Orbitz, Indeed.com, or SAP's Ariba.

- **Digital Sales**, more transformative, this is when the physical distribution of products is replaced completely by a digital version, and the entire transaction can be completed online.

- **Subscription commerce,** which utilizes pricing and consumption models for replenishment-type or repeat purchase products, key being customer retention and growth.

- **Cloud-based** or **Software as a Service (SaaS)** models for software that personalizes delivery and access to goods and services.

Direct Sales: Bricks versus Clicks

Direct sales of products online is the foundation of e-commerce. While Internet (and mobile) retailers have distinct advantages versus their "brick and mortar" retail competition, as we've discussed throughout this book, there are also many challenges. Perhaps the most important is the evolving trend for physical retailers to sell their wares digitally, trying to capitalize on the strengths of both "bricks and clicks."

Real world stores have several natural advantages over e-commerce sites. At their core, the store is a tangible and experiential, even social, experience. You can see and touch the product before buying; try on clothes or try out a television. There's the opportunity for discovery and impulse purchase created by everything from the store layout to merchandising to the human touch of a knowledgeable sales person.

Online channels, on the other hand, are independent of geography for aggregating demand, and are open 24 hours a day, 7 days a week, 365 days a year. They offer virtually unlimited inventory and sizes and are much less likely to be out of stock. The shipping delay of online can be overcome in high density areas with same day and next day shipping through sophisticated logistics; this delay can also be enough time to allow custom configuration, manufacturing, or personalization of the purchase.

The goal for traditional retailers is maximizing their embedded infrastructure of stores in communities where their customers shop, while taking advantage of the potential of e-commerce; yielding a true "bricks and clicks" strategy. Online, retailers can capture customers where they are with immediacy, service, and tangibility. But, they can also take advantage of their physical infrastructure to offer things like pickups, returns — and exchanges — at the store nearest you. This can increase satisfaction as well as cut customer service, shipping and logistics costs. Once in store, price match guarantees, easily accessible reviews and information, and even kiosks to search online for broader ranges of inventory and sizes can bring dual benefits for a digital/in-store strategy. During the 4th quarter of 2016, Macy's online sales grew at a double-digit pace even as comps at company-owned stores fell 2.7%. Target's digital sales popped 34%. Walmart U.S. e-commerce revenue leapt 29%, which included online grocery sales.[4]

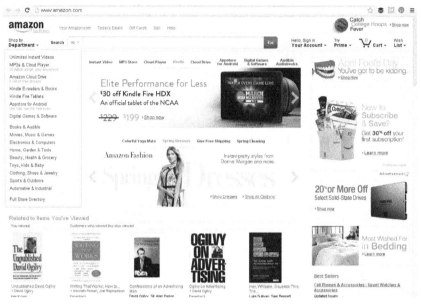

Amazon is the leader in online commerce.

Digital players do what they can to minimize the negatives of being "virtual only." Multimedia design techniques such as virtual try-ons and panoramic views of products in high definition images or video all serve to eliminate some of the advantages of in person shopping. Online retailers will almost always offer free shipping — and free returns — to eliminate sizing and fit fears and match overall price concerns. And consumers take advantage — many of Zappos's customers order several pairs of shoes fully intending to return the ones they don't like, keeping only one pair. Tennis Warehouse encourages a selection of up to 4 racquets; try them all for free, return them all or just the ones you don't want.

For startups and new brands, real world retailers are an expensive proposition to compete with. The large capital commitment to secure, staff and stock real world locations with enough density to achieve scale across marketing and operations is hugely prohibitive. It's no wonder then that most challengers in category after category are launching online first. Efficiencies in operating a simple online storefront, with centralized and limited inventory costs and staffing needs, make this route the only one that makes sense.

Interestingly, some digital retailers have launched a "bricks and clicks" strategy of their own as they grow. "Born online" brands like Warby Parker in eyeglasses and Bonobos in menswear have launched real world locations called "guideshops." A twist on traditional retail, these locations offer tangibility, service and sizing in prominent retail zones and malls. The stores feature products and merchandise, but with important differences. Guideshops are physical show-rooms that display, but do not sell, products and merchandise. Sales are completed online. A customer at a guideshop will decide on merchandise then place an order through an in store tablet on the very website of the online retailer. The product ships from the central warehouse like any online order, to be delivered to the home address. The customer doesn't go home with a product at all.

Brands like Bonobos, born online, have expanded into brick and mortar locations in high traffic areas to gain new and different customers.

Why would an online brand branch out into the real world? Many consumers, particularly older ones, are reluctant to buy without the tangible in store experience. To reach customers beyond early adopters and capture significant market share, online brands need to get into the real world. Bonobos guideshops are credited with reaching new customers and increasing the average age of their customers from 28 when they started, to 36. Bonobos has advantages over traditional retail as well — with no inventory to carry, since all sales are completed online, they have much more real estate dedicated to the selling floor. And, their sales associates focus on capturing customer information for future marketing. Once a customer has been sized and a payment method recorded, direct sales are more likely through follow-on marketing.

Amazon, the granddaddy of online retailing, is also experimenting with real world options; like lockers in other retailers (that could use the foot traffic) or in high traffic commuter areas like train stations. As we have profiled, they have also established "Amazon Pop Ups" in phys-ical locations in places like Kohl's, Whole Foods (which was purchased by Amazon), and high traffic malls. Other brands, like Harry's, have gained distribution with Target and other tradi-tional retailers.

Direct Sales: Channel Conflicts

On the flip side, manufacturers who receive just a small sliver of profit when dealing with giant, powerful retailers, are exploring digital as a way of going direct. P&G might get only $.20 on the dollar for its products sold through Walmart, but must still spend millions of dollars to capture the attention of customers for its retail partners. Mattel, despite absorbing huge licensing fees for producing action figures for a summer movie blockbuster is in a similar position. What if they could eliminate the middleman? Direct sales from their own websites happen more and more. By selling direct to the customer, the manufacturer can capture ten times the profit on a single transaction and gain a much larger lifetime value with the customer. Of course, there can be channel conflict challenges when competing directly with your biggest customers. But some creative strategies can work.

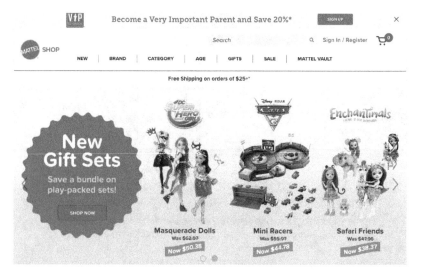

A panel from Mattel's online storefront.

One strategy for navigating conflict is "cream skimming." A toymaker can't afford to alienate Walmart or Toys"R"Us during the holidays by offering better pricing directly to online customers. But with both chains known for their discounted prices, selling direct online at the manufacturer's "suggested retail price," a list price point (the higher price that the discount giants discount off of) allows them to target a small, but significant percentage of price insensitive parents who need to get a toy under the tree. This strategy causes little channel disruption as it reinforces the discount prices of their largest partners. And, the profit margins for the manufacturer are significantly higher.

Another approach is developing a replenishment strategy. P&G tested an eStore, now called "P&G Shop," featuring its toiletries and replenishable sundries. Consumers who bought the original product from a store, can get big discounts by committing to regular purchases or bulk purchases of commonly used products directly from P&G.

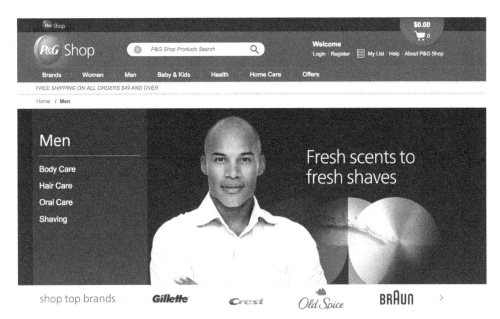

P&G Shop, the eStore home page for men. Procter and Gamble hosts home pages for products for men, women, health, baby and home. Screenshot *https://www.pgshop.com/pgshop-his/*, February 2018.

The experimentation continues as online and traditional retailers battle it out. Amazon is at the forefront with new experiments all the time. Same day delivery by drone? Stores where you simply grab products off the shelves based on your user purchasing profile, automatically charged to your account? Already being tested. Amazon's traditional style bookstores in malls? They are merchandising the store and stocking the shelves using its extensive information about what other products buyers might like. With its purchase of Whole Foods, the battle continues. Amazon now has a presence in 400 stores in the U.S. The industry is waiting in trepidation to see how this will affect existing grocery retail models.

Amazon Go is a new kind of store with no checkout required.

In their battle with Amazon, Google and Walmart are also trying to exploit their toeholds in two unsettled arenas: digital assistants and groceries. This partnership allows you to order groceries using Google Assistant at instore kiosks or online via Google Express.[5]

Disintermediated Sales

As we discussed earlier, the elimination of the middleman is a broad theme of online commerce. While some would argue it's simply replacing a real world middleman with one online, there are important differences. When the business moves online, each element of the value chain can be exposed and priced competitively. Processes can be transformed and made more efficient. Almost all of the areas where these business changes have taken place are businesses where middlemen formerly had all the advantages. As more and more information moves online and becomes accessible in new and easier ways, the middlemen will need to fight, adapt, or disappear.

Disintermediated industries have many things in common. Most seeing incredible change are those that have a high value product or service, but one that is bought infrequently. Secondly, there is generally a high penalty should a consumer make a mistake in their purchase decision. Buying real estate or a car, booking a vacation or seeking a new job are all good consumer examples. There are many similar examples in B2B markets. For a consumer, a house may be a once in a lifetime purchase; realtors, the most entrenched middlemen, sell many a month. A car may be a once every few years purchase at best; the notorious car salesmen may sell several a day. Taking the wrong job, or booking a bad choice for your once a year vacation are less costly, but equally challenging transactions without the right information or expertise.

Middlemen typically hold advantage over consumers or clients. They have developed expertise through repetition and market knowledge to provide comfort and assistance to buyers when acting on their behalf. Often, they have access to hard won local knowledge, like a realtor "from the neighborhood," or referrals based on their reputation of pleasing customers and minimizing problems. In many cases, middlemen have access to proprietary data (like the realtor's Multiple Listings Service), industry analyst reports or competitive pricing to give them an advantage over individuals.

This level of expertise and power has often resulted in decisions that were optimized for the middlemen. Travel agents booked travelers on airlines that provided the biggest commissions. Research shows that many realtors kept their own houses on the market longer — and got higher prices — than their customers. This made economic sense when middlemen got only a small percentage of the customer transaction — so a small increase wasn't worth losing the transaction.

So, with the movement of all this information online, the balance of power has changed. Now customers often know more about the prices and products they care about than the sales people who manage a whole portfolio. Before going to a car dealer, today's customers do their homework and know not only the fair price range — but often which dealer is the better place to buy. This has forced an evolution in many markets and the middlemen within them.

Travel is a great example of these changes. Travel agents used to be the experts with access to the airline databases and hotel reservation systems that drove the industry. Consumers had no access at all. Online competition has brought big changes. Over 60% of travel is now booked online by consumers in the United States (Figure 11.3). According to eMarketer, worldwide digital travel sales will total over $675 billion in 2018, a jump of roughly 18% from 2016. Steady growth is expected to continue through 2021, when worldwide digital travel sales are expected to reach $855 billion."[6]

■ Figure 11.3 Digital Travel Sales

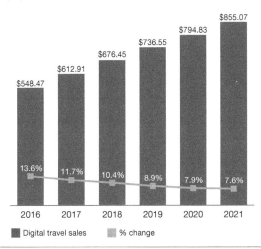

Source: eMarketer data from Digital Travel Sales Worldwide, 2016-2021.

In travel, disintermediation by online competitors has occurred in a couple main areas. First, is the movement of proprietary data (like SABRE fare data from American Airlines) into online accessible databases. This has allowed consumers the ability to compare fares from different airlines quickly and easily to make more informed decisions. The metadata around this has been put online as well — things like reviews of comfort, on time percentages, and other related travel information — to further enhance the ability of the consumer to choose. New data is created as online service companies reverse engineer the complex pricing systems of the airlines and break down volumes of consumer purchases to suggest best pricing and times to buy. Finally, new user interfaces, user-generated content like reviews or pictures, and online tools for sorting and filtering all this information has empowered consumers to make better decisions for their travel needs. That "great hotel deal" may be hiding something that someone who has stayed there can tell you — like lack of air conditioning, a huge construction project, or a bad neighborhood.

The evolution of the online travel industry reflects how disintermediation has occurred across other industries. In the beginning, websites like Orbitz, Expedia, and Travelocity simply moved the traditional business of travel agencies online — and the online travel agent was born. OTA's handled transactions, sold the plane tickets and hotel rooms, and took responsibility for the purchase and customer satisfaction. Sites competed by offering simple interfaces, *access* to detailed information, and one stop shopping for your travel needs. OTA's had an incentive to complete a transaction, but not a bias toward any one supplier.

Airlines, of course, eventually began offering direct sales on their own websites. But consumers desired the ability to choose among all their options, so the aggregator sites continued to command most of the market.

The next stage was to separate the transaction from the *discovery* process — thus the travel search engine was born. Sites like Kayak, Trivago and others offered a simple search interface and convenient ways to filter and sort information with no inherent bias. They make their money on advertising and sending you on to your eventual purchase destination.

We've now reached a maturity point in the market where specialists are peeling off pieces of the market to better serve individual areas. Last minute travel through apps like Hoteltonight; predictive fare sites, and more. Even sites with simply better interfaces are gaining traction. Hipmunk, for example, has a notable sorting feature called 'Agony" — an index of the factors that make travel pleasant or unpleasant, like comfort, on time reliability etc. — not just pricing. The interface is reminiscent of a personal calendar (Figure 11.4) and able to connect with a customer to help plan the travel, is also more user friendly. It's a certainty that innovation will continue.

■ Figure 11.4 Hipmunk Calendar Interface

Source: Hipmunk Calendar Interface, now owned by Concur Technologies Inc.

For travel agents, this has meant rethinking their role. Specialists are thriving, from corporate agents specializing in cost control, to experts in gluten free travel or family friendly vacations. For middlemen, providing clear value and expertise beyond simple access has become a necessity.

Digital Sales

Perhaps the most interesting change in the digital commerce landscape is the emergence of companies with the ability to complete the entire sales transaction online. Across industries, from music to news and games, to television, film and other types of content, a company can source potential customers, acquire interested leads, convert them to trial, and convince them to listen, view or interact with the content all online — allowing for an amazing level of data and optimization across the entire marketing funnel. The more you use, the more personalized the suggestions. From acquiring, to converting, to retaining a customer, the things that work and the things that don't can be tracked and optimized.

This model has some terrific upsides but some downsides as well. The first key upside is that by avoiding expensive physical distribution networks of the past — such as record stores and book stores — publishers and content creators can go direct to consumer and capture more revenue from each transaction. Even "content creators," musicians and writers for example, benefit by not being constrained to 'breaking through' to get distribution. The elimination of physical packaging, shipping and inventory expenses means that a product can be cheaper and easier to distribute. This opens up more pricing options and ways to target offers and promotions that wouldn't be possible in the traditional model.

The downside of the digital sales model applies mostly to the status quo in prevailing markets — cannibalization of existing sales transacted in physical formats has all but eliminated some industries as we knew them. When the tangibility of the product, such as vinyl records or compact discs, no longer matters to the buyer its value disappears. Customers also lose by forfeiting the concept of "traditional ownership." It's much more difficult to resell a digital copy, to the detriment of used bookstores and those needing quick cash. Another troubling impact is the risk of format changes. The MP3, formerly a leading digital music format, has been declared 'dead' less than 15 years after its peak popularity. What happens to the consumers who purchased music and maintain these libraries in old formats? How do they transform these purchases into new formats to retain the value of said property? And while an owner might be able to insure and replace a physical record collection — hard drive crashes with high value media might not be as easy.

For owners and creators, the risk of piracy is of course much higher when the format is digital. Illegal copying of music and movies is simple and almost impossible to stop. As bandwidth costs and cloud computing grow in accessibility and usage, obstacles to sharing files continues to drop. Indeed, the best defense against piracy seems to be accessible, simple to use, and reasonably priced subscription models like iTunes, Spotify, Netflix and Amazon Prime.

■ Figure 11.5 U.S. Recorded Music Revenue

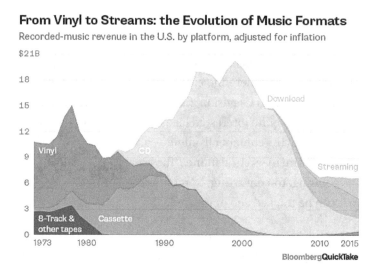

From Vinyl to Streams: the Evolution of Music Formats
Recorded-music revenue in the U.S. by platform, adjusted for inflation

A look backwards on the rise and fall of various music formats. This data was originally published by Forbes and Bloomberg, sourced from the RIAA (Recording Industry Association of America).

The music industry is a great example of "what not to do" for most other media and content-based industries. Their challenges in the face of changing technology and business model were not (and still aren't) easy to solve. The recorded music business has always grown based on superstars and their hits — driving "album sales," continuous format replacement (Figure 11.5), and the limited ability of individuals to circumvent the system.

For these reasons, the industry aggressively resisted digital distribution and even began producing singles records again instead of albums to provide consumers the option to buy just a song. Only when the emergence of simple, easy, but illegal file sharing on college campuses (beginning with the explosion of Napster usage) put the entire industry business model in jeopardy did they take action. Music companies finally licensed selected songs for digital release and got behind the model of iTunes — the emerging digital service from Apple for selling singles and albums. The success of digital sales, and its subsequent eclipse by streaming services like Spotify, Pandora and YouTube, are a "canary in a coal mine" for other media. As you can see in Figure 11.6, this pivotal action radically changed the business model (and revenue streams) within the industry during this same timeframe.

■ Figure 11.6 Revenue Models for the Music Industry

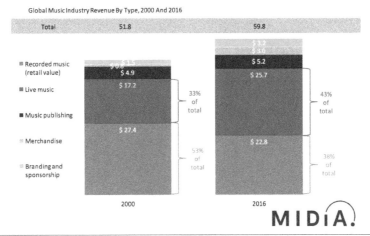

Source: Global Music Industry Revenue from MIDIA research.

One thing that has become clear is that while digital revenues appear to be the future of the recorded music industry, it's the other revenue streams of the business, from touring revenues to merchandise, that have truly blossomed. More and more artists can make a living making music — just not selling it. It's notable that although the "record business" may be dying, the music business overall is experiencing significant growth and change. While the big name artists still contribute a lot to the overall revenue in tickets and the like, a "long tail" of touring has emerged (Figure 11.7), with digital merchandise and artist revenues now accessible to the rest of the pack.

■ Figure 11.7 The Long Tail in the Music Industry

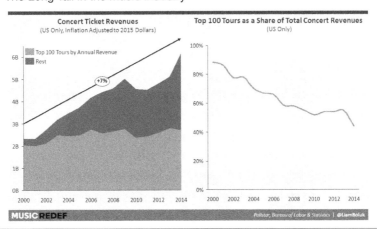

Another look back at the impact of digital, this time on concert revenues.
https://www.linkedin.com/pulse/less-money-mo-music-lots-problems-look-biz-jason-hirschhorn.

Change has come to television in much the same way. Subscriptions to traditional cable models are flat, but alternative subscription services aimed at "cord cutters" — those eschewing the bundles from the cable companies to get their consumption from Netflix (Figure 11.8), Sling TV, Amazon Prime and other Internet services — are booming.

■ Figure 11.8 The Digital Shift in Visual Entertainment

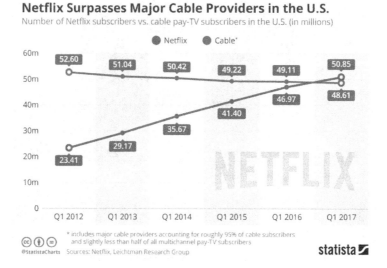

Netflix Surpasses Major Cable Providers in the U.S.
Number of Netflix subscribers vs. cable pay-TV subscribers in the U.S. (in millions)

Source: Statista, "Pay TV versus Cable"; *https://www.statista.com/chart/9799/netflix-vs-cable-pay-tv-subscribers*.

Netflix and Amazon Prime, mirroring the behavior of HBO and other early entry pay channels years ago, are also developing original content in television and film, as well as experimenting with new pricing and formats. Figure 11.9 denotes the battle between HULU, Amazon and Netflix for acquisition of original content. Live TV, sports rights, and news are very much in flux. According to Nielsen, even the venerable ESPN has lost over $13 million subscribers due to decline in cable and satellite users, despite their heavy investment in exclusive rights.

Subscription Commerce

Subscription models may be one of the most important but underappreciated innovations in digital, empowering a brand with new ways to sell products and services. One model is software as a services (SaaS). Traditionally the SaaS model works when a customer pays a *subscription* price to have continual access to digital software, products or services. Originally pioneered by magazines and newspapers, it is now used by many businesses and industries where customers want or need regular access to content or software applications. From a business perspective, revenue recognition and budgeting become much easier when you know what your recurring revenue base is each month!

■ Figure 11.9 The Race to Acquire Original Content

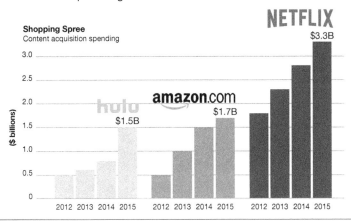

Source: Data from RBC, originally published by *The Wall Street Journal* in the article "Hulu Steps Up Its Fight Against Netflix."

This disruptive change to the economics of acquiring customers and the increase in the value of keeping them has upended many traditional industry cost structures — including marketing and customer related expenses. Subscription commerce works well for business strategies such as replenishment or repeat purchase products, like toiletries (our earlier P&G and Dollar Shave Club examples), grocery replenishment and even subscribing to marketing tools and research! In these examples businesses (marketing) attempts to capture and re-capture the small percentage of customers that may be open to something new, while reminding previous consumers to continue to subscribe or purchase again.

As we covered earlier in the book, mass media marketing is expensive, particularly brand awareness marketing to ensure that the consumer — with whom they have no direct relationship — keeps the product and brand top of mind when purchasing in category. The economics of customer acquisition costs (CAC) have to remain low given the lifetime value (LTV) of the customer is as well. The entire cost of acquiring the customer must be justified by the single purchase they make of the product.

Many digital brand launches have turned these economics on their head. Digital brands can acquire a customer once and not only market to them directly with email, social reminders and targeted remarketing, but actually sign them up for a subscription or other model for recurring purchase. The stronger and longer the customer relationship means a higher LTV for each customer. This justifies higher CAC and even lower prices within high margin categories, where the savings can be passed on to the customer in return for predictability and referrals. Products like The Dollar Shave Club's subscription razors, Blue Apron and other food products, and even underwear replenishment subscriptions all are subject to these new brand building and customer relationship economics.

Dollar Shave Club again. This time watch the YouTube video to view how it reinforces its value proposition to drive LTV. *https://www.youtube.com/watch?v=ZUG9qYTJMsl.*

Once a brand is established, offering product line extensions to a known and happy customer who already has an account (with payment information on file) becomes much easier. Providing unexpected samples of complementary products both increases the value of the primary subscription and ensures trial by the best possible target user — a happy customer. In other words, a free sample not only makes the existing customer happier and more likely to stay — extending their lifetime value — but increases the chance of them buying new products by giving them a chance to try it, coming from a trusted source.

Cloud Based Software as a Service

Software as a Service, or SaaS application models, is another rapidly growing model in the digital sector, growing roughly 20% year over year according to Gartner Inc.[7] SaaS is probably the most familiar segment of the cloud computing market (see Gartner Inc. report to view the other five primarily B2B cloud services models). For our purposes, the most common SaaS offerings regular consumers might have personal experience with are applications such as Salesforce. com, Dropbox, or some of the Google Apps. SaaS is compelling for its similarities in pricing to subscription models in addition to other reasons.

B2B enterprise SaaS models such as PaaS (Platform as a Service) or BPaaS (Business Process as a Service) or other infrastructure or security services were, and are, high value and high commitment. IBM, Infosys, Accenture and Oracle are just a few of the early leaders in this market. Companies commit to licenses and services over a period of years for a large group of employees and often pay by the seat. The decision makers — usually the IT senior management team — could and would be swayed by enterprise sales teams, events, even fancy sales dinners. New technologies had a difficult time "breaking through" given the investment and the sales cycle time needed to build relationships and penetrate the "IT Priesthood" in big companies. It took Salesforce.com a number of years to emerge into the leadership position it holds today.

Traditional sales models also leveraged organizational considerations — bureaucratic controls of who to buy from, technology and platform preferences, cost and utility and other corporate factors that could be at odds with the rank and file needs and ability to use and adopt the technology. Employees would often find themselves using hated, difficult to use technologies that weren't suitable for all their needs but were the "least common denominator" in one size fits all decisions. For a company making an organization wide, expensive, long term commitment, this made sense.

Once accessing software remotely through the cloud became feasible — through fast and reliable Internet connections among other things — a new model became possible. What if one could access the software through the Internet? SaaS software resides in the cloud centrally and is access through accounts, cutting infrastructure and support costs and making updates easy and sometimes invisible to the user. And without the need to install, customize, and maintain support for legacy systems, the pricing model is reduced to a simple per seat service and support fee. In other words, subscriptions.

With this model, free trials and freemium service levels become possible. The incremental cost of accessing a cloud service is minimal; the marketing value of capturing and educating a lead through essentially a self-guided demo is large. And perhaps equally important, the price level of a few seats for a single department is low enough that the decision can be made quickly at the line level — without need to wine and dine the IT priesthood for a major multiyear commitment. Once in an organization, the value of a tool spreads from desk to desk by word of mouth.

Subscription commerce and SaaS models have their limits of course. But by re-thinking and re-valuing the customer relationship and exploring new pricing and promotion models, digital marketers can disrupt and expand into previously inaccessible markets.

Change is the Only Constant; Business Models in Flux

As we have moved through this book and considered the many new innovations and developments in digital, it is clear that only one thing is certain: *Digital business models will continue to evolve, and marketers must keep up!*

Although all of the experimentation and new trials for doing business in new ways may not last, each innovation continues to upend decades of established models across the board.

Crowdfunding, for example, is a new business model that allows prospective products to be funded in an entirely market-driven way, through pre-orders and direct financial support from prospective customers. Kickstarter, Indiegogo, and other crowdfunding platforms allow creators — bands who want to make a new album, filmmakers with a new project, or someone with an idea for a breakthrough product — to propose their concept and create a campaign to raise enough funds to produce the product. Originally used by the creative class, many new products are finding their initial legs through this process. The Pebble Watch, for example, one of the first smart watches, was funded in this way.[8]

"Pebble Watch crowdfunding hits record on Kickstarter."

Websites like Product Hunt, which in part help identify promising new products and spread the word to early adopters and investors, help feed the process.

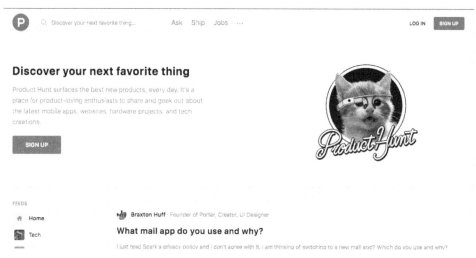

Screenshot from Product Hunt; *https://www.producthunt.com.*

Of course, it's not all Pebble watches and success. Many products succeed in raising the money but fail to deliver when the would-be entrepreneurs face the difficulties of actual physical sourcing and production of a product. Accusations of fraud and incompetence abound and there seems to be little recourse for those who were promised products that arrive late, changed or not at all. And sometimes frivolity rules the day: a posting by one wag seeking $10 for potato salad — a joke — raised more than $55,000 as people pitched in. The fortunate jokester held a "PotatoStock" festival in his hometown of Columbus, Ohio with the money, rather than simply pocketing it all.

Potato Salad
by Zack Danger Brown

Crowdsourced Potato Salad, the most expensive Potato Salad we know!

The bottom line is the bottom line: as new business models emerge and new ways of financing products take off, marketers will need to evolve with them to be successful in building and marketing the next generation of brands and products.

Endnotes

1. "3 Ways 'The Internet Of Things' Will Change Every Business," *Forbes*, August 2015; *https://www.forbes.com/sites/bernardmarr/2015/08/17/3-ways-the-internet-of-things-will-change-every-business/#3f039cb51981.*

2. Chris Anderson, "The Long Tail: Why the Future of Business is Selling Less of More"; *http://www.longtail.com/about.html.*

3. *Ibid.*

4. "Seeking E-Commerce Shoots Among Retail's Brick-And-Mortar Decline," *Investor's Business Daily*, 3/10/2017; *https://www.investors.com/research/industry-snapshot/retail-snapshot.*

5. "Google and Walmart's Big Bet against Amazon Might Just Pay Off," *Wired.com*, August 23, 2017; *https://www.wired.com/story/google-and-walmarts-big-bet-against-amazon-might-just-pay-off/.*

6. Digital Travel Sales Worldwide, 2016-2021, *eMarketer*, August 2017; *https://www.emarketer.com/Report/Worldwide-Digital-Travel-Sales-eMarketers-Estimates-20162021/2002089.*

7. Quote from Gartner Inc. "2015 Cloud Computing Hype Cycle 2016"; *http://www.zdnet.com/article/saas-in-2016-the-key-trends/.* Gartner Inc. "Worldwide Public Cloud Services Revenue, 2016–2020"; *https://www.gartner.com/newsroom/id/3815165.*

8. "Pebble Watch crowdfunding hits record on Kickstarter," CNBC, Published Mon. 30 Mar, 2015; *http://www.cnbc.com/2015/03/30/pebble-watch-funding-hits-record--.html.*

okémon GO maker Niantic says it has driven millions visitors to sponsored locations like McDonald's Japan where gamers can score a special virtual good. The sponsorships turn these locations into Pokémon GO "gyms" that players can win for their team through virtual battle, and "PokéStops" where they can gather eggs and Poké Balls to capture more pocket monsters. Pokémon GO has since signed on Sprint and 7,800 Starbucks locations as sponsors in the U.S. Pokémon GO benefits from building demand for its free-to-produce virtual goods, which users claim when they arrive at a sponsor's business. Pokémon GO is Niantic's real-world AR platform, built on a foundation proven to scale to hundreds of millions of users.

Niantic, Inc. (formerly Niantic Labs) is headquartered in San Francisco, CA.

"The idea is to offer players items at certain locations, and partners pay for each visitor attracted to the game. And, we've already attracted 500 million visitors."

— Mathieu de Fayet, Niantic

www.pokemongo.com

CHAPTER 12
Emerging Channels and Opportunities

One of the challenges of digital marketing is that it changes moment to moment and keeping up with the latest developments can be a Herculean challenge. (That's why this text has a regularly updated online component, of course.) Throughout the book our focus has been to discuss the strategies behind our marketing goals rather than just showcasing the tactics that one could execute to achieve them. In this way, a strategic marketer can apply the frameworks and techniques broadly to whatever new challenges, channels, or technologies arise in the future.

However, there are many areas where the trends are clear and data we already have shows that the impact on business will continue to be significant. In this last section, we will review the forecasts of these macro trends, touch on the most promising emerging channels, and discuss what the future may bring for the best of these cool new technologies. While experience has shown that not every one of these new areas of interest will live up to the hype, it's a good bet that being aware of them will help protect and advance any future marketers' strategic plans and provide some vision of where things are heading.

Getting Up Close and Personal

As more and more of our digital marketing efforts involve mobile marketing by default, location is emerging as a critical piece of data for marketers. Coupled with the fact that phones are personal devices, we now know where and when an individual is viewing an ad not just that it is being shown to someone on a particular website. This is a huge sea change for marketers. The existence of a powerful, location-aware personal computing device in the pockets of half the people on the planet is also leading to both new services and new methods to market within them. *Location-based services* are any information, entertainment, or marketing offer that is personalized based on the location data provided by a mobile device.

Location, Location, Location

It's important to note that most location based services utilize cell phone technologies — *multilateration technology* in the cell towers — rather than the common misconception of just GPS (Global Positioning System), which is a satellite-based technology developed for the military. Although GPS is useful, satellites are expensive to launch and maintain, and their distance from the planet provides other limitations. It's far cheaper for most services to use cell phone tower triangulation. Essentially, triangulation measures the speed of a signal between a few cell phone towers in order to pinpoint the location of the phone with a fair amount of accuracy. (WiFi allows even further accuracy.) This is the source of the "blinking blue dot" representing you on most digital maps. With some relatively simple math, the phone can be triangulated and the location determined. (And you thought you'd never use that trigonometry you learned in high school; now you can use it every day!)

For marketers, location information has already proven to be massively useful. *Geofenced advertising* — showing ads only to people in a specifically defined location, whether by a simple radius or something more sophisticated — allows real world retailers and businesses to connect digital advertising to the physical world and limit their ads to potential customers in the area. Many marketers couple this with *dayparting* (showing ads by time). Retailers and restaurants, for example, can advertise during hours when they are open or before the appropriate upcoming mealtime. With all these exciting new capabilities, the final step, as always, is closing the loop on conversion — the proverbial "door swinging and cash register ringing." Facebook and Google, with their ubiquitous presence in mobile, are already able to close this loop and attribute real world transactions to the digital marketing efforts occurring on their platforms.

Point of Sales Systems

Connecting advertising and marketing efforts to the final sale is also helped by the growth of and integration with *Point of Sale* (POS) applications. Merchants now use POS systems that are effectively the same computing platforms they need to access their marketing tools. When the cash register is a computer, this means that trackable codes integrated into advertising and promotions can be highly effective at correctly attributing a final purchase to its stimulating advertising factors.

One way to motivate this is by getting people to "check in." Pioneered by Foursquare (among others) and joined by Facebook, many apps now provide the user an option to check in, motivating them with gamification (points and badges), social benefits like knowing where their friends are, accepting information like real time relevant reviews, or even cash and discounts.

Some retailers find that going even further with *beacons* can bring both store navigation and custom promotions into play. Beacons are small devices for in-store location and navigation, or for more precise location detection in densely populated areas (Figure 12.1). By placing these devices at different positions in a store, then calibrating the internal map with their own device, shopkeepers can acquire precise aisle by aisle, shelf by shelf location data for promotions and navigation. Companies like Estimote provide the equipment and software development kits so that people and assets can be located programmatically, encouraging exploration of all the possibilities this new technology can offer.

■ Figure 12.1 Beacon Software Development Kit

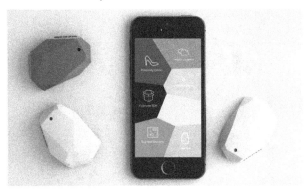

Facebook's beacon technology uses Bluetooth technology to send a one-way signal to the Facebook app on the customer's phone to show the right information while they are in their shop, or in close vicinity, without collecting any information from people or their phones. Facebook is experimenting with beacons in popular locations for selfies and posts, like Times Square and other tourist hotspots.

Many experiments are being conducted. Macy's launched an app that provides in-store navigation for its massive New York flagship store, allowing customers to make sure they are able to find what they are looking for as well as suggesting "real time" promotional items they might like (Figure 12.2).

■ Figure 12.2 Macy's Personalized Shopping App

Source: Macy's website; *https://www.macys.com/ce/splash/enhance-app*.

Another area of interest for marketers relative to location and POS connectivity is loyalty. The old punch cards of the past are being replaced by a new generation of digital trackers that can be used to stimulate repeat business, encourage loyalty and referrals, and customize incentives for individuals to do so. Growing startups like Belly are replacing the cardboard "Buy 10 coffees, get one free" cards with intelligent solutions that allow for more dynamic and sophisticated promotions and track their effectiveness.

from the old punch cards...

to this...

Belly Loyalty Program; *https://www.bellycard.com/business/loyalty/*.

Gaming Gets Serious

The video game industry has become so big and so popular that the old stereotypes of the teenage boy playing all night in his parents' basement are simply one subset of the overall gaming population. Today, everyone is a gamer. From millennials playing Pokémon GO to seniors playing "Words with Friends" on their phones, to hardcore first-person shooter clans and family console gamers, the world of gaming is now broader and much more inclusive than the early days of its inception.

Video Games: the Industry

The revenues in the gaming industry, seen in Figure 12.3, show the behemoth it's become —
with more than $100 billion in revenue across the board, and blockbuster games generating
billions across the lifetime of their franchises. These economics are eclipsed only by the sheer
amounts of time spent playing games.

■ Figure 12.3 Global Games Market Forecast

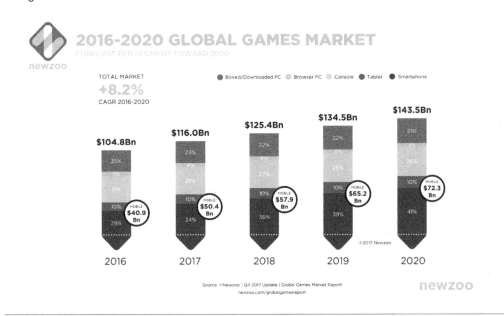

Source: Global Games Market Report, 2017, courtesy of New Zoo, a leading provider of market intelligence
covering the global games markets.

Gaming has grown for many reasons, and now reaches people in every demographic. At its
core, continuous improvement of hardware and software technology has made for better
gaming experiences and opened up the gaming world to a broader audience. Better graphics,
more immersive storylines, more exciting gameplay, and innovative controllers like motion
control, etc. have allowed gaming to cross demographic lines. With a mobile phone and some
time to kill, anyone can be a gamer with hits like Fruit Ninja and Candy Crush played by just
about everyone. More importantly, gaming has become more socially acceptable as games and
their subject matter have broadened in scope and become entwined in our culture. Gaming's
evolution from early basic shoot-'em-ups has everyone playing. Finally, gaming is now a social
activity — playing together as a family, a group, or virtually with a regular team, is common,
and the choice between gaming or being social is no longer the case. Indeed, full body motion
controllers available for the console market have made virtual dance contests an energetic
affair rather than the old gaming "couch potato" stereotype.

From a marketing perspective, gaming is a world that's been difficult for marketers to penetrate. Advertising and promoting to gamers when they are immersed in a gaming world has been difficult to do without being jarring and interruptive to the experience. Nevertheless, with the explosion of time spent in the gaming world, marketers have begun to learn ways to reach potential customers in these areas. Casual gaming on mobile devices, for example, has brought a large amount of ad inventory into the gaming environment.

"Gaming" encompasses many categories and ways to segment the industry. The various styles of play are one way to look at things. Another is the varied distribution platforms. Finally, one could divide the industry into hardware, software, and services around the industry. All have merit, but from a marketing perspective, each of these distinctions determines the options we have for reaching consumers as seen in Figure 12.4. New Zoo updates their findings quarterly, often with adjustments to nomenclature as segments change and evolve.

■ Figure 12.4 Segmenting the Gaming Universe

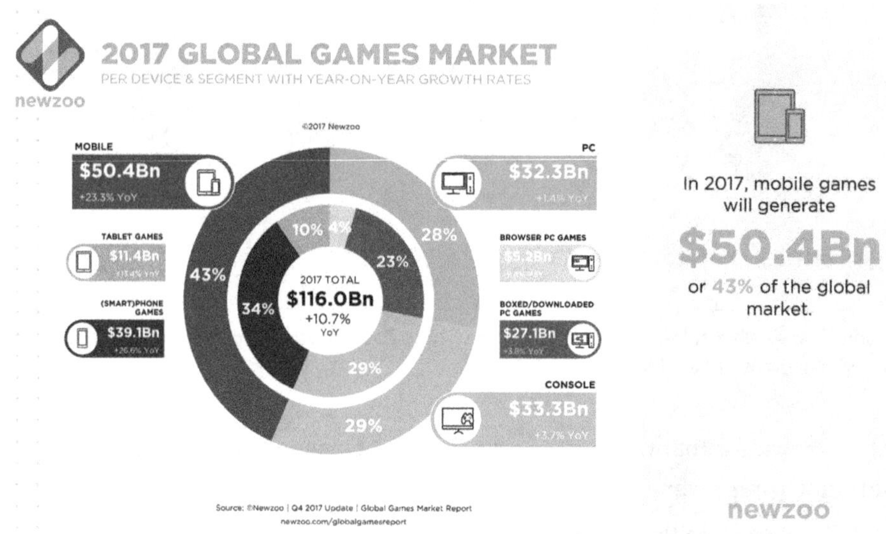

Source: Global Games Market Report, New Zoo 2017.

Gaming Styles and Users

The Interactive Advertising Bureau describes two main styles of gameplay: casual gaming, and core or enthusiast gaming. Casual games are targeted at a mass audience and are characterized by short bursts of easy to learn gameplay — "snackable" gaming. Casual games are found more and more on the mobile platform and tend to be free to play or very low cost ($1) with in game purchase and upgrades generating additional revenue. With these low price points, advertising and promotion become an important revenue stream and an opportunity for marketers to reach this huge varied audience.

Often addictive and progressing through many levels, each slice of gameplay is nevertheless a relatively low investment. Core or enthusiast games, the bigger blockbuster games, are often genre based, on consoles and computers, with deeper, more realistic gameplay. Sessions can last for hours at a time and total gameplay can be 20-40 hours to completion. Many games have no endpoint or become tournament style environments removing any limits to the gameplay lifecycle at all. These types of games are more expensive to produce, with higher production values. While core games skew slightly male, casual games skew slightly female in player demographics. Both are characterized by more and more social aspects of gameplay.

For years there were only two different distribution platforms: console gaming and consumer gaming. Consoles were and are few in number and represent proprietary ecosystems: Sony Playstation 4, Microsoft Xbox One, and Nintendo Switch are the current big players' flagships.

The PS4 and Xbox One consoles side by side.

Consoles are essentially dedicated gaming computers with custom built controllers and performance graphics processing. Some have motion detection, others use specialized controls like steering wheels or dance pads, but all are designed for and dedicated to gaming, and modern consoles are Internet connected for group play. Computer gaming, with controls on the computer itself, is the home of equally robust games and often the lines blur with dedicated gaming PCs having the power and accessories of their console cousins. Team play has made all of these gaming platforms a much more social, collaborative, and communication driven pastime than in previous generations, with teams (sometimes called clans or tribes or the like) playing together regularly and even having logos and colors. The software, whether downloaded, streamed, or on DVD, costs between $30-$50 and blockbuster games can earn billions with upgrades and peripherals over the franchise lifetimes.

From the IAB's perspective, there are three main types of game marketing, shown in Figure 12.5. *Around game ads* are ads that target the user outside of the gaming experience. This is very common in the casual gaming environment where numerous opportunities present themselves. *In game ads* take advantage by placing ads and promotion into the actual gameplay and gaming worlds. This entails a bit more complexity in integration but with more potential for higher engagement. Finally, *custom branded games* can make the entire experience all about the brand (sometimes called advergames).

■ Figure 12.5 IAB Game Marketing Model

Around Game Environment Ads

Display
• Ex. banners, digital video ads, downloadable content on console services

In Game Environment Ads

Display
• Ex. banners, digital video ads, billboards, retail store fronts

In Game Immersive Ads

Interactive Elements
• Ex. computer terminals, branded racing cars, cell phones, downloadable items within game

Advergames

Interactive Elements
• Ex. game specifically designed around product or service being advertised

Source: IAB Games Advertising Ecosystem Guide. *https://www.iab.com/news/forecast-2017-brands-take-fresh-look-game-advertising/*. © 2018 Interactive Advertising Bureau. All rights reserved.

Around Game Ads

Around game ads come in a variety of types, but from a marketers' perspective are perhaps the easiest to understand and create. Many of these ads are simply standard IAB display or video ad units in the game itself; banners or video across the bottom, or interstitials showing up as pre, post or between level ads in progressive games, or between games for short games. Some games will allow for total brand re-skinning of the entire gaming environment, "taking over" its look and feel for a period of time, often for a big event or short-term promotion.

Display ads *around* a game environment.

As these ads are IAB standard and dynamically inserted, there is no additional cost of creation for marketers and no need for any additional planning in most cases beyond the simple media buy. Marketers can often just treat the around game ads in the casual gaming environment as another way to reach a target audience in their media plan. Many of these ads are in a mobile app, so the environment may be more suited for brand impact than conversion. However, there are obvious benefits if the marketing goal is to get someone to download your own app!

In Game Ads

More difficult and varied are *in game ads*. These might be the only way to reach the core gamers in the more immersive environments where they spend so much time. These ads began as static advertisements that had to be planned and inserted into the games during the development process. But now they can be dynamically inserted as games are developed with specific marketing revenue streams in mind.

Product placement in games is a powerful area for engagement. The integration of branded clothing or equipment into the game can be very powerful. Indeed, the integration can make the game more realistic. For example, initial versions of NASCAR racing and other sports games had to use made up brands in the game to mimic the real world to avoid legal issues. Now, virtual branding is an important part of overall brand licensing — can you imagine a NASCAR racing environment where the car isn't covered by sponsor logos? As the IAB says:

> *Some of the first examples of in game advertising were static, or unchanging, consisting of simple in game product placement or virtual billboards. Artists or programmers placed these brands and advertisements directly into a game, after which they could not be altered. Nowadays brands can be deeply integrated into the game experience and storyline, adding value and realism to the game while also evoking the brand's core values. For example, the inclusion of Gatorade into EA's Madden 25 console game title mimics the real-life usage and sponsorship of Gatorade in the NFL, and adds authenticity to the gameplay experience.*

> *Although many of these types of ads and integrations are still programmed into the game during the development process, they can also be added after the game is released via a game update or content download.*
>
> — IAB Games Advertising Ecosystem Guide.[1]

One of the biggest challenges of static product integration is similar to that of movie placements, predicting the hits. Paying a large amount of money early enough in the development and production process to be integrated into a game generally requires a bet on its success. With many franchise type games (Tom Clancy, Call of Duty, etc.) success can be predicted. But with a lead time of a year or more, it's often difficult for a brand to feature a current product. However, in some cases this can work very well. Cadillac paid to include its then new sedan in a game with its peer group (BMW, Audi, etc.) as a driving option — hitting a perfect target of potential customers in its demographic with a virtual opportunity to meet the model.

More and more commonly available, *dynamic integration* into the game environment, can work even better. These placements are offered up in real time using an ad server, in the same way that banner ads are served on websites and blogs. Examples are racing games with billboards, cityscapes with posters and other "natural" integrations.

A political dynamic ad integration using a billboard.[2]

The clothing the player wears in some skateboarding games, for example, also mimics the real life lifestyle marketing of the brand. Ultimately, the "natural feel" of the integration is key. This makes it difficult, for example, to integrate modern products into swords and sorcery, and fantasy world environments.

Quicksilver clothing featured in a skateboarding game; Ford ads in a racing game.

Real Legal Issues for Brands in Virtual Worlds

More importantly, real legal and contract issues have been raised as sponsors insist they own the rights on the hood of a car or a player's jersey — in both the real world and the virtual. For example, what happens if the NBA licenses a player's likeness to a sports game — but the player has a contract with a clothing or sneaker company to appear in their clothes? If a virtual stadium appears in a game environment, do the sponsors in the real stadium have the right to appear in the virtual arena as well — or can their rivals replace them? Many of these questions are still being worked out.

Even if the integrations are intended to speak to the player more than the in game environment — these are often jarring and may even be lambasted — they are still effective. The heavy handed integration of the "Nissin Cup of Noodles" brand into a *Final Fantasy XV* game — with characters in the game even commenting on its' deliciousness — has been ridiculed (and rightly so...).[3]

Nissin Cup of Noodles "In Game" Integration.

The Value Exchange

Another form of marketing that has shown promise in many games is the *value exchange* or *incentivized promotion.* This is an interruptive scenario, where the user gains in game credits or items of value in return for engaging with ad content. These ads are usually optional and clearly delineated from, but integrated with, the game play itself. Maxis' Sim City Buildit, for example, allows items and in game currency prizes in exchange for watching 15-30 second video commercials or interactive ads.

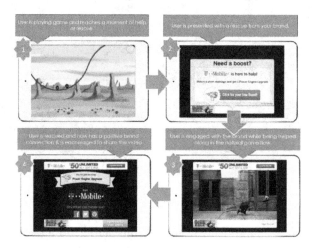

Example of brand value exchange from IAB/Mediabrix.

Custom Branded Games (or Advergames)

The most immersive and often most expensive way to integrate a brand into a game is to attempt to blend the brand seamlessly into the gaming experience. The challenge here for the brand is that game design is a complex and unique skill set. The best games should be integrated well, but the game itself needs to be playable and enjoyable to the point that people would play it without the brand's presence.

The Sims computer game has an entire add on to the game sponsored by IKEA. The game, which revolved around players living virtual people's lives, essentially allowed them to furnish their virtual world with the same IKEA furniture they might be sitting on in the real world.

IKEA's SIMS living room scene.

Other brands have simply created their own games to emphasize a brand value. Chipotle created a scarecrow game to play that illustrated the farm to table goals of its locally sourced ingredients. Still other brands avoid the risk of developing their own enjoyable game by partnering. The movie *Rio* licensed the Angry Birds franchise game and created its own levels and gameplay featuring characters from the movie as well as incorporating information about when and where to see it and how to get tickets. Ten million copies were downloaded for free by the game's enthusiasts.

Chipotle Scarecrow Game. Created by Moonbot Studios.

Rio Branded Angry Birds Game.

Given the bewildering array of games already available in the app stores as well as the difficulty of producing a game with high quality gameplay, many brands are following a new model: repurposing existing games for their own use.

Similar to what *Rio* did with the Angry Birds franchise, but using perhaps an overlooked game that nevertheless plays well, an economic *advergame* can be made. An example might be an auto marketer digging through the many driving games that never broke through to long term popularity, making a deal to reskin it for the brand, and leveraging this known property against its customer base.

Voice, Visual Assistants, and Beyond

The way we interact with both the mobile and digital Internet continues to change and evolve. Voice and visual interfaces to the web are increasing as artificial intelligence, virtual assistants, and photo apps increase their penetration in the broader consumer and personal electronics markets. Google notes the number of searches conducted by voice — voice search queries increased *over 35× between 2008 and 2016*, coinciding with the rise of smartphones.[4] And companies like Pinterest and Snap are devoting teams to making visual matching technology — picture inputs to search — more and more effective.

Voice search is now being used at least once a week by more than 25% of all mobile users. From the most basic perspective, working with OK Google on Android or Siri on iOS is no different than traditional search — you need to appear in the search listings. However, one real question marketers need to understand is: where do the ads go?

In a typed search, the ads appear around and near — and are complementary to — the natural search listings. Right now, there is no comparable way to reach voice searchers. This problem is likely to increase as we move from *voice search* — trying to simply find something — to *voice act* — trying to do something. Typical searches can be seen in Figure 12.6. That something, whether ordering a pizza, an Uber, or something more complex, puts commercial transaction out of reach of Google's (and marketer's) ability to reach and monetize that consumer.[5]

■ Figure 12.6 Google Mobile Voice Survey Results

Source: *https://googleblog.blogspot.com/2014/10/omg-mobile-voice-survey-reveals-teens.html*.
Google and the Google logo are registered trademarks of Google Inc., used with permission.

Another area of growth is visual search, where one can use an image or picture to find similar images or pictures. The commercial applications of finding a similar item when shopping are as obvious as browsing in a store; it makes the experience of reviewing the possibilities more seamless and natural. Google began to experiment with visual search through a variety of methods — one was an app called *Google Goggles*. Goggles matched fairly standardized, iconic, or well-structured items, like product labels, landmarks, artworks, or business cards, and retrieved information about the item for the user. (The functionality is now incorporated into Google Lens, a similar product that works with the voice functionality of the Google Assistant.) Now you can scan a restaurant and be instantly connected to reviews and information about the venue.

Pinterest, with its legacies of image-based content, is also working on visual search tools. For example, Pinterest has a new tool that allows you to find similar objects to one in another picture. They use the example of a perfect lamp in a picture of someone's room; the Pinterest search tool finds items that are visually similar.[6]

Screen Shot of New Pinterest Matching Tool.

When you spot something in a Pin that you want to learn more about, tap the search tool in the corner. Then select the part of the Pin you're interested in, and they'll show you Pins just like it. You can even filter your visual search results by topic so you find exactly what you're looking for. So, if you zoom in on that lamp, you can discover what it's called ("Antiqued Metal Funnel Pendant"), and where you can find it (Restoration Hardware). If you want to know more—like how to get a table like that—just resize your selection and move it around to instantly see more Pins.

With the ability to buy something directly from a recommendation made by the tool, a new avenue becomes available for a marketer to present a recommended option that meets the visual cues — much like keywords for search. This has already started. Domino's actually allows people to buy pizza simply by texting an emoji. While primitive as a visual tool, the leap to taking a picture of a desired product and using it to make a purchase is actually not that big at all.[7]

Domino's Emoji Ordering App.

New Outputs: Augmented, Mixed, and Virtual Reality

While voice and visual search are new ways to enter information into the digital world, newer outputs like augmented, mixed, and virtual reality are emerging ways to overlay digital information into your real and virtual environment. All are showing growth and promise, with experiments appearing all the time, with new, dramatically improved hardware debuting regularly.

How are they different? There is a lot of overlap, but all involve projecting digital data and environments into a realistic setting. *Augmented reality* is when digital information or data is overlaid in real time on top of a view of the real world: directions on a phone screen that adapt to the location and streets you see on the screen, or even just a funny face altering filter from Snapchat. *Mixed reality* is incorporating virtual world and environmental features in with the real world view seen by the viewer — like an "x-ray" view of a person by a doctor or medical professional, or being able to look "through" walls to see ductwork or wiring. Both are usually used with devices like phones, glasses, or the like, and the effects are overlaid by apps or software.

Marketers are beginning to use augmented reality and mixed reality to demonstrate products and other uses. LEGO, for example, has in-store cameras that use their boxes as triggers to show a virtual version of the fully assembled model in the box. A *trigger* is a known object that can serve as the virtual one's real-world stand-in to produce the effect.

IKEA, with flat packed products available at a limited amount of giant stores, is using its catalog as a trigger to allow app based virtual reality directly into the consumers' homes. With its app, one simply places the catalog where the product would go, and the app depicts it as if it's part of the room already, allowing a customer to cycle through potential "end tables" in virtual reality to find the best fit. For marketers, using the product or catalog as a trigger is a simple way to place the object in the real world. Some companies have moved beyond this in interesting ways.

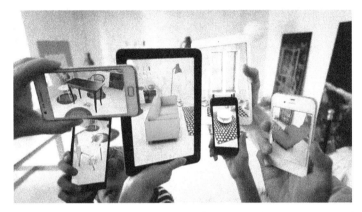

IKEA's virtual reality app brings furniture comparison directly into the consumers' home.

Another great Augmented Reality app that I just introduced to my classes is "Living Wine Labels." From swirling vortexes to grim confessions, this app brings wine labels to life — and reveals the story behind every bottle. Start by scanning an AR-enabled label to watch its story unfold.

Beringer Bros. takes viewers on a journey back to 1895 to help the Brothers capture a moment in history.
"19 Crimes" brings you face-to-face with infamous convicts as you hear their side of the story.
Rick Grimes takes "The Walking Dead" drinkers on a dangerous supply run, dodging the grasping hands of a zombie or uses bottles to unlock the ultimate battle for survival: a showdown worthy of the apocalypse.

Ink Hunter is an app for the smartphone allowing users to "try on" a tattoo — directly on their bodies — using the augmented reality function of the app to place it on their arm or body part. The app can then refer the user to a tattoo parlor where they can get the more permanent "ink." (Ink Hunter has the user draw a square smile to serve as the trigger.)

Ink Hunter lets you virtually try on a tattoo in AR — before you get inked!

Virtual reality (VR), on the other hand, is an immersive, simulated environment that nevertheless seems to respond to real physics, gestures, and the like, enabling virtual gesture control, interactivity, and intuitive understanding. Virtual worlds do not have to be completely realistic, but they generally have to have enough functionality and realism for it to be an environment that a user can act naturally within — moving, walking, etc. — as well as fun actions such as flying or riding magic carpets!

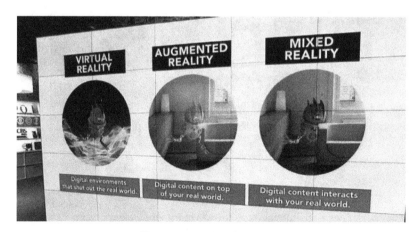

The spectrum of digital reality.

VR generally requires headsets or goggles costing hundreds or thousands of dollars for full effect. Additional hardware, like walking platforms, can run even higher. The realism can be enough to induce nausea. VR seems to be taking hold primarily in entertainment areas like gaming or for certain types of corporate training exercises.[8] Magic Leap, a well-funded, secretive, and much-hyped virtual reality company, recently announced their lightweight VR goggles.

The Magic Leap One system; oversized cyberpunk-y goggles, a Lightpack, and handheld controller.

For marketers, using VR is still an open question. When the world is virtual, perhaps the first step is rendering the appropriate product for use in that world. Virtual objects, modeled after brands and their iconic designs, are likely to be a point of contention from the start. If I am in a virtual environment, must I pay to place my avatar (me, as a VR character) in designer clothes? Do I have to pay to take a ride on my virtual Harley or Segway?

Wearables, Cars, and Homes

Wearable devices like Google Glass, Snapchat Spectacles, along with watches and fitness devices, etc., are becoming more and more common, but we have barely tapped their potential. These new and emerging devices provide more and more places to send and receive digital information. Much of this information is commercial in nature — from refrigerators and appliances, to the cars and homes themselves, "smart" devices will be able to signal when (and what) action needs to be taken.

How this impacts marketers is difficult to discern, but as more people get selective information from dedicated devices, the possibilities for targeting and the complexities in reaching them increase dramatically. Someone wearing a Fitbit is clearly interested in his or her health — but how should you reach him or her effectively with a marketing message?

Snapchat's Spectacles never took off — thousands of unsold pairs are in a warehouse.

Similarly, new questions are being raised by the emergence of connected cars and homes. With connected cars, many of the same challenges of mobile and location based marketing can apply — but now with the added ability of the car itself stimulating a purchase. For example, if the car can signal its location and that it's in need of gas, the marketing opportunities for the fill up are obvious. An enterprising advertiser could simply pay to have directions to their gas station sent to the car's onboard mapping system. Similarly, passengers in need of a pit stop could be extolled the virtues of a local restaurant's cherry pie and clean bathrooms.

With connected homes, replenishment strategies have begun to be a prime mover. Marketers in the near future will need to contend with smart refrigerators that can re-order supplies, appliances that can order new parts or materials, and the like. Getting a foothold in this chain of replenishment and re-ordering will be key.

Smart appliances remind consumers to order the products they use —
will brands be able to muscle in on these relationships?

Marketing in the Face of Change

The transition from traditional mass media marketing techniques to digital and now to the mobile world has disrupted the way marketing operates at every level. From the channels selected to reach a new customer, to the ways we create loyalty, new methods of measuring effectiveness rooted in data and constantly emerging technology have taken firm root in our landscape. The only constant going forward will be change itself.

Emerging technologies, for example, always present a bewildering array of challenges to the marketer (see Figure 12.7). Think about the paradigm shifts in marketing that took place with the advent of broadcast television and the personal computer! What can be done to prevent future shock? Thinking strategically, understanding the fundamentals, and starting out with a sound set of marketing goals is a great place to begin. New channels, new inputs, and new outputs are simply the medium to get out the message.

■ Figure 12.7 Which Devices are Most Popular for Internet Searches?

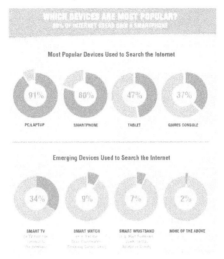

Source: "Why you need a mobile strategy now more than ever"; *https://www.beargroup.com/ideas/why-you-need-mobile-strategy-now-more-ever*. Original art, *http://insight.globalwebindex.net/device*.

Your approach should always begin at the highest level of strategy: who are your potential customers and where can we communicate our marketing message(s) efficiently with greatest impact? From this determination marketers can then identify where they're going — short- and long-term goals and the performance metrics we will measure against — then track and optimize all our activities against them.

With digital channels we can be more flexible, nimble, and creative. We can learn, we can experiment, and we can quickly know what works and what doesn't — and act accordingly. Clear strategies lead to testable tactics and provable success. This simple framework and the tactics and channels we use to test and optimize our ideal digital marketing mix — will make our journey far more exciting and successful.

John Wanamaker famously said:

"Half the money I spend on advertising is wasted; the trouble is I don't know which half."

Marketers cannot simply absorb the new methods described in this book and put it on a shelf for reference. Everything in this text (unfortunately for me!) will continually be changing and evolving. New methods, new channels, and new best practices will emerge for us to explore and improve upon. Only after seeing how the general population adopts and uses these new tools and technologies will we be able to build on stable ground.

And as another great observer of life said:

Well we know where we're going
But we don't know where we've been...
And the future is certain
Give us time to work it out

— "The Road to Nowhere," Talking Heads

While the tools and strategies will keep changing, the role of the marketing professional remains critical as long as we keep learning. We must embrace the journey and not simply seek the final destination. Enjoy!

Tools and Resources

■ [Final Videos — Corning's "A Day Made of Glass 1 and 2] Corning, the glassmaker, made a video for its shareholder meeting a few years ago to show how the glass it makes would be part of the incredible technologies that are becoming available in our homes, cars, schools, and offices. The video became the most viral industrial video of all time — version 1 has more than 26m views, and the second version almost 6m. *https://www.youtube.com/watch?v=6Cf7IL_eZ38, https://www.youtube.com/watch?v=jZ-kHpNnXLB0.*

■ Virtual Reality Projects and Design Ideas
http://community.foundry.com/?_ga=2.63233319.989181735.1515763881-1281914348.1515763881

Endnotes

1. IAB Games Advertising Ecosystem Guide:
    https://www.iab.com/insights/iab-games-advertising-ecosystem-guide/.

2. "Six of the best product placements in video games," *The Guardian*: *https://www.theguardian.com/technology/2014/jul/03/six-of-the-best-product-placement-video-games*. Photo, Burnout Paradise with Barack Obama's 2008 campaign billboards. Observer.

3. "The most shameless product placement in video games," *Geek.com*:
    https://www.geek.com/games/the-most-shameless-food-product-placement-in-video-games-1682634/.

4. "Google voice search queries in 2016 are up 35× over 2008" according to Google trends via Search Engine Watch *https://www.branded3.com/blog/google-voice-search-stats-growth-trends/.*

5. "Voice search becomes voice action," Andreas Rieffen, *SearchEngineLand*:
    http://searchengineland.com/voice-search-becomes-voice-action-key-talking-point-smx-london-276186.

6. "Oh, How Pinteresting," Pinterest Blog: *https://blog.pinterest.com/en/our-crazy-fun-new-visual-search-tool.*

7. "Now you can text a pizza emoji to order Dominos":
    http://creativity-online.com/work/dominos-text-ordering-with-emojis/42287.

8. Foundry, Imagination Engineered:
    https://www.foundry.com/industries/virtual-reality/vr-mr-ar-confusedvirtual.

Index

Page numbers with an *f* refer to a figure.

CPSIA information can be obtained
at www.ICGtesting.com
Printed in the USA
LVHW060648280120
645022LV00004B/56